NOT WITHOUT
A FIGHT

NOT WITHOUT
A FIGHT

THE STORY OF A POLISH JEW'S RESISTANCE

D.W. DUKE
WITH THOMAS BIEBERS (BIEBERSTEIN)

NOT WITHOUT A FIGHT
THE STORY OF A POLISH JEW'S RESISTANCE

iUniverse books may be ordered through booksellers or by contacting:

iUniverse
1663 Liberty Drive
Bloomington, IN 47403
www.iuniverse.com
1-800-Authors (1-800-288-4677)

ISBN: 978-1-5320-2667-6 (sc)
ISBN: 978-1-5320-2669-0 (hc)
ISBN: 978-1-5320-2668-3 (e)

Library of Congress Control Number: 2017911661

Print information available on the last page.

iUniverse rev. date: 08/03/2017

ACKNOWLEDGEMENTS

Editors:
Victoria Wright
Zach Brown

Consultant for Close Quarter Fighting Segments:
David Kahn, Esq
Chief US Instructor for the Israeli Krav Maga Association

Thank You:
Jewish Family Services

Thank You:
Robert Sylk
Businessman/Philanthropist

Thank You:
Steven Spile, Esq
Spile, Leff & Goor, LLP

Thank You:
USC Shoah Foundation

Cover photo of D.W. Duke by Michael J. Elderman

PREFACE

MY FATHER USED to ask, "At a time when entire families were being murdered during the Holocaust, why was I so lucky not only to have survived personally, but to have done so with my entire immediate family intact?" You see, my father, Casimir Bieberstein, was a survivor of the Holocaust and a Resistance fighter, and because he so freely talked to his family about his experiences as a child in the Warsaw Ghetto, his story is easily told.

While many books tell the story of how the Jewish people died during the Nazi reign, there is very little mention of how and why some survived. This book, which has been masterfully written by the attorney and author D. W. Duke, is not just about the atrocities committed upon the Jewish people. It is about one family's skillful method of survival. A family who defiantly refused to die under the terms of their German oppressors. My father often said, "If we were going to die, we were going to die on our terms."

From their prewar aristocratic status to living and fighting in the ghettos, the story of the Bieberstein family is a story that needs to be shared. While many books have been written about personal survival in the Holocaust, to our knowledge, there has never been one in which the entire Jewish family remained intact throughout the war years. Whether it was divine intervention; the skillful disobedience of Irena Bieberstein, the family matriarch; the mistakes of the oppressors; the protection granted by the Soviet army; or as my father used to say, "just good old-fashioned luck," the entire immediate family survived.

My father passed away on April 7, 2014. His lifelong question was, "Why did we survive?" Perhaps that question was answered at his funeral. Among those who came to pay their respects were several generations of families. Attending in a kaleidoscope of religions, cultures, ethnicities, ancestries, and other variations, they came not as individuals representing their respective backgrounds but as people pledging to never let hate dictate how we live or die. That answers the question why they survived. How they survived is a different question, the answer to which is found within the pages of this book.

While the uprisings may not have appeared successful on the surface, the reality is that the Nazis were often forced to bring in real combat troops from the front lines to quell the Resistance. In doing so, they left exposed flanks on the Eastern and Western fronts. This in turn exposed the German army to the assault of the Allies. So while the uprisings may not have appeared successful, they were likely an important event that created a breach in the militia of the Reich, which made victory more easily achievable for the Allies.

This book is dedicated not only to the memories of the Bieberstein family, but to everyone who fought back and lived to share with the world the evil that mankind can inflict on itself. With that said, I want to thank D. W. Duke, who spent countless hours reviewing my father's interview tapes, courtesy of the Shoah Foundation, interviewing him personally, and translating his words into this biographical novel. Thank you, or as they say in Hebrew, *toda*.

Thomas Biebers (Bieberstein)

CHAPTER

1

IT WAS FRIDAY afternoon, August 7, 1937, in Warsaw, Poland; the Bieberstein family was preparing for Shabbat. In the dining room of the mansion, Adelajda, the young nanny, reverently placed the solid-gold Shabbat candelabra on the marble-top table, under the window that opened onto the beautiful multitiered garden. She smiled at six-year-old Casimir, who sat on the floor on the burgundy Persian rug, next to the Shabbat table. Cass quietly observed her graceful actions and found her appearance pleasant and lovely. He was fond of her. Jewish by birth and upbringing, Adelajda always observed Shabbat with the Biebersteins. She often lit the candles. She was pretty with her long dark hair and hazel eyes. She was kind. She was gentle. And Cass adored her. She was the best nanny he could ever have.

He leaned his head against the table. Adelajda smiled, wagged her index finger at him, and then touched him gently on the forehead. He did not understand the reason the Shabbat table was so important or what distinguished it from any other table; he only knew that his grandmother called it the Shabbat table and that it held special significance for her. She often said that it had been passed down through the family for several generations and was hand built by her great-grandfather, a rabbi. Cass knew that the table was very important, much like the Torah scroll that

1

was kept wrapped in a *mitpahat* in a wooden case with glass windows, also built by his grandmother's great-grandfather. The scroll was said to have been handwritten in Hebrew by her grandfather, a project that began at his bar mitzvah and lasted his entire life. The marble-top table was never used for any purpose other than to hold the Shabbat candelabra.

Cass studied the stern expression on the face of his uncle Bernard Szyncer, seated at the dining room table. Uncle Bernie, as he was called, was a man of distinguished appearance. His dark eyes seemed focused; his features revealed stress. Cass glanced at his father, Sigmund, and his maternal grandfather, Dr. Szyncer, also seated at the same end of the table. Dr. Szyncer's gray hair and long gray beard reminded Cass of the pictures of the old Chassidic rabbis that hung on the wall in the *shul*. While studying these men, who were great patriarchs in his eyes, Cass was distracted by the sheer linen curtains that caressed his face as they billowed in the oak-framed window, embellished by the warm afternoon breeze. He gently rubbed his fingers through the soft, heavy fiber of the burgundy Persian rug.

Looking at the ceiling, hovering twenty feet above his head, Cass noticed the dark oak supporting beams that spanned sixty feet, the length of the room. He wondered if the ceiling would fall if the beams were removed. The beams were sturdy and strong like his father. He noticed the leaded-crystal teardrops that hung from the massive chandelier. They were delicate and refined like his mother, Irena, who was seated at the opposite end of the table from the three men. Irena was known throughout Warsaw as a woman of tremendous beauty, the wife of one of the wealthiest men in Poland. Her medium-dark hair and thin figure accented her pretty features. Gazing at his family, a symbol of authority in the community, Cass wondered, *Why is Uncle Bernie angry? This isn't like him. I have never seen Uncle Bernie angry before.*

The three men, wearing imported Brooks Brothers tailored suits, had removed their suit coats and placed them on the backs of their chairs. They sat together at one end of the dining table, in their white shirts, ties, and suspenders. Between the men, but closest to Uncle Bernie, was a bottle of slivovitz, an expensive Eastern European plum brandy, popular among wealthy Jews. Sigmund and Bernard were wealthy businessmen, and Dr.

Szyncer was a dentist. Though he was the father of Cass's mother, everyone in the family called him Grandpa Szyncer or just Grandpa.

"I'm telling you, we need to get out of Europe. Germany is under the control of a madman who plans to conquer the world. He is building a huge army and is going to invade Poland. When he does, Poland's Army has no reasonable chance of defending itself," Uncle Bernie said.

"You're paranoid. Germany is not going to invade Poland. We're too powerful. We're safe here," Sigmund replied, waving his arm in the air for emphasis as his voice became louder. "Hitler would not dare invade Poland." Cass noticed that his handsome father, with his bright-blue eyes and brown hair, seemed less confident than usual. He was perspiring, which Cass rarely saw him do.

"You're wrong," Bernard said, also raising his voice. "The Nazi party has become very powerful and plans to impose its hateful ideology on all of Europe. Hitler has been heard to speak openly against the Jews, and he blames them for all of Europe's woes."

"Who is telling you these things?" Grandpa Szyncer asked.

"I hear it everywhere—at the university, at the temple, at the market. Everyone is saying it."

"I hear that too," Sigmund replied. "It's just fear talking. Hitler is not stupid enough to invade Poland. Besides, where would we go if we left?"

Bernard glanced at the open window. "Anywhere is better than Europe. We could go to the United States or Palestine."

"And give up everything? Our homes, our businesses, our community? Besides, how do you know we can even get into the United States or Palestine? They have limitations on the number of immigrants."

Bernard leaned forward in his chair, placing his arms on the table. "If we don't get out now, we will lose everything anyway, including…maybe even our lives. We could liquidate everything and take our funds with us."

"Maybe we should listen to him," Irena said. "I know that everything is very strange now. We have never seen times like this before. Even a fire sale would be better than losing everything."

"Are you buying this crazy talk too?" Sigmund asked. "I thought you would be the last person to succumb to Bernie's fantasies."

"It is not fantasy," Bernard said loudly, slamming his fist on the table. "If we don't get out, we are all going to be dead."

"Poppycock," Sigmund replied. "Hitler is not going to invade Poland, and no one is going to die."

Located in Mokotow, an affluent district of Warsaw, the Bieberstein mansion was a white Mediterranean structure on Pulawska Street with over thirty rooms. Surrounded by a tall wrought-iron fence in the front and an eight-foot concrete wall in the back, the large structure seemed like a fortress. A balcony overlooked the sunken gardens in the rear yard, and the window of the dining room opened out upon the balcony. The garden, filled with bright red, pink, blue, and purple flowers, provided a colorful fantasy for Cass whenever he looked out. One of the few houses in Warsaw with indoor plumbing, central heating, and electricity, the home was often visited by the singer Jan Kiepura and other famous musicians, who performed for the Biebersteins and their guests.

The Bieberstein family had two nannies, one for Cass and one for his older brother, Thaddeus; three maids; a chauffeur; a gardener; and a wine keeper who lived in an area called the wine cellar. Cass and Thaddeus called the wine keeper Baba Yaga because they had never met him but had seen him from a distance in the cellar, and they were afraid of his dark and foreboding appearance. In addition to the home in Mokotow, the Biebersteins owned a summerhouse in a little town called Sopot on the Baltic Sea, a winter house in the Carpathian Mountains, and two other homes in the city, in addition to several apartment buildings.

Casimir Bieberstein was born in Warsaw, Poland, on March 16, 1931. Some say he was born to be a Resistance fighter in the Warsaw Ghetto. Others say he was simply a tragedy of the times, reacting in the only possible way to the evil that was thrust on his doorstep. He was the son of a wealthy publisher and maker of fine china who employed his adult family members as managers in his businesses. From his earliest memories of childhood, Cass was a happy boy. He knew that his father was very wealthy and powerful in Poland. Once, when his father was awakened in the middle of the night by the sound of the trolley that ran past the mansion, he ordered that the trolley be rerouted to a line several blocks away, an order with which the city officials eagerly complied. Proud of his father and his influence, Cass had no doubt of his security in his place of affluence in society—that is, until the day he learned what it means to be a targeted minority in a world filled with hate.

Often described as adorable by his mother's friends, Cass, with his dark hair and blue eyes, appeared average in height and weight for a boy of six years. He had come to expect deferential treatment from his father's employees and found it unsurprising when shown respect by others as well. Already understanding that this deference was a result of his family's prominent position in society, he viewed it, quite simply, as the proper order of things. Yet, firmly disciplined by his father, he showed no signs of becoming a spoiled child. Popular among the other children, he knew a good life. He enjoyed his studies, and he exercised regularly in the gym his father had built in the basement of the mansion. Honesty was a virtue of particular importance to his father—one that Cass learned was narrowly interpreted if he ever embellished a story.

1937 was a troubled time in Europe. Clouds of despair hung from every turret and roofline. Sadness filled the eyes of the inhabitants of these once-proud people. The Polish-Lithuanian Commonwealth, established in 1569, had enjoyed prosperity until fierce fighting destroyed its sovereignty in 1795. The Second Polish Republic was established in 1918, at the conclusion of the First World War. For the first time in a century, the city of Warsaw had displayed a genuine hope for the future, a hope that was soon smothered in fear and despair. Rising from the rubble of the First World War, Poland stumbled, shocked and dazed, toward the hopelessness and tyranny of the Third Reich. Such a climate creates dependency, and dependency is the tool of Moloch, the ancient child-sacrificing Ammonite god, who appears in many forms to persecute the Jews as he deems necessary to achieve his objective at any given time. In this instance, his name was Adolf Hitler. At least, that's what Cass learned in *yeshiva*.

Almost two decades had passed since the conclusion of World War I, then simply called the Great War. The Treaty of Versailles promised peace, but fear gripped the soul of Europe. The war had shattered the tranquility that once filled the nations, and the air was still clouded with a sense of impending doom. The world had learned that a military conflict could reach international proportions and that a second world war was possible. Immediately to the west of Poland, Hitler had established a tyrannical regime and was amassing a huge army. Although he had been elected by popular vote, he soon placed a stranglehold on the people of Germany, and his rhetoric included plans for world domination. Dissenters were imprisoned or executed. This concerned some inhabitants of Poland. Others felt that he would not dare invade the neighbor immediately to the east. This was the topic of discussion in the Bieberstein home on this fateful day in August, right before Shabbat.

The argument between Sigmund, Bernard, and Dr. Szyncer continued until late in the afternoon, with Bernard becoming more frustrated as they talked. Finally, he stood to his feet, pulled his coat off the back of his chair, and walked briskly from the room. "I came to tell you that I am leaving Poland. I am getting out while I can. You can come with me, or you can stay here. If you are smart, you will come with me," he shouted as he walked down the hall toward the front door of the Bieberstein home.

Bernard left that night, and they did not see him again for many years. Later they received letters from him saying that he had arrived in the United States and that they should join him. Cass missed Uncle Bernie, who always had a candy treat for Cass and Thaddeus. Bernie never seemed to become upset about anything, at least not until this day of the argument between Bernie, Sigmund, and Dr. Szyncer.

As fall approached, Cass registered at the small yeshiva where his brother, Thaddeus, also attended. The yeshiva operated almost exclusively on donations from Sigmund Bieberstein, and it was one of a few yeshivas where both girls and boys were allowed to attend, a requirement imposed by Sigmund. Thaddeus was six years older than Cass and usually associated with older children.

The chauffeur, named Lech Wagner, was married to a woman named Patrycja who helped with cleaning in the house. They had a daughter slightly younger than Cass, named Zofia. She also attended the yeshiva, even though she was not a Jew, and she was permitted to ride to school with the Bieberstein children in their chauffeured automobile that her father drove. She would sit next to Cass in the back seat, and they would talk all the way to and from school. The Wagners lived in the servants' quarters in the Bieberstein mansion.

One morning, as they rode to school, Cass looked at Zofia. *She is so pretty*, he thought. He noticed her blond hair and her light-blue eyes. *She is my best friend.*

Thaddeus asked, "Why are you staring at Zofia, Cass? If you think she is so pretty, why don't you kiss her?"

Cass looked out the window. Zofia giggled. "I wasn't staring at her," Cass said in an effort to overcome his embarrassment.

Zofia leaned over and whispered, "I know you weren't staring at me, but even if you were, it's okay." Thaddeus, who overheard her comment, chuckled softly to himself and gently tapped Cass on the back of the head, causing his yarmulke to fall forward. He whispered, "Go for it, Shlomo," as he readjusted Cass's yarmulke. Cass did not know what he meant.

Cass really liked Zofia, and maybe she was even his girlfriend, but he knew such affection was not permissible among children in Orthodox Judaism, particularly since Zofia was not a Jew. Cass had often heard his family talk about Orthodox Judaism—they said that it was better than modern Judaism but more difficult to observe. Dr. Szyncer always studied the Shulchan Aruch in Hebrew before Shabbat, but Sigmund seemed impressed by the teachings of Rabbi Abraham Geiger, termed Reform Judaism. Orthodox Judaism strictly follows the 613 laws given to the Israelites by Moses; whereas, Reform Judaism teaches that adherents are free to observe only the laws that increase their relationship with God. Dr. Szyncer called the followers of Reform Judaism "porkers," which always caused Sigmund to laugh and to call Dr. Szyncer "Grandpa Moshe." While the beliefs were deep, the joking was fun, and there was no ill will between the men. Cass did not really have an opinion about Orthodox or Reform Judaism, though he loved the traditions. He was not old enough to form an opinion, but he knew he liked Zofia, and he did not believe Hashem would oppose such pleasant emotions that made him feel so happy inside.

One weekend Zofia's parents were planning to be away for a holiday, and Irena invited them to let Zofia stay with the Biebersteins until they returned the following Monday. Cass was so excited he could barely contain himself during the ride home from school on Friday afternoon. The children rode in a 1935 Chevrolet Mercury, considered a luxury automobile in Poland, where most of the wealthy families drove the less desirable Mercedes-Benz. After all, the Mercedes-Benz was common in Europe but a General Motors vehicle was from America, where the world's wealthiest people lived. The Chevrolet was far more expensive than the Mercedes, due to import costs, but Sigmund always said it was well worth the investment. The car pulled into the driveway of the Bieberstein home. Though taught to wait for the chauffeur to open the car doors, Cass and

Zofia jumped from the vehicle and ran inside the house before Lech had turned off the ignition.

Zofia and Cass ran upstairs and began moving Zofia's clothing from her room in the servants' quarters and into Cass's room and putting her clothes in the chest of drawers. Adelajda walked by and asked, "What's going on in here?"

"Didn't Mama tell you? Zofia is going to stay here with us while her parents are on a holiday," replied Cass with a smile beaming on his face.

Adelajda laughed. "Maybe she is staying with us, but she isn't sleeping in here."

"Why not?" asked Cass. "My cousin Michael always sleeps in here when he stays the weekend."

"That's different. Michael is a boy," replied Adelajda. She began carrying Zofia's clothes back to Zofia's room.

Cass and Zofia looked at each other with disappointment. "I don't understand," Cass said.

"Someday you will. For now, all you need to know is that boys and girls don't sleep in the same room unless they are married."

Cass could hear his mother in the hallway trying to hide her giggle. "Well, okay. But it would be a lot more fun if Zofia slept in here," he said.

"No doubt," replied Adelajda with a laugh, "but it isn't going to happen this weekend. Follow me, Zofia." She carried Zofia's clothes down the hall to her room.

That night Irena let Zofia light a Shabbat candle. Zofia said a blessing. Because she was a child, and unmarried, she was only permitted to light one candle. Cass watched with fascination as Zofia covered her head with her scarf then drew the warmth of the flame toward herself.

Later Cass asked, "Where did you learn to light the Shabbat candle?"

"Your mama showed me. She always lets me light one in my room on Shabbat."

"Don't your parents care?" asked Cass. "You're Christian."

"No, they don't care. Sometimes Mama lights it with us."

"I didn't know that," replied Cass. "So that's why you disappear every Friday evening at the same time Mama disappears."

Zofia laughed. "Yes."

Cass and Zofia stayed up as late as they could, joking and laughing until they became sleepy. Finally Adelajda said, "Okay, kids, it's time for bed. You can play again in the morning."

Cass and Zofia picked up the toys and placed them in the toy box then went to bed. The following morning Cass awakened to a light tapping sound on his door. He quickly put on his pants and opened the door to be greeted by Zofia, smiling from ear to ear. "Cass, there's a big bird in the garden."

Cass and Zofia ran to the steps at the end of the hall then down the steps and out onto the balcony that overlooked the sunken gardens. There in the garden was a wild peacock, strutting about as if it were the proprietor of the premises. He spread his tail and exhibited a beautiful array of multicolored feathers.

"She's so pretty," said Zofia.

"That's a he," said Cass. "I wonder where he came from and how he got in."

"How do you know that is a boy?" asked Zofia.

"Because boys are the ones with all the pretty colors."

Cass and Zofia ran down the steps into the garden toward the beautiful bird, which seemed unconcerned with the approaching children. Suddenly, the back door swung open and Rex, Cass's German shepherd, burst into the yard to investigate the commotion.

"Rex," called Cass in an effort to calm the dog, to no avail.

The barking dog was too much even for the brave peacock, which half ran and half flew up the steps to the balcony, over the wall, and onto the street beside the mansion.

"Rex," Cass said loudly, "you scared away the bird." Rex ignored Cass's stern voice as he ran up the steps to the balcony, sniffing the deck where the peacock had been.

"I think Rex doesn't like birds," Zofia said with a laugh.

"I think maybe so," Cass said. "Let's go inside and get something to eat."

After breakfast the children decided to explore the mansion. Sigmund and Irena said they had to go out for a while, and Adelajda was busy reviewing Cass's homework, which he had to turn in on Monday.

"I want to show you something in the attic," Cass said. "We aren't allowed up there, so we have to be very quiet. It's my favorite room."

"If we aren't allowed up there, then we better not go up," Zofia said.

"No, it's okay. No one will know."

Cass opened the door to the attic, and Zofia followed him up the wooden steps. At the top of the steps was a huge room that spanned from one end of the house to the other. The uncarpeted hardwood floor sounded loudly underfoot as the children walked toward the other side of the room, which had windows on both ends providing sufficient light to see. There was no furniture, and it was obvious that the area was used primarily for storage. They walked across the floor and up to a wall. Then they stopped in front of it. Zofia looked at Cass, who smiled and pushed on the wall, which opened like a door, leading into a long hallway. Cass put a box in front of the opened wall to keep it from closing, which would have caused the hall to become too dark to see.

"What is this?" Zofia asked.

"It's a secret passageway."

They entered the hallway, and after walking for about forty feet, they came to another wall. Cass pushed on that wall, and it swung open into another room almost as large as the first one.

"Wow," Zofia said.

Unlike the first, this room was fully furnished and carpeted with many chairs, couches, and several beds. A large candle chandelier hung from the center of the room, and candelabras lined the walls. At one end was a beautiful mahogany dining table. Cass took ahold of Zofia's hand. "This is the hiding room. This is where we will hide if Poland is ever attacked by the Nazis. If that ever happens, you can come up here with us, and we will hide up here. You can't ever tell anyone about this room."

"I won't tell anyone," Zofia promised.

Cass and Zofia stayed in the hiding room for about twenty minutes. From a window at one end, they could see all the way up the street in both directions. Soon they saw Irena and Sigmund walking toward the house. "We better go back down now," Cass said.

The children ran through the secret passageway to the first room, across that room, and down the steps. They slipped out of the attic and quietly shut the door behind them. They trotted down the steps to the first floor and sat on the couch in the parlor as if they had been there all morning. Sigmund and Irena came into the house through the front door. "Hello, children," Irena said. "Where's Thaddeus?"

"I think he's out on the balcony," Cass replied.

Irena and Sigmund walked through the house toward the balcony. Cass and Zofia followed.

Irena asked, "Thaddeus, are you out here?" She saw Thaddeus standing next to the banister, looking out toward the garden.

He did not respond. He looked upset.

Sigmund asked, "Is everything okay, Thad?"

Irena took him by the shoulders and turned him around, though he tried to avoid her gaze. "Yes," he said looking downward. Cass could see that his face had been bloodied and his eye was swollen. "What happened to you?" Irena asked.

"Nothing, Mama," he replied.

Cass asked, "What's wrong, Mama?" She was troubled. Her jaw was tight and her eyes worried.

"Nothing, Cass, go back inside." Cass followed his mother's instruction and went back into the house. Zofia followed.

"Who did this to you?" Irena asked Thaddeus.

"Nothing happened. I just got skinned playing soccer. Why do you think something is wrong?"

"Thad, Tzipi told us what happened. Her son, Zeb, saw it. She said those boys beat you and called you 'filthy Jew' and other names. Did that happen? Do you know who they were? We'll report them to the police."

Finally Thaddeus said, "Yes, it happened. It is getting worse every day. Everyone picks on Jewish kids, but we can't report them. That would only make it worse. One of the boys in my class reported it to the police, and now the boys beat him up every day."

Irena took Thaddeus in her arms. "You need to tell us when something like this happens. There is no benefit in bearing this pain alone."

Sigmund said, "Thad, tell me who did this. I can make sure it doesn't happen again."

Thaddeus shook his head. "No, it's all right."

Cass and Zofia overheard the conversation but did not understand what was being discussed.

"What are they talking about?" Zofia asked.

"I don't know. Mama is sad."

Cass and Zofia soon forgot about Thaddeus's troubles and began playing again. They enjoyed their time together, and both thought the weekend went too fast. They were close friends. They rode to school together every day and saw each other all day long at school because they were in the same class. They shared everything, including their lunches and homework. In the fall of 1937, they began to notice something they had not seen before. People would walk or drive past the yeshiva and shout obscenities at the students or call them "dirty Jews." Sometimes they would throw objects at them, and sometimes they would threaten them. On an afternoon in early December 1937, Cass and Zofia were standing at the edge of the playground. Cass was six, and Zofia was five. They were talking about the holidays.

Suddenly, Cass was struck in the face by a cold object. At first he did not know what had happened, but then he saw some boys standing on the other side of the street, laughing and pointing at him. One of the boys had hit him in the face with a snowball. The right side of his face burned like fire. Cass was embarrassed and did not know what to do. He picked up a handful of snow and made a snowball, which he threw at the boys across the street. The boys began throwing snowballs back at Cass. Soon other boys at the yeshiva saw what was happening, and they came over to join Cass in throwing snowballs at the boys across the street. Due to the larger number of boys in the yeshiva, they quickly demonstrated greater throwing power, and the boys across the street ran away. This day marked the beginning of tension between the Jewish children in the yeshiva and the other children in the neighborhood. It was a tension that would grow worse every day.

A few days after the snowball incident, Thaddeus, Cass and Zofia arrived at school. As Lech pulled the car up to the curb, Thaddeus said, "Look at that." He sounded disturbed.

Cass and Zofia looked out of the car window and saw a giant swastika painted on the building above the Star of David that was engraved above the front door of the school. "Why did somebody paint that on the school?" Cass asked.

"That's the symbol of the Nazis," Thaddeus said.

"What is a Nazi?" Zofia asked.

"A Nazi is someone who hates Jews," Thaddeus replied.

"Why do they hate Jews?" Cass asked.

"Some people feel more powerful if they have someone they can hate," Thaddeus said.

Cass had a sickening feeling in the pit of his stomach, but he could not understand why. He looked at the front of the school, shocked at the vandalism. The school was a beautiful three-story synagogue that had been purchased by Sigmund to serve as a Jewish school. On each side of the tall doors were pillars that supported a second-story balcony. Above the balcony, engraved into the stone, was the Star of David. The swastika was painted on the wall above the Star of David.

"Somebody had to put a ladder on the second-story balcony to reach that high to paint the wall," said Thaddeus. "That means they must have broken into the school to come out on the balcony."

Lech, the chauffeur, said nothing. He got out and opened the door for the children, who climbed out of the car, walked up to the school building, and entered the door beneath the star that was under the painted swastika.

CHAPTER

2

C HANUKAH CELEBRATIONS BEGAN on November 29 in 1937, with the Holiday of Lights. Grandpa always encouraged everyone in the family to have their own Chanukah menorah, which each of them would light each night of Chanukah. The candle lighting always took place in the dining room with the main menorah sitting on the Shabbat table. Each of the other menorahs sat on the dining room table, one in front of each member of the family. The main lights were turned off so the only lights in the room were the candles of the menorahs. On the first night of Chanukah one person would light the candle on the main menorah while the others lit a candle on their own menorahs. The flickering flames soothed the atmosphere, and watching the figures that the flames cast on the walls, Cass imagined that he saw ancient Israelites dancing sacred dances before the God of Abraham.

On the second night of Chanukah, another family member would light the second candle of the main menorah, while everyone else lit the second candle on their own menorah, and so on each night thereafter. Cass loved the beautiful flickering lights that cast dancing shadows on the walls around the room. As the candle lighting progressed through Chanukah, with more candles being lit each night, the brilliance of the lights became more pronounced. By the last night the menorah candles created a festival of lights that dazzled even the most cynical of the faith.

One day Cass asked Grandpa why each person should have his own menorah. Grandpa said that if a family uses only one menorah, when the children grow older and move away, they will not keep up the tradition of lighting the menorah; but if everyone has their own, then they will take their menorah with them and will always light it, even when they are alone. The largest menorah was in the living room windowsill opposite the mezuzah on the doorpost near the window. The mezuzah is a small scroll mounted on a doorpost that contains the Shema, a prayer written in Hebrew as required in the Torah in Deuteronomy 6:9. "And you shall write them on the doorposts of your house and on your gates." Grandpa had told Cass that this is proper because when the family gathers around the menorah, they will be surrounded by the two mitzvot of mezuzah and Chanukah. Cass did not understand what that meant.

The Bieber steins loved Chanukah. It was a time of celebration and gift giving. They were a unique Jewish family in that they also had the Christmas tree for the Christian staff. Around the second week of December, Sigmund would take Thaddeus and Lech into the forest to find a tree. The tree had to be small enough that they could dig it out of the ground by the roots. The Biebersteins would not allow a cut tree to be brought into the house because the tree becomes a cut idol of wood, as described in Jeremiah 10:2–4. However, a living tree is not the same as a cut tree, and therefore, it does not become an idol.

The Christmas tree would be placed in a pot on the landing to the second story. The landing was nearly two hundred square feet and was the place where the employees would gather each day to receive their instructions. Because the landing was so large, it was the perfect place for the tree. The tree was placed in the center of the landing nearest the wall. The beautiful oak woodwork of the landing floor seemed to glow with the multicolored lights of the tree shining down on it. "That's a very nice tree," Adelajda said as Sigmund and Thaddeus carried a tree up the steps to the landing late one Sunday afternoon.

"Thad found it," Sigmund replied. "He has a talent for selecting the right tree. We looked for over a half hour."

Sigmund and Thaddeus set the potted tree down on a piece of cloth on the floor of the landing. The tree stood nearly twelve feet tall. The household staff all came to see the tree with its thick green branches. The smell of pine permeated the house. Lech trimmed several of the branches off the bottom. "I love the smell of pine," he said.

"I do too," Adelajda replied as she placed a large box of ornaments on the floor next to the tree. She pulled a string of lights from the box and gave one end to Lech. "Can you reach the top and then wind the string of lights around the tree?"

"Of course." Lech retrieved a wooden stepladder from a closet at the top of the stairs and placed it next to the tree. He climbed on the ladder and placed the end of the string of lights at the top of the tree then wound it downward. After the lights had been placed on the tree and tested, they began to place the ornaments. The maids each had an ornament that had been given to them years ago by Irena. They were placed on the tree first. Eventually, all of the ornaments had been placed on the tree. The lights were dimmed in the house, and the tree lights were plugged in. Cass and Zofia sat on the steps, looking down at the tree with the colorful lights that glowed brightly.

Zofia whispered to Cass, "The lights are very pretty. I like the way they sparkle."

"I'm glad we have the staff living with us. We get to have Chanukah, and then we get to have Christmas too."

"Me too. I'm glad I got to be with you this Chanukah, Cass."

"I know. Me too," replied Cass.

"What are we going to do with the tree after Christmas?"

"We plant it in the yard."

"Oh, I remember we did that last year," said Zofia.

Cass nodded.

After admiring the decorated tree for several minutes, the staff went about their work. Cass and Zofia continued to sit on the steps, talking and looking at the tree for over an hour. Then they climbed to the top of the steps and lay down on the carpeted floor. A short time later, Sigmund, Irena, and Thaddeus came upstairs to go to bed.

"Cass, you and Zofia can stay up for a little while and look at the tree, but not too late," said Irena as she walked past the children.

"We won't," replied Cass. Soon the house was quiet. The servants had gone to bed, as had the Bieberstein family. Cass and Zofia fell asleep on the floor at the top of the steps. Cass found himself awakening to the chimes of the grandfather clock as it struck twelve. He leaned over and shook Zofia gently. He whispered, "Zofia, it's twelve o'clock."

Zofia whispered, "Twelve o'clock, I've never been up this late before."

"I haven't either. It is kind of exciting. Let's do something fun."

Zofia sat up. Cass could see her silhouette from the lights on the tree. "You look like an angel," he said.

Zofia laughed. "You don't look like an angel; you look like a devil. You look nice, though. What do you want to do?"

"I don't know," Cass replied. "Something we're not supposed to do."

Cass and Zofia both put their hands over their mouths to muffle their laughter. Cass stood up and took Zofia's hand in his. "C'mon."

Zofia stood up and followed Cass down the stairs. "Where are we going?"

"You'll see," replied Cass as he led her down the steps through the living room and into the kitchen. He then opened the basement door, turned on the light, and led her down the stairs, closing the door behind them.

The basement of the Bieberstein mansion was nicely finished and had over a dozen rooms. They walked through the game room, with the shuffleboard court and ping-pong tables, then through the entertainment room, with the indoor barbecue and the spotlights for stage performances. At last Cass opened a door and led Zofia into a room filled with exercise equipment consisting of weights, a pull-up bar, and a stationary bike. "What is all of this?" she asked.

"This is our exercise room."

"I have never seen this before."

Cass walked over to the free weights. He picked up a barbell with twenty pounds of weight and began doing curls. After doing a set of twelve, he set the barbell on the floor and asked, "Do you want to try?"

Zofia walked over to the barbell. "Okay." She bent down to pick it up but was only able to move it a few inches off the floor.

Cass laughed. "I come in here all the time to exercise."

"You better be careful, or you are going to be like one of those muscle-bound guys." Zofia filled her cheeks with air then held her arms out as if she was trying to look bulky. Waddling, she walked toward Cass. Suddenly he tackled her onto the wrestling mat on which they were standing. Holding her down, he began tickling her.

Zofia laughed uncontrollably as she tried to tickle Cass, but he was on top of her, making it difficult. "No, no," she said, laughing until her eyes watered. Finally Cass stopped, and she sat up, looking at him as if she was angry.

"What, you don't like being tickled?" he asked.

"You touched me without my permission."

"I thought you were having fun," Cass replied.

Suddenly Zofia jumped on Cass and laughed. "I was." She began tickling him as she tried to hold him down on the floor. He quickly overpowered her and rolled over on top of her, tickling her again. After several minutes of wrestling and tickling each other, they stopped and sat on the mat. Zofia looked at Cass.

"Why are you looking at me like that? What are you thinking?"

"Hmm," she replied as she shook her head.

"What does *hmm* mean?"

Zofia laughed again. "I can't tell you."

"Why can't you tell me?"

"It's a secret."

"What's the secret?" Cass persisted.

"I can't tell you because then it wouldn't be a secret."

"You can give me a hint," Cass replied.

"No, I can't. Okay, I will give you a hint. I don't like you anymore."

Cass looked stunned. "You don't like me anymore?"

"Nope," Zofia replied. "I feel something else."

"You hate me?" Cass laughed.

"No, what is the opposite of hate?"

Cass blushed. "Uh, I don't know. What is it?"

"You do too. You know exactly what I mean."

"Well, if it means what I think, then I opposite of hate you too."

Cass and Zofia looked at each other for a moment.

Zofia asked, "Do you want to kiss me? You can kiss me here if you want to." She touched her right cheek with her index finger.

"We better go upstairs before we get in trouble."

"Get in trouble? How could we get in trouble? Besides, you said you wanted to do something we aren't supposed to do."

"Yeah, but I didn't mean that." Cass laughed nervously. "We better go to bed now."

"Okay," Zofia replied with a pout. "I hope you don't act like this when we are twenty."

Cass laughed. "We're a long way from twenty. I'm six, and you're only five. Does it seem really hot in here to you?"

Zofia laughed. "No, Cass, it isn't hot in here. We are in the basement, in December. It's cold in here."

"It's heated."

"But it's still cold."

Cass and Zofia were startled when someone opened the door to the exercise room. Thaddeus stuck his head through the door. "What on earth are you two doing in here?"

"We were exercising," Cass replied.

Thaddeus entered the room. "Exercising? At one o'clock in the morning?"

"We fell asleep at the top of the steps looking at the Christmas tree lights and woke up when the grandfather clock struck twelve," Cass replied.

"Well, you better go to bed now, or Adelajda is going to make it difficult for you to sit tomorrow," Thaddeus said with a laugh.

"What are you doing?" Cass asked.

Thaddeus replied, "I came down to exercise."

"Why are you going to exercise at this time of night?"

"I always do. It's the perfect time when everyone is asleep. I only sleep about four hours a night. I have always been like that."

Cass and Zofia got up to leave the room.

"You better be quiet when you go upstairs. You don't want Mama to know you were up this late."

"Okay," Cass said.

Cass and Zofia went upstairs. As they prepared to go to their rooms, Zofia said, "I don't like you anymore."

Cass laughed. "I don't like you anymore either."

Zofia kissed Cass on the cheek. Then she giggled, ran into her room, and quietly closed the door behind her.

Christmas morning was an exciting time in the Bieberstein mansion. Although the Biebersteins did not celebrate Christmas, the household staff always bought Christmas presents for Cass and Thaddeus. The Biebersteins always bought Christmas gifts for the household staff but not for the Bieberstein family members. They exchanged their own gifts as part of the Chanukah celebration.

Cass woke up early on Christmas morning, got out of bed, dressed, and knocked on Zofia's door. A few moments later, Zofia opened the door, still in her pajamas. "Let's go look at the presents," Cass said.

"Okay, in just a moment," Zofia replied as she closed the door. She emerged a short time later in a new dress. "I'm ready," she said. "Let's go down and watch the celebration." She took Cass's hand, and they walked down to the landing.

They looked at the tree, covered with lights and ornaments. Under the tree were dozens of wrapped gifts that had not been there the night before. Cass and Zofia walked up to the tree and got down on their knees to look at the presents. Zofia said, "Hey, Cass, this one has your name on it."

"Let me see." Cass picked up the large box and shook it. "I wonder what this is. Look, here is one for you. It says it is from Saint Nick." Cass and Zofia both laughed.

"All righty, then," Zofia said. "Santa came to visit me last night."

Suddenly, the quiet was interrupted by loud knock at the door. Cass looked at Zofia. "Who would that be so early in the morning on Christmas?" Zofia shrugged.

Cass and Zofia ran downstairs and to the front door. They opened the door, but no one was there. On the porch was a box with the name Bieberstein written on it.

Cass picked it up. "Somebody left us a gift. It must be from a Christian since today is Christmas." They went back into the house and closed the door behind them as Sigmund came down the steps.

"What's that?" Sigmund looked at the box in Cass's hands.

"Someone left us a gift," Cass replied.

"Oh, that was really nice. I wonder who did that," Sigmund said as he took the gift from Cass. "We'll put it under the tree and open it with the rest of the gifts." He carried the gift upstairs and placed it under the tree on the landing.

Gerek, the gardener, walked into the living room with Lech, followed by the maids. "Merry Christmas everyone," he shouted.

"Merry Christmas," Cass called. Sigmund laughed as Irena and Thaddeus came down the steps followed by Adelajda.

Irena asked, "Who knocked on the door?"

Cass replied, "Someone left a gift on the porch but they didn't stay, so I don't know who it was."

"The package just says 'Bieberstein,' so Cass, why don't you go ahead and open it?" Sigmund said as he took the gift from under the tree and gave it to Cass. Cass opened the cardboard box and found a wooden box inside. He threw the cardboard box and wrapping on the floor and opened the wooden box. He looked inside but didn't say anything.

"What is it?" Irena asked. Cass did not respond.

Zofia and Thaddeus walked up and looked inside the box. Zofia screamed and ran down the steps from the landing.

"What is it?" Sigmund reached for the box.

Cass replied, "It's a dead rat wearing a yarmulke and a yellow star."

Sigmund took the box from Cass and closed it as others walked up to see.

"Why would someone leave something like that at our door?" Irena asked.

Sigmund shook his head. "There are some very sick people in the world. I will be right back." He took the box out into the back garden and threw it in a trash container on the back deck. When he returned everyone was sitting around the tree. No one was talking. Cass wanted to break the silence but could not think of anything to say. Finally he asked, "I don't understand what that means. Why was there a dead rat in the box? Why did it have a yarmulke, and why was it wearing a gold star?"

No one answered.

The family and the staff opened the presents, but few words were spoken that morning. Zofia asked Cass why someone would do that. Cass said he didn't know. The adults didn't want to talk about it. Cass noticed that Lech had become very quiet. *This must bother Lech*, Cass thought. Christmas this year was different from anything Cass had ever experienced before.

CHAPTER

3

O N A SNOWY January day in 1938, five-year-old Zofia and six-year-old Cass were sitting on the soft burgundy Victorian couch in the parlor of the Bieberstein mansion. They were not permitted to sit in the living room, so the parlor had become their favorite place of refuge and conversation. Zofia leaned back against the right arm of the couch facing Cass. Her legs rested on the seat cushions. Cass sat at the opposite end, leaning back against the left arm of the couch, facing Zofia. His legs were also resting on the seat cushions so that his stocking feet were barely touching Zofia's stocking feet. He felt it slightly exciting to touch her foot with his. Sigmund, Irena, and Thaddeus were seated in the dining room, listening to a woman singing on the radio. Cass chuckled. "Everybody says she's a great singer. She sings on the radio all the time." He leaned forward and whispered, "It just sounds like someone screaming to me."

Zofia nudged Cass's foot with her foot. "I think she is good. You just don't like opera."

"Well, maybe not," Cass replied. "Papa got a gramophone recording of a guy named Glenn Miller from a friend of his who works at RCA. Glenn Miller plays jazz music. The recording hasn't been released yet, but it's coming out this summer."

"What does released mean…and who is RCA?" asked Zofia.

"When someone makes a recording for gramophones and you can buy it in the stores, that is called 'released.' RCA is a company in America that makes recordings."

"So you like jazz?" Zofia asked.

"I love jazz. Did you know that the Nazis aren't allowed to listen to American jazz music? They are really missing out."

"I didn't know that. I wonder why they aren't." Zofia paused then looked at Cass. "What do you think is going to happen with the Nazis?"

"What do you mean?"

"Well, do you think they are going to invade Poland like some people say? I'm really scared." Zofia pulled her knees up to her chest and hugged them. "Your papa says the Nazis are really bad, and they're really mean to people."

Cass put his right arm on the back of the couch. "Well, I really don't know. Uncle Bernie said they're going to."

"What will your family do if that happens? Have you talked about it?"

"Uh-huh, we will go to the house in the mountains if we have time to get there. Then we will find a way to get out of the country and to America. Papa will go ahead of us and get things arranged, and then he will send for us. How about you?"

"We haven't talked about it. My papa says that he doesn't believe they will invade Poland. If they do, maybe I can come with you to America. Papa says the Nazis aren't as bad as everyone says."

Cass looked at Zofia with a puzzled expression. Then he said, "That would be wonderful if you came with us." The back of the couch was adjacent to the parlor window facing the front street. The heavy drapes were tied back revealing the front yard. Cass looked outside at the snow-covered ground and watched the snow falling gently. "I hope they don't invade. I would hate to leave, and I wouldn't want to be separated from you."

"Do you think we will always be friends?" Zofia asked.

"I hope so. We have known each other since we were tiny little children. I think we will always be friends. You are like a little sister to me."

Zofia laughed. "Sister? I don't want to be like a sister. I want to be something different."

"I didn't mean sister. I just meant we have always been together."

"Do you think we will be more than friends? Do you think someday I will be your girlfriend?"

Cass laughed. "Maybe you will. Maybe you already are. I really like you."

"I really like you too. I mean I don't like you anymore."

Cass laughed. He jumped off the couch and said, "Let's go outside and play in the snow. We can make snow angels."

"That sounds like fun."

Cass and Zofia bundled up in their winter coats and hats. They put on their boots and their mittens. Cass shouted, "Adelajda, Zofia and I are going outside to play in the snow."

Adelajda replied, "Okay, but don't stay out too long. It's going to be dark in about an hour. I don't want you out after dark."

Zofia and Cass ran out the front door and down the steps into the front yard. The ground was covered with fresh snow that was about one foot deep. There were no tracks anywhere. They fell on their backs in the snow, and each made a snow angel. Then they stood up to examine their work.

"Those are nice snow angels," Cass said.

Zofia replied excitedly, "They are. Let's make some in the neighbors' yards too."

"Okay, let's do that. Everyone will be excited to see the snow angels in their yard."

Cass and Zofia ran to the next-door neighbor's yard and made snow angels there. Then they went to the next house and made snow angels in that yard and so on until they had made snow angels in every yard on the street, for several blocks in each direction. Cass had forgotten about Adelajda's warning to come in before dark, and soon they were several blocks away. It was getting dark. The children were laughing hysterically. They were so engrossed in the task of making snow angels that they failed to notice three teenage boys who had stopped on the other side of street to watch them. They did not even notice when the boys crossed the street and walked up to them until one of them said, "Stupid Jew pigs. What are you making snow angels for? You Jews are all going to hell anyway."

Cass turned quickly and saw the teenage boys. Before Cass could even respond, one of them stepped forward and struck him in the face with his fist so hard that Cass fell to the ground and was rendered momentarily unconscious. The boy then grabbed Zofia, and another of the boys smashed snow into her face. She screamed, and the first one held her while another struck her in the face with his hand. They began shoving her back and forth between them. Then one of them tackled her and held her face in the snow. She began waving her arms and struggling frantically to get air. Cass regained consciousness barely enough to see what was happening. Dazed, he staggered to his feet and ran toward the boy who was holding Zofia's face in the snow. He kicked the boy in the head with all of the force he could muster and then jumped on him and shoved him off Zofia. As he struggled to overpower the much larger boy, Cass could hear someone yelling in the distance. He recognized the voice of Adelajda. "Hey, you leave those children alone. Stop it now."

Cass looked up to see Adelajda running toward them.

"Let's get out of here. She might recognize us," said one of the boys as they began running down the street away from Adelajda.

Adelajda ran up to Cass and Zofia. Zofia was crying, and Cass and Zofia were both bleeding. Adelajda helped Zofia to her feet. "What's going on?"

Cass replied, "I don't know. We were in the yard making snow angels when they started hitting us."

"Do you know who they are?"

"No, I don't think so. But they acted like they know you. One of them was afraid you would recognize him."

"I think I did recognize one of them," said Adelajda. "I think one of them was Rajmund Litynski. Why did you stay out so late? I got worried when it started to get dark, so I came looking for you. You know you aren't supposed to go this far from home."

"We were playing and didn't know how far we had gone," Cass said. Zofia continued to cry as they walked back home. When they arrived at the Bieberstein mansion they walked to the front door and took off their boots to avoid tracking snow on the floor. Adelajda led them to the bathroom so she could dress their wounds and clean them. While she was tending to Zofia's wounds, Sigmund came to see what was happening.

"What's going on?"

Adelajda continued washing the blood off Zofia's face. "The children were attacked by some neighborhood teenagers. There were three of them.

I think one of them was Rajmund Litynski. They ran away, so I couldn't see who they were for sure."

"Is he any relation to Josef Litynski?"

"Yes, Rajmund is his son."

"Cass, where were you? Why did they attack you? Did you say something to them?" asked Sigmund.

Zofia tried to answer in between sobs. "They…they…they came up behind us. We didn't even know they were there. One of them called us 'Jew pigs' and said we're going to hell. When we turned around to see who they were one of them hit Cass in the face with his fist." Zofia paused as she continued sobbing. "Then they jumped on me and pushed my face in the snow. I couldn't breathe. I thought I was going to die. Cass pushed him off me. Then Adelajda came, and they ran."

Adelajda said, "Actually, Cass was quite heroic. The boys were a lot older and twice his size. When I came up, I saw one of them on top of Zofia holding her face in the snow. I started yelling at them. I was running in snow so I couldn't get there very fast, but I saw Cass kick the one in the face who was holding Zofia down. It looked like his head was going to fly off. That was a really hard kick. Cass jumped on top of him. The other boys just stood there. I think they were afraid of Cass even though they were much older."

"Who is Josef Litynski?" Cass asked.

Irena and Thaddeus came to the bathroom to investigate. "Oh no," said Irena. "What happened?"

"The kids were attacked by some neighborhood boys. Adelajda thinks one of the attackers might have been Josef Litynski's son, Rajmund," Sigmund said.

Irena began cleaning Cass's bloody nose. "Are you going to talk to Josef?"

"I am going over with Cass as soon as we get his nose to stop bleeding."

"Who is Josef Litynski?" Cass asked a second time.

"He owns a restaurant over on Hipoteczna Street," replied Sigmund. "It's in the business district. We go there all the time for business lunches. He will be angry to learn what his son has done."

After Cass and Zofia were cleaned up, Sigmund and Cass drove over to the Litynski home to talk to Josef Litynski about the incident. They parked the car in front of the house and walked up to the door. When they stepped on the front porch Cass looked through the window, where he could see three boys in the living room. One of them had a bruise on the left side of his face. Cass immediately recognized him as the one who was holding Zofia's face in the snow.

"Those are the boys who attacked us," Cass told his father.

Sigmund rang the doorbell, and Mr. Litynski opened the door.

"Good evening, Sigmund," Mr. Litynski said. "What a pleasant surprise. How may I help you?"

"It seems we have a little problem. My son Cass and his friend Zofia were beaten up by three boys. A witness said that one of the boys was your son, Rajmund."

Still looking through the window, Cass saw the three boys trying to listen to the conversation. They abruptly stood to their feet and prepared to run out of the room.

"Are you sure it was Rajmund?" Mr. Litynski wore a disturbed expression on his face. "Rajmund," he shouted. "Get in here."

Rajmund and the other two boys came in and stood beside Mr. Litynski, who asked, "Are these the boys who fought with you, Cass?"

Cass looked at Rajmund and then the others. "Yes."

Mr. Litynski turned toward Rajmund and asked, "Is this true? Did you fight with Cass and his friend?"

"He started it," said Rajmund. "He kicked me in the face."

Mr. Litynski looked sternly at Rajmund and raised his voice. "What do you mean he kicked you in the face? How could he get his foot up that high? You are almost twice as tall as him. He just walked up and kicked you in the face for no reason? He attacked three of you?"

"We were just playing," one of the other boys said.

"What do you mean you were playing? Cass has a bloody nose and a bruise on his face, and Rajmund has a bruise on his face. It doesn't look like you were playing to me. Were you playing, Cass?"

Cass was concerned that the boys would retaliate if he incriminated them. He paused for a moment then decided to tell everything for Zofia's sake. "Zofia and I were making snow angels when Rajmund called us 'Jew pigs' and said we were going to hell. When I turned around to see who said that, he hit me in the face with his fist. It knocked me down, and when I looked up he was holding Zofia's face in the snow, so I kicked him to try to get him off her."

Mr. Litynski looked at Rajmund. "I am going to give you one chance to tell me the truth. If you tell me a story different from Cass, I am going to go to every door on the street to find witnesses. If they tell me the same story as Cass, I am going to beat you with a belt. Now, I suggest that you think long and hard before you answer my next question. Is Cass telling the truth about how this happened?"

Rajmund was silent for a moment; then he looked down. "Yes, he is telling the truth."

Mr. Litynski slapped Rajmund in the head forcefully. "You apologize to Cass. All of you."

Each of the boys mumbled an apology, though Cass doubted their sincerity. He wondered if they would retaliate later when they found Cass alone or with Zofia. "Okay," Cass mumbled.

"We'll talk about this later," Mr. Litynski said to the three boys. "Rajmund, you go to your room. You other boys go home and tell your parents what you did. I will ask them later if you told them, and if I find out you didn't, you are really going to be in trouble. Civilized people don't behave this way."

Rajmund went upstairs, and the other boys put on their coats and left. No one said anything further until they were gone. Finally Mr. Litynski said, "I am so sorry, Sigmund. I had no idea my son would ever behave that way. I hope this doesn't hurt our friendship. You know how much I appreciate that you bring your business associates to my restaurant."

Sigmund nodded.

Then Josef said, "Come on in for a minute. I would like to ask your opinion about something, Sigmund. I just made some hot chocolate. I know Cass would like some, wouldn't you, Cass?" Mr. Litynski smiled at Cass.

Hot chocolate sounded good to Cass. "Yes, please."

"Thank you," Sigmund said. "That would actually be very nice."

Cass and Sigmund entered the home. The Litynski home was nice, though it was not a mansion like Cass was accustomed to. They walked through a hallway leading to the kitchen. Cass noticed a large golden retriever lying on a rug in the dining room as they walked by. They went into the kitchen, and Josef invited them to sit at the table. Josef served hot chocolate to Cass and gave Sigmund a glass of whiskey. Then he sat at the table with Cass and Sigmund.

"So what did you want to ask me about?"

"I wonder if you know what is going on with the Nazis. I never believed my son would do something like he did today. He is getting ideas at school. I have been thinking about pulling him out of that school, but he is already thirteen. I don't know that it would do any good at this point."

"What is he hearing at school?"

"Apparently, all of the students are talking about Jews and saying that they are the cause of all of our problems. They are saying that our country would be much better off if there weren't any Jews here. Some of the teachers are saying the same thing. It is difficult for me to convince Rajmund that those teachings are wrong when all of his friends and even his teachers are saying they are true. I don't know what to do, Sigmund."

Sigmund's gaze was focused on the table as he nodded his head. "Some of my non-Jewish employees have been telling me the same things you are saying. They are telling me what their children are hearing at school and among their friends. Some are saying that they hope Germany invades Poland so the Jews will be forced to leave."

"I have a very big favor to ask of you, Sigmund."

"Okay," Sigmund replied. "What is it?"

"I don't want Rajmund to grow up hating Jews or anyone else. I thought that maybe he and your older son Thaddeus could get to know each other. Rajmund will learn that what he is hearing about Jews just isn't true. I have known you for a long time, and Thaddeus has come with you to my restaurant on many occasions. He is a polite young man."

Sigmund nodded. "I might be able to help you with that. Is Rajmund going to be working at the restaurant any time soon?"

"Yes, he will be there Monday evening."

"Why don't I bring Thaddeus by for dinner that evening? You and Rajmund can join us when we get there. The boys can get to know each other, and if they get along, we can arrange for them to get together to do other things."

Mr. Litynski said, "I think that's a nice idea. We'll plan to have dinner with you and Thaddeus that evening."

As Sigmund and Cass drove back to the Bieberstein mansion, Cass asked, "Why are you and Thaddeus going to have dinner with Mr. Litynski and Rajmund?"

Sigmund replied, "Rajmund is confused about some issues. He believes that Jews are bad people. Mr. Litynski thinks that if he gets to know a Jew his own age, he will learn that Jews aren't bad."

"But he beat us up a little while ago. I don't understand."

As they pulled the car into the driveway next to the mansion and under the porte cochere, Sigmund said, "For Mr. Litynski this is very important. He believes he is losing his son to the hatred of Nazi ideology. He is asking us to try to help him. It's the right thing for us to do."

"But what if he does something mean to Thaddeus?" Cass asked.

"Thaddeus can take care of himself." Sigmund laughed. "Besides, if he gets out of line, we'll have you go whip him like you did earlier today."

Cass joined in the laughter. "You always know best, Papa."

The following Monday evening, Sigmund and Thaddeus were driven by Lech to the restaurant owned by Josef Litynski, called Litynski's. They entered the restaurant and were seated at a table in a private loft near the rear of the dining room. The room was very large, with fifty tables. It was busy that evening. A short time later Mr. Litynski and Rajmund came into the dining area and joined Sigmund and Thaddeus at the table.

"I'm glad you could come this evening," said Mr. Litynski as he sat at the table. "Thaddeus, this is my son, Rajmund. I don't believe the two of you have ever met."

"No, we haven't, but I have seen him here at the restaurant. It is nice to meet you, Rajmund," Thaddeus said as he reached out his hand to Rajmund. Rajmund shook his hand slowly and with reservation.

"It's good to meet you too," Rajmund replied.

"So, Rajmund, do you enjoy sports?" Thaddeus asked.

"I play soccer."

"You do? So do I," Thaddeus replied. "Are you in a club?"

"I play on my school team."

"I do too. What position do you play?"

"Midfield, how about you?"

"I play forward."

Mr. Litynski said, "I thought you two might have something in common. That's why Mr. Bieberstein and I planned for us all to get together."

Throughout the evening the table conversation revolved around business and the European political climate. Thaddeus and Rajmund broke off into private conversations on several occasions. Soon Thaddeus and Rajmund were joking and laughing as if they were old friends. After several hours of dining and conversing, Sigmund said, "Well, I suppose we better call it a night. These young men have school tomorrow, and we have to work."

"Before we go I have to say something," said Rajmund. "I had a really good time tonight. I wasn't expecting this. Because of what happened last week, I wasn't sure what to expect. But I am glad we got together tonight. Everywhere I go, I hear how bad Jews are and that they have always held Europe in a financial stranglehold. Even some of the teachers are saying it at school. I didn't know what to believe, but I believed what I was being told."

"We never hear those things," Thaddeus replied, "at least not until the last year or two. But we still don't hear it in our neighborhood."

"I fear that there is some evil force arising in Poland. A force like the Nazism that arose in Germany," Mr. Litynski said. "I hope I'm wrong, but it just seems like it."

After a moment of silence, Sigmund said, "Hey, next weekend, Thad, Cass, and I are going to our home in the mountains for a hunting trip. We will go up on Friday afternoon and come back on Sunday night. Why don't you two come with us? Do you ever go red deer hunting?"

"We have never gone hunting, but we've always wanted to go," Rajmund said. "We don't have any guns."

"We have plenty of guns you can use," Thaddeus said.

"We would love to come with you," Mr. Litynski said.

"Okay, why don't we pick you up at your house on Friday afternoon around two o'clock?"

"That will be perfect," Mr. Litynski said. "We will be ready. Will you be in for lunch tomorrow, Sigmund?"

"Yes, I will. Good evening, my friend." Sigmund shook Mr. Litynski's hand.

Sigmund and Thaddeus left the restaurant and drove back to their home.

CHAPTER

4

E ARLY FRIDAY AFTERNOON Cass, Thaddeus, and Sigmund
arrived at the Litynski home in a Polski Fiat 621 L military truck,
with a canvas-covered bed. The truck was painted a light-green-
and-brown camouflage. Sigmund parked the vehicle by the curb in front
of the house. Mr. Litynski and Rajmund walked out the front door and
down the sidewalk toward the truck. Each was carrying a bedroll. Sigmund
got out, went to the rear, and opened the tailgate.

"Good afternoon, gentlemen," he said, leaning against the tailgate of
the truck.

"Hello, Sigmund." replied Mr. Litynski. He shook Sigmund's hand.

"Good afternoon, sir," replied Rajmund, shaking Sigmund's hand.

Thaddeus and Cass got out of the passenger side and walked around
to the rear of the truck. When Cass saw Rajmund he felt a mild sensation
of panic. *This is the guy who pushed Zofia's face in the snow.*

"Hi, Cass," Rajmund said.

"Hello, Rajmund."

Sigmund said, "The front will hold three. Two will need to ride back
here. Actually, it's probably more comfortable back here. There is a wood-
burning stove for heat."

"Rajmund and I can ride back here. Cass, Mr. Litynski, and you can ride up front," Thaddeus said.

Mr. Litynski laughed. "That sounds good. By the way, you boys can called me Josef. Mr. Litynski is too hard to say."

"Okay, there's firewood over there in the front of the bed so you can keep the fire going," said Sigmund. "Don't worry about smoke. The stove has a vent that goes out above the roof."

Thaddeus and Rajmund climbed into the back of the truck while Cass, Sigmund, and Josef walked around to the front and climbed in. Cass was sitting in the middle between Sigmund and Josef.

"Where did you get this military truck?" asked Josef with a laugh. "Are we going to invade Germany?"

Sigmund laughed. "I borrowed it from the army. Actually, my father dropped it off this morning. He's in the army."

"Oh, are you talking about Major Bieberstein? I didn't know he's your father. I haven't met him, but the officers often talk about him in the restaurant."

Sigmund nodded. "We often take officers to our mountain home to hunt deer. We use the military trucks to bring the deer back. So when I need a truck, they let me use one."

The drive up to the mountain home took four hours. Once they arrived at the foothills, the road became winding and less maintained. Soon they were driving on a muddy dirt road that wound through the forest and into the mountains. The truck bounced in and out of deep ruts. As they neared the crest, they found snowdrifts covering the road in some areas. But the snowdrifts were no match for the military truck, which plowed through them as if they were feathers. When they arrived at the mountain home, Sigmund pulled the truck alongside the house under the porte cochere. They opened the doors and exited the vehicle.

The chalet was a seven-thousand-square-foot wooden structure painted white, with red trim around the windows and doors. The front porch deck spanned from one end of the house to the other then wrapped around spanning the length of both sides. The yard was maintained by a gardener, who lived in the rear of the house during the summer. He had come up earlier in the week and plowed the half-mile driveway leading to the house.

"Gentlemen, come inside," Sigmund said as he unlocked the front door to the house. "Make yourselves comfortable."

Cass walked over to the wood-burning stove in the living room and opened the door to see if there was wood inside. He noticed that it was well stocked with hardwood the gardener had probably chopped when he plowed the driveway. There was a large pile of wood next to the stove. Under the hardwood were little branches with dry leaves. Taking a match off the mantel, Cass struck it against the stone floor under the wood-burning stove. He lit the small branches and dry leaves. The leaves smoked momentarily then ignited. Cass closed the door of the stove.

The men and boys sat down at the wooden table in the dining area. It didn't take long before the stove was warming the rooms comfortably. Sigmund went down into the basement and lit the oil furnace. Thaddeus made a pot of coffee, and Cass made hot chocolate. Cass and Rajmund both acted a bit awkward because they had not seen each other since the afternoon of the fight. They drank hot chocolate, and the others drank coffee.

"So this is your first hunting trip then, is that right?" Sigmund asked.

"Yes, it is," Josef replied. "It was very kind of you to bring us along. How do you find the deer?"

Sigmund replied, "We build a blind near the deer trails; then we wait as quietly as possible. We have to be careful not to have anything with us that has a scent that is not natural to the forest, or the deer will recognize that we are here. The blinds are built downwind of the trail to minimize the chance of being detected. We wait until the deer get close enough, and then we shoot."

"Do you know where all the deer trails are?" Rajmund asked.

"We know where most of them are because we have been coming up here for years," Sigmund replied.

"How do we build the blind?" Rajmund asked.

Sigmund took a sip of his coffee. "We actually have several already built in the forest. Most of them are in trees. A tree blind is best because a deer never looks up."

Rajmund looked puzzled. "They never look up?"

"No, they only look horizontally or down to the ground."

"Why is that?"

"Because they are herbivore grazers like cows or sheep," Thaddeus replied with a laugh. "Grazers only look in a horizontal direction or down."

Rajmund nodded. "Oh, I didn't know that. Do these deer have antlers?"

"Among the red deer, only the stags have antlers. They start growing them in the spring and shed them around the end of winter," Thaddeus said. "Rajmund, have you ever shot a gun before?"

"No, I haven't."

Thaddeus walked over to the gun rack and took down a rifle. Bringing it back to the table, he said, "I will have you shooting like a sharpshooter in no time. This is a Karabin wz. 98a bolt-action rifle. It is my favorite for hunting deer." He pulled back the bolt. "You insert the cartridge here. Then you close the chamber." He pushed the bolt forward, closing the empty chamber. Lifting the gun to his shoulder, he pointed it toward the window. "One important thing to remember: unless you are using it as a military weapon, you never point the gun toward a person." Thaddeus handed the rifle to Rajmund.

Rajmund pulled back the bolt, opening the empty chamber, then closed it. Mimicking Thaddeus he put it up to his right shoulder, closed his right eye, and pointed it toward the window.

Sigmund smiled. "If you are a right-handed shooter, you sight with your right eye. I mean, you keep your right eye open and close the left. Do you see the little bump at the end of the barrel?"

"Yes."

"At the other end of the barrel, closer to you, there's a piece of metal that forms the shape of a V. Do you see that?"

"Yes, I do."

"What you want to do is line up the bump at the end of the gun so it is right in the center of the V. Then you set the bump on the center of the object you intend to shoot. That is called sighting the gun. The 98a holds five rounds. A skilled shooter can accurately shoot fifteen rounds per minute. This is a state-of-the-art weapon for a sniper. With a telescopic sight you can shoot a very long distance. Fewer than five hundred of these guns have been made so far. We have ten of them, so there are plenty for each of us."

"It's too dark to learn to shoot tonight, but I will show you in the morning," Thaddeus said. "Don't be disappointed if you don't get a deer on your first hunt. Very few people hit a deer on their first few hunts, even if they already know how to shoot. The deer are very fast, and they will spook at the slightest sound. On your first hunt, you just want to learn how to find them without scaring them."

"Do you hunt on Saturdays? I thought Jews don't do anything on Saturdays," Josef said.

"We are reform Jews. Our observance is not as strict as Orthodox. We don't work on Shabbat, but deer hunting would not be work to us. Orthodox Jews would not hunt on Shabbat. They would not even shoot a gun on the Shabbat because they are prohibited from starting a fire. Igniting the cartridge by releasing the firing pin would be considered starting a fire."

While listening to Sigmund explain Jewish customs and practices, Cass remembered that they had not lit the Shabbat candles. He walked over to the window, where the candleholder was kept, and lit a candle. Everyone became silent as he said a prayer in Hebrew that he had learned from his grandfather. Rajmund watched and listened intently.

A few minutes later, Sigmund stood up and motioned everyone toward the fire. "Why don't we move to the chairs around the stove?" Near the wood-burning stove were two mission chairs imported from San Francisco, a wingback chair with a hassock, and two soft Victorian couches. Everyone followed Sigmund into the living room and seated themselves around the stove. A comfortable warmth emanated from the fire. After sitting around the stove for several hours, the hunters went to bed.

The next morning the boys awakened before dawn. Thaddeus and Cass took Rajmund outside and taught him how to shoot a rifle. Rajmund learned quickly and within a half hour was shooting accurately. The boys went back inside and enjoyed a breakfast of eggs, potatoes, pancakes, and coffee. By seven o'clock they were walking in deep snow through the forest, each of them carrying a gun. Sigmund had shown Josef how to shoot while the boys were eating breakfast. They walked with the rifles pointed to the sky held by a strap across the shoulder. When they saw deer tracks in the snow, Sigmund took his rifle off his shoulder and held it with the barrel pointed toward the ground. Motioning for everyone to be quiet, he crouched in the snow as he surveyed the terrain. Everyone followed his lead, removing the rifle from their shoulders, and crouched in the snow.

Suddenly Cass lifted his rifle and fired a shot down into the open valley. He always took great pride in the ability to withstand the recoil of a K-98 at the young age of six.

"What are you shooting at?" Josef asked.

"I didn't see anything," Rajmund said.

"I didn't either," Thaddeus said.

"Down there by the river." Cass pointed down into the valley.

"I still don't see anything," Sigmund said.

Thaddeus laughed. "I see it. Look into that clump of brush next to the frozen river." He pointed toward a clump of brush in the direction Cass had pointed.

"Merry Christmas," Rajmund shouted. "There's a deer lying in the snow down there. How did you even see that, Cass?"

Sigmund laughed. "*Oy vey.* I must be losing my eyesight. I didn't see a thing down there. Cass, you have amazing eyesight. That will be of great value to you if you ever go into the military."

"I hope I won't ever have to shoot a person."

The hunting party descended into the canyon to retrieve the deer. Sigmund showed Rajmund and Josef how to dress the deer and clean it with snow. Cass and Thaddeus dragged the deer back to the cabin so the others could continue hunting. As Cass walked back to the cabin with Thaddeus, dragging the deer by the antlers, he felt a sense of pride. He thought, *I wonder what Zofia would have thought if she had seen me shoot the deer. She probably wouldn't have liked it, but she will be impressed to hear that I got one.*

As they neared the cabin, Cass and Thaddeus heard a rustling sound in the forest behind them. They paused momentarily to listen but did not hear or see anything. Thaddeus said, "We'd better get the deer inside. That might be a wolf." They took the deer around to the back of the cabin and into a skinning area in the basement, where they cleaned it.

When they had finished, they changed out of their soiled clothes and went back out to find the others. While they were skinning the deer it had snowed heavily, and the tracks were completely covered. When they arrived at the location where Cass had shot the deer, they saw no sign of the other hunters. "The snow has covered their tracks. We probably won't

37

find them," Thaddeus said. "Why don't we go to the blind by the fork in the river to see if I can get a deer?"

"Good idea."

When they arrived at the tree blind, they climbed the ladder and took their positions in the blind. Cass had done this dozens of times. He knew to speak as little as possible and only in a whisper. He also knew to hold perfectly still. After several hours, Cass felt Thaddeus nudge him. Thaddeus nodded his head toward the fork. About a hundred yards away was a Monarch stag with a sixteen-point antler, standing on the ice.

"Oh," whispered Cass.

Thaddeus put his sight on the deer. "He is coming this way. I am going to let him get closer," he whispered. Whenever they were in the tree stands, they always kept a cartridge in the chamber ready to shoot. Cass knew that Thaddeus wanted a clean shot.

Within 10 minutes the deer was only 150 feet away. Thaddeus fired, and the deer dropped in the snow. Quickly Cass and Thaddeus climbed down and ran over to the fallen animal. They stopped a few feet away to make sure the deer was dead. Thaddeus field dressed it as he had Cass's deer. They dragged the deer back to the cabin and skinned it. Then they went upstairs, cleaned up, and started another fire. They drank hot chocolate, and Thaddeus cooked venison and vegetables to feed the hungry hunters when they returned. About an hour later, they heard voices outside. They looked out the window to see Sigmund, dragging a deer behind him.

Cass opened the door. "Who got that one?"

"Rajmund shot it," Sigmund said.

"Seriously?"

"Yes, he made a great shot."

Rajmund smiled. "I was really surprised. I just learned how to shoot this morning. We were in the blind, and he walked right up to us. Mr. Bieberstein helped me line up the sight. Got him on the first shot."

Cass and Thaddeus came out to drag the deer down into the skinning room, where they skinned it. After dinner, they sat in the living room near the fire and talked about their lives in Poland. "Where did your ancestors come from?" Josef asked.

"The Biebersteins came from Switzerland to Poland several generations ago," Sigmund explained. "Historically, Jewish people have moved about as different communities became hostile to them. They have had varied relationships with different populations, but they have learned that they cannot trust anyone completely. A certain community might be very kind to them in one generation then hostile the next. During the Habsburg dynasty, our ancestors had appointments of nobility, though we were required to keep our Jewish faith secret. Some of them went by the name von Bieberstein and some spelled it Biberstein, but we believe most of us are of the same family."

"That is fascinating," Rajmund said. "I had no idea Jews ever held titles in Europe."

"You would be surprised to learn the whole story," Sigmund said. "For example, did you know that European royals claim descent from King David of Israel? In fact, that is the sacred secret of the divine right of kings."

"Do you mean King David in the Bible?" Rajmund asked.

Sigmund nodded. "One and the same."

The men and boys sat around the fire and talked until late that night. The boys drank hot chocolate, and the men enjoyed a bottle of merlot that Josef had brought with him. Soon Cass had fallen asleep, and Sigmund carried him into his room and put him to bed. Then he came back into the living room and sat in one of the mission chairs by the fire.

"So what are you going to do if the Nazis invade Poland?" asked Josef.

"I hope we don't ever have to cross that bridge. Do you think they will invade?"

Josef looked at Rajmund. "I sure hope not. But we really don't know."

"Well, we may all have to fight. Truthfully, I have been told by my father, Major Bieberstein, that if Germany does invade, our military doesn't stand a chance. All we could do would be to surrender," Sigmund said.

Rajmund said, "If Germany invades Poland, I am going to become a terrorist and kill as many Germans as I can."

"I will fight them too," said Thaddeus. "We might as well, because we will all be slaves anyway if we don't."

The thought of Germany invading Poland made everyone uneasy. There was enough talk about it in the schools, and many were saying that they would just become Nazis. This is what Rajmund had thought until he became acquainted with the Biebersteins and decided he liked this Jewish family.

When the hunting party returned to Warsaw on Sunday night, Cass did not feel well. He had a cough, his eyes burned, and he was feverish. "You must have caught a cold," said Irena. "Let's get you right to bed."

Cass walked up to his room, took off his clothes, and climbed into bed. Within an hour he had chills and could not stop shaking.

Irena went into Sigmund's library. "Sigmund, I think Cass is really sick. He has a very high fever and can't seem to stop shaking."

Irena and Sigmund went upstairs to Cass's room. Cass was lying on his side with the covers pulled up over his head. Sigmund pulled back the blanket put his hand on Cass's forehead to check his temperature. "Cass, can you hear me?" he asked. Cass did not respond.

Irena left for a moment then came back with a jar of Vicks VapoRub. Sigmund turned Cass over on his back, and Irena put the ointment on him.

"What do you think it is?" Irena asked.

"I don't know. I don't think I have ever seen him this sick before. He seemed fine all weekend. I will check on him throughout the night."

The following morning Cass seemed almost lifeless. Zofia wanted to go in to see him, but Irena would not let her in. "We don't know what he has yet. It could be contagious, and we wouldn't want you to get it."

"But you and Mr. Bieberstein are in there. Won't you get sick too?"

"Adults have much stronger resistance than children. We will probably be okay, but it is too dangerous for you. Sigmund went to get the doctor. If the doctor says it's okay, then you can come in."

Irena sat by the bed as Cass slept. Zofia left with her father and Thaddeus for school. A short time later Sigmund returned with the family doctor, Dr. Janda. The doctor examined Cass with a stethoscope. He opened Cass's mouth, held the tongue down with a tongue depressor, and shone a light inside of his mouth. Cass was barely able to comply with the instructions to keep his mouth open. Dr. Janda stepped to the side and motioned with his head for Sigmund and Irena to look down into his throat. "Do you see that second layer of yellow membrane in the back of his throat? That looks like diphtheria."

"Isn't diphtheria serious?" asked Irena.

"It can be."

"How is diphtheria transmitted?" asked Sigmund. "Can you catch it in the air?"

"No, we do not believe it is airborne, but it can be spread by sneezing on someone. In other words, it is spread by bodily fluids. You should probably put on surgical masks. I have some in my bag." The doctor took out three surgical masks and gave them to Sigmund. "I thought I might need these so I brought them along."

"Will you stay with him?" asked Sigmund. "I will pay you three times your normal daily income."

"I have other patients to tend to, but I can probably get someone else to cover them some of the time. I can't be here all the time, but I will stop by as often as I can. We may want to take him to the hospital. I will check on him in a few hours to see how he is feeling." Dr. Janda walked over to the window and opened it all the way. Then he walked over to a second window and opened it all the way as well.

"Won't that be too cold?" asked Irena.

"No, we need to put lots of blankets on the bed so that he will stay plenty warm, but he needs to breathe the fresh cold air. That will help to keep his lungs clean and will help prevent the spread of bacteria, much like a refrigerator prevents the spread of bacteria. I will take some cultures for testing, but I'm fairly certain it's diphtheria."

After taking some cultures, Dr. Janda said, "I will take these to the hospital, test them in the lab, and let you know what we find. Keep the windows open and keep lots of blankets on his bed. You don't want his body temperature to drop too low, or he will suffer hypothermia."

Dr. Janda picked up his bag and walked toward the bedroom door. "Be sure to call me at the hospital if there are any changes. Keep everyone out of here except yourselves and don't let him sneeze on you. Keep your surgical masks on at all times when you are in here. I will bring a box of them. You should change them every four hours and take them off whenever you leave the room. Wash your hands thoroughly every hour or so."

"Is he going to be okay?" Sigmund asked.

"We will know within the next day or so."

Sigmund walked Dr. Janda to the front door, where they paused. "He's a strong boy. He should make it," Dr. Janda said.

Sigmund nodded. "How did he catch diphtheria? What is it?"

"Diphtheria is bacterial. An epidemic started in England and Scotland about three years ago, and it arrived here about a year ago. But as I said, don't worry. He's very strong. The mortality rate for children his age is five to ten percent. Those who die are usually already weak before they catch it. I will be back in a little while." Dr. Janda walked out the door then closed it behind him.

Irena and Sigmund stayed with Cass throughout the day. They kept the windows open and heavy blankets on the bed. Cass remained asleep. Adelajda brought in warm towels throughout the afternoon. Several hours later, Dr. Janda returned with an ambulance and a driver. They let themselves in through the front door and walked up to the bedroom. "I have brought an ambulance," he said. "The cultures confirmed it's diphtheria. I decided to go ahead and take him to the hospital. That way he can have twenty-four-hour care."

"Okay," said Sigmund.

Cass awakened as they moved him from the bed to the gurney. "What are you doing?"

"We're taking you to the hospital so you can get better," replied Irena.

"What is wrong with me?" Cass could barely keep his eyes open.

"You have something called diphtheria," Sigmund said.

"Is it bad?"

"We are going to take you to the hospital so it doesn't get bad," replied Dr. Janda. "Don't worry, we will take good care of you."

Lech drove Irena and Sigmund to the hospital following behind the ambulance. "Should I bring Thaddeus here when I pick him up from school?"

"No, just take him on home then come back and pick up Irena. I am going to stay with Cass tonight."

Lech nodded then left to pick up the children from school. When he arrived at the yeshiva to pick up Zofia, she climbed in the car and asked, "How is Cass?"

"They took him to the hospital," Lech replied.

"Is he going to be okay?"

"He has been sleeping all day. The doctors think he will be all right, but they are going to give him twenty-four-hour care to make sure."

"What's wrong with him?" she asked.

"It is something called diphtheria. I have heard of it. They had a lot of cases in England, and now it has spread to Poland."

After picking up Thaddeus, Lech drove them to the Bieberstein mansion. They went inside where they were greeted by Adelajda and Patrycja, Zofia's mother. "How do you children feel?" asked Adelajda.

"Okay," Zofia said.

"I'm fine," Thaddeus said.

"I want to go see Cass," Zofia said.

Lech looked at his daughter momentarily then said, "It is too dangerous. Mr. Bieberstein said it would be better if you children didn't come to the hospital. Cass will be home in a few days."

Zofia started to cry. "But I want to see Cass."

Adelajda took her in her arms and held her. "Cass is going to be okay," she said. "We just don't want anyone else to get sick." She exchanged glances with Patrycja, who looked at her daughter as she continued to cry softly. The extent of her grief surprised everyone.

Patrycja whispered to Lech, "Zofia loves Cass."

Adelajda overheard the comment and nodded. Lech looked at Zofia with a troubled expression. Zofia walked over to her mother, who hugged her. "Zofia, what is this? Cass will be okay. You need to be strong."

Zofia nodded.

Patrycja continued, "Adelajda prepared a wonderful dinner. Let's go eat." Ordinarily, the Biebersteins ate separately from the employees, but on this occasion, since Thaddeus was the only Bieberstein at home, they all ate together.

Cass remained in the hospital for six days. When he finally came home, he seemed tired but otherwise well. Dr. Janda told Sigmund that they'd almost lost him. He slept most of the time in the hospital, but he finally turned around. Within a few days of returning home, Cass was back to his normal self. When Cass heard how Zofia had cried, he realized for the first time how much she really cared for him.

CHAPTER

5

SPRING CAME EARLY in Warsaw in 1938. By mid-March most of the snow had melted from the streets, and the days were bright with sunshine. The melting snow, combined with heavy rains in April, caused the rivers and streams to flow swiftly through the streets. Thaddeus and Rajmund had become good friends, though Rajmund's friends tried to discourage this friendship. Thad was a Jew, after all. As the weather began to warm, sometimes Rajmund and Thaddeus would tell the chauffeur not to pick them up after school so they could walk home with Cass and Zofia and enjoy the warm weather.

On a Wednesday afternoon in April, all four were walking home together after school. Strolling down the sidewalk, they saw a group of boys approaching. Cass recognized some of them as Rajmund's friends who had been with him when they had assaulted Zofia and Cass several months earlier. Three other boys, who appeared to be much older than Rajmund's friends, accompanied them. As they neared, Rajmund said, "Hey, guys."

"What are you doing walking with the Jews?" one of Rajmund's friends asked.

"We're just walking. Why?"

"Are you becoming a Jew too?" the same teenager asked.

Rajmund did not reply.

"Is this your little Jew girlfriend?" one of the other boys asked, pointing at Zofia.

Zofia lowered her head in embarrassment. In an effort to protect her, Cass moved between her and the older boys as they passed.

"I wonder how she kisses. Does she kiss good?" another teenager asked.

"She wouldn't kiss you," Cass said. "Besides, she is not a Jew."

"Oh, the little Jew boy talks." One of the older boys laughed. "Is she your girlfriend, little Jew boy? How do you say in Hebrew, 'my girlfriend is a little Jew whore'? If she is your girlfriend and she lives in your house, then she is a Jew."

Rajmund and Thaddeus both stopped simultaneously. "That's enough," Thaddeus said.

"Why are you being such a kraut?" Rajmund asked.

"Why are you being such a Jew lover? Let's kiss the little Jew girl," the boy said as he walked toward Zofia. "She's a pretty little Jew whore, isn't she?"

Suddenly, Rajmund stepped forward and pushed the older boy off the curb, shoving him on his back in a stream of running water. "You shouldn't have done that," the teenager said as he started to get up from the water. "Now you're going to be sorry."

Before he could get to his feet, Rajmund kicked him in the face, knocking him back into the water.

"Lighten up, Rajmund," said one of the boys Rajmund knew. "We're just playing."

"I don't consider that playing," Rajmund shouted. "All we are trying to do is walk home. Leave us alone."

The teenager got out of the stream a second time, though he didn't say anything. He walked a wide circle around Rajmund. The older boys walked past the Biebersteins but made no further comments. The teenager who had been knocked in the stream was holding his jaw, and blood was running from his nose. As they walked away, Cass heard one of them ask, "Are you going to let him get away with that?" He did not hear a reply. One of them shouted back, "You have changed, Rajmund. I feel like I don't even know you anymore."

When the boys had gotten out of hearing distance, Thaddeus laughed. "Why did you kick him in the face?"

"Because I knew he was going fight me if I let him up. He's a lot bigger than me."

"But how did you know that kicking him in the face would stop him? It might have made him really mad."

Rajmund laughed. "I learned it from Cass. That time he kicked me in the face hurt worse than any pain I ever felt. So I know it works."

"It looked like you were doing a bicycle kick," Thaddeus said.

"I almost did, but then I decided I didn't want to kill him…plus I didn't want to crack my own head on the concrete."

"What's a bicycle kick?" asked Cass.

Thaddeus replied, "That's a soccer kick where you have both feet off the ground and literally kick the soccer ball over your own head." He laughed and shook his head. Cass and Zofia didn't laugh. This was a frightening event for them.

As the season turned to summer, Thaddeus and Rajmund continued to socialize with each other. Rajmund no longer associated with his former friends, who were decidedly hostile toward Jews. He attempted on several occasions to plan activities where Thaddeus could meet his former friends, but they wanted nothing to do with a Jew. Thaddeus and Rajmund both enjoyed fishing. When the time arrived for the Bieberstein family to go stay at the summer cottage on the Baltic Sea, they invited the Litynskis to join them for the summer. The home was sufficiently large to accommodate several families while providing necessary privacy. Due to the business, the Litynskis were unable to stay the summer, but it was decided that Rajmund would stay the summer; Josef would stay for a week. Josef was pleased that Rajmund and Thaddeus had developed a close friendship. He no longer feared that Rajmund would develop Nazi sympathies, and he was grateful to the Biebersteins for helping his son learn to be empathetic to those from other cultures.

Often Sigmund would take Rajmund and Thaddeus out on the Baltic Sea to fish. One day, he decided to invite Josef, Cass, Thaddeus, Rajmund, and Zofia with them for an overnight fishing trip. They loaded the boat with tackle and bait and set out on the water in the early morning. The boat was a sixty-foot luxury yacht with sleeping quarters below. Cass, Zofia, Thaddeus, and Rajmund sat on the deck as the boat moved swiftly across the sea in a northerly direction toward Sweden. Sigmund had fished in these waters on many occasions and had often fished near the coast of Germany. Now, however, given the rise of Nazism, he avoided the German coast. Although they did not expect a confrontation with the Germans, it seemed that the farther from the German coast they remained, the safer they would be. After traveling for several hours at about half speed, they came to rest in the middle of the Baltic Sea.

As Cass looked around, he could not see land in any direction. "Are we going to put down the anchor?"

"No point," Sigmund replied. "The water is too deep for an anchor."

"Why is it too deep?"

"Because the anchor wouldn't reach the bottom. The chain isn't long enough. It's probably a thousand feet deep here."

The thought of being in water so deep that the anchor would not reach bottom gave Cass a feeling of fear mixed with excitement. As he looked over the side of the boat into the water, he wondered what was down there. Because of the sun high overhead, he could see a fair distance below the surface but saw no fish.

"Do you think there are sharks down there?" Zofia asked.

"Sure there are," Josef said.

"If someone was swimming in the water, would a shark attack him?" she asked.

"It is always possible but unlikely. Sharks rarely attack humans," Sigmund said.

As Cass and Zofia looked into the water watching the red bobbers on the end of their fishing lines, they suddenly heard a loud splash. They turned around to see Thaddeus swimming in the water off the starboard side of the boat. They saw Rajmund standing on the top deck, preparing to dive. Sigmund and Josef were seated at the stern, manning their poles as they each drank a beer.

"Do you want to swim?" Cass asked Zofia.

"I kind of do, but it's scary to go in water that deep."

Zofia and Cass both laughed. "You can swim, so it doesn't matter how deep it is," said Cass.

"I'm not afraid of drowning. What if something comes up and grabs us from down below?"

Cass laughed even harder.

Zofia laughed again. "Well, I don't know," she said. "It's scary."

Cass reeled in his line then pulled off his T-shirt, stepped up on the edge of the rail, and dove into the water. He turned around, swimming away from the boat. "Come on in, Zofia."

"No."

Cass, Thaddeus, and Rajmund swam around the boat for about twenty minutes. Suddenly, Sigmund shouted, "Boys, get out of the water."

"What?" Thaddeus shouted.

"Get out of the water quickly," Sigmund said.

"Why?" Cass asked.

"Don't ask questions. Just do it." Sigmund walked quickly to the boat's helm and started the engine.

The boys climbed out of the water as instructed. "What's going on?" Rajmund asked.

Josef replied, "We just spotted a German U-boat about a hundred yards starboard. It surfaced just a few minutes ago. Don't look in that direction long, they are looking at us with binoculars."

Sigmund directed the boat to the portside and moved the boat slowly away from the U-boat, but the U-boat changed directions and began following.

"Why are they stalking us?" asked Thaddeus.

"That's a good question. We're at least a hundred miles from the coast of Germany," replied Sigmund. Sigmund slowly began to increase speed. But the U-Boat seemed determined to keep up.

"Can this boat outrun the U-boat?" Josef asked.

"Yes, easily, but we can't outrun a torpedo."

"Why would they torpedo us?" Josef asked.

"I don't know. Why would they stalk us at all? Everybody sit down. If you have a line in the water, bring it in."

Zofia reeled in her line, and everyone sat on the lower deck. Sigmund suddenly pushed the throttle into full position and turned directly toward the coast of Lithuania. Cass looked back at the U-boat and noticed that it seemed to be falling behind. He heard what sounded like a rapid-firing of the 88-mm deck gun of the U-boat.

"Are they shooting at us?" he shouted.

"Yes. Stay down."

As he watched, Cass noticed something approaching rapidly under the surface of the water. "Papa, what's that in the water? It's moving really fast."

Sigmund looked into the water then turned the wheel sharply to starboard, throwing everyone off balance. As they fell to the deck, Sigmund said, "That's a torpedo."

The torpedo exploded about fifty yards from the boat.

Sigmund explained, "That was a magnetic torpedo. An abrupt change in the magnetic field causes it to detonate."

The U-boat continued to pursue them for several miles, though falling farther behind. Then eventually the U-boat fell out of sight. Sigmund pushed the boat at full throttle for two hours. At last he slowed the boat to an idle and turned off the engine. They sat silently for several minutes, attempting to absorb what had transpired.

"Has that ever happened before?" Josef asked.

"Never," Sigmund replied.

"Are you sure they were pursuing us before we fled?" Thaddeus asked.

"Absolutely. There's no question. We were probably a hundred miles from the nearest shore. They didn't just happen to surface near us. They surfaced because we were there. When I looked at them with the binoculars, I could see them looking back at us with theirs. Then, when we began to leave they stayed right behind us. It was only when I pushed the throttle into the full position that we got away."

"Why did they fire the torpedo?" Thaddeus asked.

"I guess they didn't like it that we were escaping. They wouldn't ordinarily waste a torpedo on a small yacht," said Sigmund. "They probably followed us all the way from Poland and were planning to attack us."

"What are we going to do now?" Cass asked.

"We'll keep fishing, but we will fish closer to the Lithuanian shore," replied Sigmund. "I doubt they can find us now."

As evening approached, the boat was near enough to the coast of Lithuania that they could see lights on the shore in the distance. "What do you think they would have done if they had caught us?" asked Cass.

"I don't know what they were planning," Sigmund said, "but I didn't like it. We were out in the middle of nowhere, so there was no one to help us. They could've done anything they wanted because there were no witnesses. Those boats carry a lot of men and heavy artillery. They would easily have overpowered us if they had caught up to us."

The group stayed up late that night, fishing. Due to the tension of the events that day, there was very little conversation. Finally Josef asked, "What do you think is going on, Sigmund? Why would a U-boat chase us out in the middle of the Baltic Sea?"

Sigmund replied, "I really don't know. We don't have radio contact, so it's hard to tell if anything has happened."

"Do you think it's possible that Germany declared war against Poland?"

"Oh, I hope not. I don't think that happened, but who knows for sure? We are cut off from communication out here. Our boat clearly has Polish markings and a Polish flag, and the name *Irena* is written in large letters on the side. They knew we were from Poland."

"Is there any reason they might pursue this particular boat?"

Sigmund put his hand on his neck. "Well, possibly. For the last two years I have been helping Jews escape from Germany. Often we use this boat to pick them up on the coast and take them to Poland or another coastal destination. I also spend quite a bit of money to help them get out of Germany. The Germans know I do this, and I suppose it's possible they know that this is my boat. It's also possible they have actually seen this boat pick up the Jews along the coast."

"What would happen if Germany invaded Poland?" Zofia asked.

"It would be bad," Thaddeus said. "We don't have a military that can withstand a German invasion. Germany is a war machine today. Hitler is building a military for something."

"I'm scared," Zofia said. Cass, who was sitting to her right, took ahold of her hand. He would not have done that in the daylight, but he found courage in the dark. Zofia responded by squeezing his hand tightly. Cass felt warm feelings for her. He leaned over and whispered, "I don't like you," remembering the game they had played months earlier when "I don't like you" actually meant the opposite.

"I don't want to play that game anymore." Then she whispered, "I love you, Cass." She squeezed his hand tightly.

"I love you too," he whispered.

The group put on jackets and slept on the deck that night with their poles in the water. They were awakened many times by fish tugging on the lines, and they each caught several fish. The following morning, they prepared to return to the summerhouse. While they tried to enjoy the fishing trip, all felt a little unnerved by the experience with the U-boat. Sigmund kept the yacht within two miles of shore out of concern of encountering the U-boat again if it had come looking for them. After traveling southward along the Lithuanian coast for about an hour, they came to an unpopulated coastal region.

Looking toward land with the binoculars, Josef said, "Sigmund, look at this. What is going on up on that hill?"

Sigmund took the binoculars and looked at the shore. "Do you know what that is?"

"It looks like a military unit, but those are not Lithuanian uniforms," replied Josef.

"Are they Soviet?" Thaddeus asked.

Sigmund reduced the engine to an idle and turned toward shore north of the location of the troops. "They look like German navy to me. I don't think they saw us."

"What are we doing?" asked Josef.

"I am going to dock out of sight and go up for a closer look. We need to know what's going on."

Within thirty minutes Sigmund had found an area well concealed by brush where he docked the boat and set the anchor. "We should be well concealed here. Josef, why don't you come with me. Thaddeus, you and Rajmund stay here with the kids. We shouldn't be more than an hour or so. You can fish here for a while."

Sigmund and Josef jumped to the shore and climbed the hill into the thick forest. Strapped to Sigmund's belt was a German Luger that he always carried on the boat for protection against pirates. When they reached the top of the hill, they fell prone on the ground and remained motionless for several minutes as they scanned the terrain for evidence of military personnel. Seeing no movement, they stood to their feet and ran quietly toward the location where they had seen the troops assembled. Eventually, they neared the edge of the forest. They could see a group of approximately twenty men in German naval uniforms sitting on the ground, smoking cigarettes and talking.

Josef looked closely with the binoculars in an attempt to see what the men were doing. "They're German, all right. What do you think they're doing here?"

"That's a good question. Even more important, how did they get here? I don't see any vehicles."

"They must have come by boat. Those are navy uniforms."

Sigmund took a camera from his backpack and snapped several photos of the men. Josef and Sigmund ran down the hill to the shoreline and began walking along the shore under cover of the trees. Eventually, they came to a heavily wooded area.

"Look," Sigmund whispered. "There's a U-boat."

Josef nodded. "Do you think it is the same one we saw yesterday?"

"I don't know. It could be." Sigmund took his camera and snapped several photos of the U-boat. They then turned to go back to their own boat. They ran through the woods for about twenty minutes until they came to the boat they had docked in the brush along the shore. As they started to climb down the hill toward the boat, they heard voices speaking German. Peering through the trees, they saw two German navy officers standing on the boat with their guns pointed at Thaddeus, Rajmund, Cass, and Zofia, who were sitting on the deck with their hands on their heads. Josef and Sigmund dropped to the ground to avoid being seen.

"They found the boat," Josef whispered. "One of them has a radio. He probably radioed for assistance. What are we going to do?"

"We can't rush them. They might shoot the kids."

Josef took off his hat and rubbed his head. "We can't sneak up in the water. They'll see us when we try to climb up onto the boat. But we can't wait very long. If they did call it in, someone will be coming from the U-boat."

Sigmund said, "Obviously, their intentions are hostile; they're holding guns on the kids. But they shouldn't even be in Lithuania. Look, only one is holding a gun on the kids. The other is looking around on the deck. They don't act like there is anyone else with them." He took several photos. "We may need this for evidence."

"We have to shoot them," Josef said.

"Are you serious?"

"What other choice do we have? Do you see any other options? Here give me the gun. Remember, yesterday they shot at us and fired a torpedo at us. They have already tried to kill us."

Sigmund looked at Josef with a perplexed expression. "We don't know for sure that's the same U-boat."

"Do you want to take that chance? Besides, how many U-boats do you think are cruising around the Baltic Sea? They obviously came here looking for us." Josef held out his hand and said, "Give me the gun. I'll do it."

Sigmund looked at the men on the boat. The officer with the gun kicked Thaddeus in the shoulder with his boot as he shouted something in German. He could hear Zofia crying. Sigmund pulled out his luger and said, "No, I'll do it. I'm probably a better shot. I practice often. I will hit the first and then immediately shoot the second before he knows what happened. Be prepared to run as soon as I shoot the second officer. We have to get out of here before others arrive."

Sigmund carefully aimed the pistol at the officer holding the gun on the children. When he knew his shot was true, he fired. Before the first man hit the deck, Sigmund fired two more shots into the second, who also crumpled to the deck. Zofia screamed and began to cry. Cass held her and tried to comfort her. Sigmund and Josef ran down the hill. As they ran, they could hear men behind them, shouting in German. Thaddeus kicked the gun away from the officer who had held the gun on them. He ran to the cockpit and started the engine. Rajmund untied the boat and threw the line into the water. Sigmund and Josef reached the bottom of the hill and leaped into the boat. Thaddeus pushed the throttle to full speed while Sigmund and Josef threw the Germans overboard. They heard gunfire behind them, and Sigmund returned fire until the Luger's chamber was empty.

As the boat sped out into the Baltic Sea, Sigmund saw through his binoculars the men running to the U-boat and descending one by one down the hatch. Before the U-boat's diesel engines started, the yacht was several miles from shore. "Head straight out from shore for about an hour then directly south to Poland," said Sigmund. Thaddeus nodded.

After traveling for several hours, they finally reached the shore of Sopot, Poland, and tied up at the pier of their summerhouse. Inside the house, after they had described the situation to their families, Sigmund called his father, a major in the Polish army, and told him everything that had happened. "What do you think is going on?"

"I don't know, but it's troubling. Lithuania has been concerned about a Soviet occupation, not German. I have no idea why Germans would be there. You saw no Lithuanian military personnel?"

"No, and we looked. All we saw were German navy men who apparently arrived by U-boat."

"Do you think they got a good look at your yacht?" "I know they did. It has *Irena* right on the side of it."

"Get the boat out of the water and into a marina right away. Have it painted and the name removed. They might be sending spy boats along the shoreline to watch for the *Irena*."

"Okay, I'll do that. Thanks for your advice."

"Thank you for letting me know what happened. I'll file a report and tell you if I learn anything about what's going on."

"Okay. Have a good afternoon."

"You too. Bye."

Sigmund called a local marina and asked the proprietor to come and get the boat. He then went into the dining room, where the family was sitting, and sat down. "The past twenty-four hours have been a horrific experience for all of us," he said.

"Indeed," said Josef. "What did the army say?"

"I spoke with my father. He said he doesn't know what's happening. He's as puzzled as we are. He said there aren't supposed to be any Germans in Lithuania as far as he knows. He recommended that we get the boat into a marina right away and get it painted. I called the marina. They'll be by this afternoon to pick it up."

The marina retrieved the boat that afternoon and returned it two days later, freshly painted without the name *Irena* on the side. Nothing further was said about the fishing trip and life returned to normal. Several days later, the Biebersteins heard a knock on the door. Adelajda opened the door and was surprised to see Kuba, the Sopot chief of police.

"May I speak with Sigmund?" he asked.

"Please come in and have a seat," Adelajda said. Kuba complied. She left the room and returned a few moments later with Sigmund.

"Good afternoon, Kuba. How can I help you?" Sigmund asked.

Kuba stood up. "May we speak privately?"

"Excuse me," Adelajda said as she left the room.

Kuba said, "Sigmund, I came to warn you. There has been an uproar in town. Some strangers from Germany have been asking around about a yacht named *Irena*. They came past the police station for permission to investigate. I didn't have much choice. If I decline, it will seem suspicious. Of course, I know your boat is called the *Irena*, but I told them I didn't know of such a boat. They claimed that some people on a yacht called *Irena* killed two German officers who were on the coast of Lithuania. They said that someone had once seen a yacht here in Sopot called *Irena*, and they asked me to identify the owners and arrest them. They want to extradite the owners to Germany to stand trial. They are going door-to-door, asking if anyone knows who owns *Irena*. I don't think anyone here is going to tell them, but I wanted to warn you."

"Did they tell you what happened?"

"They said that two German officers and some sailors were in a small VP-boat several miles out from the coast of Lithuania on routine patrol when they had engine trouble. They were able to get to the Lithuanian shore, where they were going to look for assistance. The two officers said they were going to go for a short walk. A little while later the sailors heard gunshots. When they got to the location of the shots, they found the two officers lying in the water and a boat named *Irena* speeding away. Someone on the boat began firing at the sailors on shore."

"That's what they told you? They lied. Just so you know, I already filed a report with the army."

"So what really happened?"

"We were a hundred miles out to sea with no land in sight. The boys were swimming when we saw a U-boat. We decided to get out of there. They opened fire with a machine gun and then fired a torpedo at us. We were able to reach the Lithuanian shoreline and dropped anchor. We spent the night there. As we headed back home, we spotted some German navy men on the shore. They didn't see us so we docked north of them and went ashore to investigate."

Sigmund led Kuba into the kitchen, where he retrieved the photographs, which had already been developed by a local film processor. He handed them to Kuba. "We knew we needed evidence that they were on the

Lithuanian shore, so we took these." Sigmund pointed at the photo of the submarine. "That is what they really came in. It wasn't a little VP-boat. We believe it was the same U-boat that fired a torpedo at us." He then pointed at the photo of the officers standing on the *Irena* pointing their guns at the children. The name was clearly visible on the side of the yacht. "See the officers on our boat pointing their guns at our children? We were in Lithuania. They had no authority to board our yacht, and they had no authority to attack us in international waters. We had no choice but to shoot."

"I wonder what's going on," Kuba said. "These Nazis are going crazy. I'm concerned. I think they are going to invade."

"You do? My brother-in-law said that. He left Poland. He said it is just a matter of time before Germany invades."

"Where did he go?"

"We aren't sure because we haven't heard from him in several months, but he was talking about going to the United States."

Kuba turned and started walking toward the front door. "Well, thanks for letting me know what really happened. I knew they were lying when they told the story. I know you would never kill someone without necessity."

"Thank you for giving me a heads-up about the people looking for the *Irena*. Do you think there is anyone who will tell them it's ours?"

Kuba scratched his head. "I think everyone here hates the Nazis. But you never know what some people will do for a little excitement or when they're frightened. This is a small community, and probably only the people near you know that the *Irena* is yours. You know just about everyone near you, and you are well liked. Just the same, I would recommend that you bring in security for the rest of the summer. I will have officers patrol several times each day. I noticed you already took the name off the boat. That was a wise decision."

"It was the first thing we did when we returned from the fishing trip."

Kuba opened the front door to let himself out. "Well, as I said, I will let you know if I hear anything further."

Sigmund took Kuba's advice and brought in two military-trained security guards from the factory to live at the summerhouse for the rest of the summer. They were equipped with M1918 Browning automatic rifles. For several months they heard nothing further about the incident. Generally,

Sigmund would be away at the factory for much of the summer while the family stayed at the summerhouse, but because of the events on the fishing trip and the fact that Germans were actively searching for the *Irena*, he decided to spend most of the time with the family at the summerhouse.

One day, shortly before they were preparing to return to Warsaw for the fall school session, the children were sitting in the living room, reading books. The parents were in the kitchen, drinking tea and talking. They heard the doorbell ring. Adelajda opened the door, and Cass overheard someone ask for the man of the house. One of the security officers hid near the front door, and the other went outside and hid at one end of the porch. Sigmund went to the door and asked, "May I help you?"

"Yes," said one of the men. "We are with the German Reich Criminal Police Office. We are investigating a crime that occurred in Lithuania a few months ago involving a yacht that had the name *Irena* written in Polish on the side of it."

"What kind of crime?" asked Sigmund.

"Someone used the yacht to murder two German naval officers. That's all I can tell you."

"By what authority are you going door-to-door in Sopot?"

"We have cleared it with the Sopot police. They know we are here. Do you know anyone who has a boat called *Irena*?"

Sigmund put his hand on his neck to give the appearance of pondering. "I don't remember ever seeing a boat like that. Why do you think it is owned by someone in Sopot?"

"A witness from Germany said he believes he saw a boat called *Irena* docked somewhere on this shoreline. We have spent the whole summer going door-to-door, but no one has ever seen it. The witness must have been mistaken." One of the men gave Sigmund a business card. "If you ever see a boat like that, would you call me? These criminals need to be brought to justice."

Sigmund nodded. "If I see a boat like that, I will call you."

After they left, everyone came to the front door. "Wow, that was scary," Thaddeus said.

"I can't believe they identify themselves as officers with the German Reich Criminal Police Office and expect anyone in Poland to help them. They must think people will be intimidated," Sigmund said.

"Is that who they said they are?" Irena asked. "That would be like the Polish police going into Hamburg and searching door-to-door for information involving a crime. They're lucky someone hasn't shot them. But it does show how bold the Nazis have become."

On the last Saturday evening at the summerhouse before returning to Warsaw, Cass and Zofia sat on the deck looking out over the Baltic Sea. The crisp air gave them both a slight chill, notwithstanding the jackets they were wearing. "I'm always sad when we go back to the city at the end of the summer," Cass said.

"I can see why," Zofia replied. "It's so nice here."

"This summer has been strange, though. All the time I have been expecting someone to come to try to arrest us. That made it a little less fun than most years."

"Do you really think those Nazis were going to kill us?" asked Zofia. "I mean when they had the gun on us on the boat."

"Papa says he thinks they would have if they hadn't come back to the boat. I think it's probably true. Nazis are really bad."

"That was the scariest thing ever. There have been a lot of strange things that have happened this last year. Everything is going crazy. I don't feel safe like I used to," Zofia said.

Cass nodded. "I know. It feels like something bad is going to happen. I would feel safer here than in Warsaw if it hadn't been for that day on the boat. But now I feel safer in Warsaw."

"Do you think Rajmund's old friends are going to give us trouble when we get back to Warsaw?"

"Papa isn't going to let us walk to school now. He said we are going to have to go with the chauffeur from now on. So I don't think we will see them anymore."

"What's going to happen to us, Cass? Do you think the Nazis are going to come here and kill us?"

Cass put his arm around Zofia, and she rested her head on his shoulder. "No, I don't think that will happen. I think when we are old people we will look back and wonder why everything was so crazy when we were little."

Cass and Zofia stayed on the dock until long after dark. Finally Irena came out and said, "Cass, you and Zofia better come in now. It's getting late."

"Okay, Mama," replied Cass. "We will be in shortly."

As they stood up to go into the house they held hands. Zofia stopped and hugged Cass. "I want to be with you for the rest of my life, Cass. I know people aren't supposed to feel this way at our age. I think maybe we are growing up too fast. I saw two people killed this summer. Mama said children our age are not supposed to see things like that. Do you think we will always be together? I am so scared."

Cass responded nervously, "I hope so. I can't imagine life without you."

Cass and Zofia walked up the dock and then the steps and entered through the back door of the summerhouse. In the living room, they sat down in front of the fireplace, where a warm fire danced erratically, casting flickers of light around the room. They sat silently watching the fire, until finally they lay down on the soft rug and fell asleep. They slept in front of the fireplace that night. Irena slept on the couch in the living room and kept the fire burning all night long to keep the children warm.

CHAPTER

6

AFTER THE TERRIFYING events of the summer, the children felt relieved to be back in school. Although Rajmund was not Jewish, Sigmund persuaded the yeshiva to allow him to transfer to the school. Josef had thought that taking Rajmund out of the public school and placing him in the yeshiva would help prevent him from learning anti-Semitic speech and behavior. Rajmund was a good student who did well in all of his classes except for Jewish studies. He knew nothing of Judaism until he began spending time with Thaddeus. He was quickly absorbing the traditions but particularly enjoyed Jewish history and law, so he soon caught up in Jewish studies as well. Because the yeshiva was small, students were permitted to study at their own pace, provided they met certain minimum class requirements. Cass and Zofia always studied together, so they progressed at the same pace.

The students at the yeshiva accepted Rajmund and welcomed him into the school. Perhaps the inevitability of being a novelty Christian in a yeshiva, a member of the forbidden faith, was that he fascinated the young Jewish girls. He soon became popular among the students. One pretty girl in particular caught his attention, and he caught hers. Neither would jeopardize their education by showing a romantic interest in public, but the attraction was real. Her name was Sarah, and she was the prettiest girl Rajmund had ever seen.

Sarah had a sister named Rachel who was pretty like Sarah. She had captured Thaddeus's affection, and he had captured hers. Sarah and Rachel thought Cass and Zofia were adorable, and they invited the children to eat lunch with them. In truth, Sarah and Rachel thought that by inviting Cass and Zofia to eat with them, perhaps Rajmund would join them and introduce them to Thaddeus. The four of them would often have lunch together and sit together in assembly. Cass and Zofia's classmates admired their association with older children, something all of them would have cherished.

Rajmund and Thaddeus both joined the soccer team at the school. Sometimes Cass and Zofia would attend the soccer games to watch Thaddeus and Rajmund play. Rachel and Sarah were at every game and always chaperoned Cass and Zofia. Because the non-Jewish schools played on Friday nights and Saturdays—Shabbat for the Jewish students—the yeshiva only played Jewish schools in competitions. Sometimes the Jewish teams would play non-Jewish teams for practice, in preseason games, but the Jewish teams could not participate in the non-Jewish league because scheduling would be too difficult. For the non-Jewish schools, the soccer season began in March, but for the Jewish schools, the game was played year round, and only snow would cause the postponement of a game. Because the Jewish teams played year round, the Jewish league was generally more talented than the non-Jewish teams, and they usually won the preseason games. Most of the students at the non-Jewish schools respected and admired the talent of the Jewish soccer players, though they generally told everyone that the reason they lost to the Jewish schools so often was that they were only practice games, and they didn't put forth much effort.

In time, Sarah and Rachel began riding home in the Bieberstein automobile so their parents would not have to pick them up after games. Eventually, they began riding home from school even on nights there were no games. Rachel and Sarah would be dropped off first, then Rajmund. After everyone had been dropped off, the Biebersteins would go home. It was not long before Rachel and Sarah began coming to the Bieberstein home to study with Thaddeus and Rajmund. Because Rachel and Rajmund did not disclose their romantic interests to their parents, the parents had no concern that they were studying together. The parents simply saw it as a study group.

On a cool October evening, Rajmund, Thaddeus, Rachel, and Sarah were sitting at the dining room table in the Bieberstein mansion studying European history. Cass and Zofia were sitting on the floor by the fireplace. "So what really caused the Bolshevik Revolution?" asked Sarah. "That's one of the questions Rabbi Lieberman says is going to be on the essay portion of the test tomorrow."

Rajmund replied, "The short version is that the czar was too nice a man. He believed that war between Russia and Germany was unlikely because of the close family relationships between the leaders of those countries. But Russia got into the war against Germany, and he felt that he needed to be on the battlefield himself to support his troops. The people didn't want the war, and in his absence, the complaining grew. Lenin's party was actually very small, but in the vacuum created by the absence of the czar—"

Sarah interrupted, "Why did they kill the Czar's whole family? That was so terrible. What harm were the children going to do?"

Thaddeus replied, "They always kill the ruling family to prevent any future heirs ever claiming entitlement to the throne. It's harsh, but it's what people have always done when they overthrow a hereditary government. Lenin was awful. He was a monster, and he encouraged that kind of brutality. The Bolsheviks were cruel, just like the Nazis."

The room became quiet when Thaddeus mentioned the Nazis. Everyone knew that the threat of a Nazi invasion was real, and they were all frightened. Finally Rachel asked, "If the Nazis decide to attack Poland, do you think they'll declare war first, or do you think it will be a sneak invasion?"

"I don't think they will give a warning. They are too evil for that. We will just wake up one day, and they'll be here," Rajmund said.

"But how can they get here without us knowing they're coming?" Rachel asked.

"I don't know," Rajmund replied. "They'll probably just invade at a specific location on the border between Poland and Germany and move east, killing everyone in their path who does not surrender."

"But people have telephones. Wouldn't they call and tell us what is happening?" said Sarah.

"I don't know. Maybe they will attack with airplanes first," Rajmund replied.

"Why can't they just leave us alone?" Rachel asked. "Why do they have to conquer everyone?"

"Hitler is a crazy man. He wants to own everything," Thaddeus said. "And he hates Jews, and I hate Hitler. Hitler is worse than the dog poo that gets on your shoe when you walk in a dog yard." Everyone chuckled.

"He is dangerous," Rachel said. "I wish he would just die."

Although they did not say anything, Cass and Zofia were sitting on the floor listening to every word. Zofia looked at Cass to see if he would react to what was being said. Cass said nothing, but he knew that the situation was serious.

The next morning in Cass and Zofia's Torah class, the teacher said, "Okay, students, in the Torah we learn that there is good and evil in the world. When Eve took the apple from the forbidden tree, that was evil, right? Why was it evil? Isaac?"

Isaac was a quiet student in the class, and the teacher hoped he would participate more if she could draw him out. Isaac flushed with embarrassment and said, "Because Hashem said that they were not to eat of the tree. She did it anyway, and that was evil."

"That is very good. It's evil when we disobey Hashem. Can anyone give another example of evil?"

"When someone steals something, that's evil," another child said.

"That's correct," said the teacher. "The commandments that we were given through Moshe tell us that we are not to steal. Can anyone else give us an example of evil? How about you, Cass?"

"Nazis are evil," Cass said.

The teacher was silent for a moment then she looked down at the desk. "Why do you say Nazis are evil?"

"Because in Germany they kill people, and they won't let Jews do things that other people can do, like have shops and teach in schools. And Nazis make Jews go away to concentration camps."

The teacher again grew quiet for a moment then asked, "Who told you these things, Cass?"

"Everybody knows it," he replied. "My papa told me, my mama told me, my grandpa told me. My uncle Bernie told me that the Nazis are going to invade Poland."

All of the students began talking at once. "Is that true?"

The teacher replied, "What Cass is saying might be true, but we won't talk about that at school. Each of you should ask your parents about it."

"What will happen to the school if they attack us?"

"I don't know, but I think it is better that we not talk about it," said the teacher. "You should talk to your parents about these things. They may feel that it is better for you not to know."

"Why wouldn't they want us to know?"

"These are matters for a family to discuss," the teacher repeated. "I am not going to answer any more questions about this."

After class, the teacher asked Cass and Zofia to stay for a moment. When the other students had left, she said, "Cass, Zofia, your parents told me what happened to you this summer. Are both of you doing okay?"

Cass replied, "Yes."

Zofia said, "I'm not sure. I've been pretty scared."

The teacher replied, "If there is anything we can do to help you, just tell me. You went through something very frightening. You don't have to go through it alone. Do you understand what I am saying?"

Zofia nodded.

Cass replied, "I think so."

"Okay, your ride will be waiting. You better go. I will see you in the morning."

Cass and Zofia went out to the car and climbed inside. Later that evening Sarah, Rachel, and Rajmund came over to study with Thaddeus. They took their usual places at the dining table with Sarah next to Rajmund and Rachel next to Thaddeus. Adelajda brought in hot chocolate. Sarah opened her copy of the Torah and asked, "Okay, the question we are supposed to answer tomorrow in Jewish history class is what happened to the bodies of the brothers of Joseph. Rabbi Lieberman said that Exodus 13:9 tells us that Moses took the bones of Joseph from Egypt." She looked up Exodus 13:9. "Yes, it says right here that he did. But it doesn't say anything about his brothers."

"I think Joseph's tomb is in Israel," said Thaddeus.

"I think that's right, but what about his brothers?" asked Rachel.

"Think about it for a minute," said Sarah. "Joseph was in a tomb in Egypt, probably Goshen, for hundreds of years. Wherever he was buried, his brothers were probably buried too. So unless they were taken from Egypt with Joseph, their bodies are still in the tombs they were in."

Thaddeus said, "One day Rabbi Lieberman said that if the bodies of the brothers of Joseph were ever found, maybe scientists could someday determine who is descended from what tribe."

Rajmund closed his book reflectively. "Wow, can you imagine that? But wouldn't the bodies deteriorate after all those years?"

Sarah replied, "No, the embalming was so good, and the sarcophagi so well sealed, that Egyptian mummies are preserved to this day."

"I wonder if that is why Rabbi Lieberman wants us to think about where the bodies of Joseph's brothers are," said Rachel. "Is it a mitzvah to find the bodies of Joseph's brothers?"

"I don't think so. I wonder if the Talmud tells us if their bodies were taken from Egypt," said Sarah.

Thaddeus shook his head. "I looked, but I couldn't find anything. The Talmud is harder to read than the Torah. The translations are funny. I think the Talmud says something about the casket of Joseph floating to the top of the Nile River or something like that."

"I know, I have a hard time reading the Talmud too," said Rachel.

Cass walked into the dining room and overheard Thaddeus say that the casket of Joseph floated. "Do people always float after they die?"

Thaddeus replied, "Only if they are dead." Everyone laughed.

Cass continued. "When Papa and Josef threw the bodies of the Nazis off the boat, they floated. I wonder if dead bodies always float. Why did they throw them in the water?"

"Who wants to drive all over the Baltic Sea with a bunch of dead Nazis?" Thaddeus said. Everyone laughed again.

"Why are you asking these questions, Cass?" Rachel asked.

"I don't know. I keep thinking about those men."

Rachel reached out and took ahold of Cass's arm and pulled him to herself. She hugged him. "Are you okay, Cass?"

"I'm okay. I just keep wondering what's going to happen. I feel like something bad is going to happen. Everybody seems so scared."

"Everything is going to be okay." Rachel kissed Cass on the cheek.

Everyone around the table became quiet for a few moments. Cass left the room and went upstairs to bed.

"I heard that in Germany, they are putting Jews in prisons. They call them concentration camps," Sarah said. "Why would they put someone in prison just for being a Jew?"

"Because they're idiots," Rajmund said.

"What are you going to do, Rajmund, if they invade Poland and take over?" asked Rachel. "Are you going to help us if you can, or are you going to pretend you don't know us?"

"I would never do that," Rajmund said. "I will do whatever I can to help you if that happens. I will get a gun and fight the Nazis."

"That's easy to say now. But if they start arresting Jews and sending them away, you'll be putting yourself in danger if you try to help us. You aren't a Jew, so you won't be in any danger unless you try to help us."

"I won't do that, Sarah. I will fight for you until they either shoot me or take me away." He reached over and took ahold of Sarah's hand.

She looked in his eyes and gently squeezed his hand. "I believe you."

Later that night Thaddeus and Rachel were talking alone with each other while Rajmund and Sarah were talking alone. Sarah told Rajmund, "I'm so happy we met, Rajmund. Even though we are from different cultures and religions, I have really become close to you."

Rajmund replied, "I feel the same way, Sarah. I enjoy being with you so much. You know, just a year ago I thought Jews were strange people with weird ideas who were cruel to everyone who wasn't a Jew. It wasn't until I got to know Thad and his family that I realized how wrong I was. I think the reason so many people don't like Jews is because they have those same ideas about Jews that really aren't true." Rajmund became silent for a moment then said, "Sarah, I really want to start seeing you, but I promised when I came to the school that I wouldn't go out with any Jewish girls."

"I am so happy to hear you say that, Rajmund. I want to start going with you too, but if we do, we have to keep it secret. My parents would disown me if they found out I was seeing a goy."

"A what?"

"A goy. That means a gentile."

"Is it a bad thing to be a goy?" Rajmund asked.

"No, not at all. But the thing is, in my religion we are not supposed to date anyone who is not Jewish."

Rajmund nodded, "And in my religion we are not supposed to date anyone who is not Catholic. Isn't it weird that everybody only wants to accept people who are just like them?"

"I suppose the reasons make sense," replied Rachel. "I think it would be difficult for a Christian and a Jew to be married. How would they raise their children?"

"I think you would expose them to both religions and let the children choose which is better," Rajmund said.

The next day in school Rabbi Lieberman, who was the yeshiva's headmaster, called all of the students and teachers into the gymnasium for an assembly. The students walked in single file and took their seats. Rabbi Lieberman walked onto the platform and said, "Good morning, students. I asked all of you to come in here to discuss a new protocol we are implementing. We are going to start having safety drills. At exactly ten o'clock, five minutes from now, you are going to hear the new emergency alarm. That alarm will be what you'll hear if there is ever a threat to the school like a tornado or a bomb. All of your teachers are going to have a specific route to take you to the basement for shelter. When you get to the basement, your teacher will show you where to go. You are to walk up to the wall single file, and stand next to one another with your face to the wall. We are going to start having these drills every week. This is to practice in case there is ever a real emergency.

"If it is a real danger, and not a drill, the danger may be several hours away. In that situation we may permit you to leave the premises, but only with your parents or someone designated by your parents. It is important that you discuss with your parents what should happen in the event of an emergency and that they inform us what they would like for you to do. If your parents or their designated representatives don't pick you up, and we don't believe that you can reach your home safely, then you will have to stay here with the rest of the students. Does everyone understand?"

The students listened intently as Rabbi Lieberman explained the new protocol. The younger children were having trouble understanding what he said, but the older children knew. Zofia and Cass were sitting in the third row from the front. "Why are they doing this, Cass?" she asked.

"I don't know," Cass said.

Rabbi Lieberman continued, "Okay, now the alarm is going to ring in thirty seconds. Just remain in your seats. Today we only want you to learn what it sounds like."

Suddenly, there occurred a loud buzzing sound. For most of the students, the sound was terrifying and deafening, as it should have been. They had never heard such a sound before. After the alarm stopped, Rabbi Lieberman explained the process again and then excused the assembly to their respective classes.

That afternoon on the way home in the limousine, Cass said, "Now I know what will happen if the Nazis invade."

"What will happen?" asked Rachel.

"There will be a loud, ear-shattering buzzing sound. Then they will be here."

"That's only if you are at school," said Thaddeus. "If we're at home or at the summerhouse, there may not be any warning. If we are in the mountains, we will probably know from people we see before we come back down."

As the car drove past Park Dreszera, established in the summer of 1938 by the mayor of Warsaw, they noticed a large group of protesters partially blocking the road. They were holding signs that had a symbol Cass had seen only twice before, once above the front door of the yeshiva and once on the German officers on the boat, but he knew it was called a swastika. It was a strange image that he would never forget. One protester was holding a large sign that read "National Socialist Party." Visibility was clear in the afternoon daylight.

"Who are all these people?" asked Rachel. "What are they doing? There must be two hundred of them."

"They are Nazis," Thaddeus said.

"But what are they doing in the streets?"

"This is a protest."

The protesters blocked the streets, forcing the chauffeur to stop the car and wait. They were chanting, "National Socialist." In the distance, they could see a large number of trucks and police officers approaching. The chauffeur tried to back up to get out of danger, but the limousine was blocked by other cars. They were forced to sit and watch. As the police drew closer to the crowd, some of the protesters broke rank and ran up the street. Others stood and shouted louder. Cass could see that some of them had guns.

Thaddeus said, "If they start shooting, duck down."

Soon the police and the protesters were fighting with clubs and knives. Someone started shooting. Then there were dozens of people lying in the streets. As the police continued to advance, the protesters retreated. Eventually, they had retreated all the way back to the Bieberstein automobile. The children locked all of the doors. Someone fell backward with a loud thud against the car next to where Rachel was sitting. He turned around and looked into the car. He was covered in blood. Suddenly, two police officers ran up to him, turned him around, and began beating him. As they hit him repeatedly, he screamed in anguish. They then dragged him away in handcuffs. By this time, the car was surrounded by protesters, running to get away from the police. Some pounded on the car and pleaded for Rachel to open the car door.

"Don't open the door," Rajmund said.

"But they're going to kill them," replied Rachel.

"If you open the door, they'll crowd into the car, and the police will think we're part of the protest."

"He's right. We can't open the door," said Thaddeus. "It's too dangerous. They might even try to kill us and steal our car."

The fighting around the Bieberstein car continued for ten minutes with people repeatedly bumping into the car, pounding on windows, and trying to open the doors. The police clearly had the upper hand, given that they outnumbered the protesters three to one. The police were brutal, striking the protesters, who appeared to be mostly young people in their early twenties. Cass wondered, *Why do they want to be Nazis? Do they know something that I don't know?* He didn't like them because of what they stood for, but at the same time, he felt sorry for them because of the severe beatings they were receiving. He saw a young man pull a knife on one of the police officers, who simply pulled out a revolver and shot him.

The fighting began to subside. Most of the protesters had been taken into custody or fled. Slowly, the traffic started to move. Several police officers assisted by directing the traffic away from the congested area. No one said anything all the way to Rachel and Sarah's house. When they got out of the car, Rachel said, "I can't study tonight. I will see you in the morning when you pick me up."

Thaddeus replied, "That's okay. I don't feel like studying tonight either."

"Me neither," said Sarah.

They dropped off Rajmund, and Zofia, Cass, and Thaddeus rode home in silence. Cass had much to think about. This was the second time he had seen people killed. First he saw two men die right in front of him on the boat. On that occasion he felt sick. Today he saw at least a dozen people die. This time he didn't feel sick. He tried to understand it. He noticed that both times when he saw people killed, the people killed were Nazis. *Is that what Nazis are supposed to do? Are they supposed to die?* These were difficult questions for a young boy who was only seven years old. But this was the world in which Cass had found himself. It was the world in which he would have to live.

He made up his mind that if the Nazis invaded, he would become a Resistance fighter. He was not impressed with the courage of the protesters at all. They seemed foolish to him. The police dealt with them harshly; maybe the police knew something he didn't know. But most important, the Nazis want to kill Jews. *I am a Jew, my family are Jews, and Rachel and Sarah are Jews. That means I have no choice.* He had to fight them as long as they wanted to kill Jews. He decided on that day that when the Nazis invaded, he would be a Resistance fighter, and he would kill the Nazis.

CHAPTER
7

I N NOVEMBER OF 1938, Josef Litynski opened a jazz club in the rear section of his restaurant. He called it Litynski's Speakeasy. Named after American jazz clubs, the facility boasted a large dance floor, a sitting area with tables, and a stage large enough to hold a small orchestra. Previously serving as a warehouse, with minor modifications, the area easily transformed into a dance club with a table seating capacity of two hundred. A live eight-piece band, consisting of a saxophone, drums, three trumpets, a clarinet, a bass, and a six-string guitar, created an exciting atmosphere that became popular within weeks of opening night.

Yet, there was a new tension in the air after *Kristallnacht*, the "Night of Broken Glass" when all over Germany and German-occupied territories, the windows of Jewish businesses and synagogues were shattered by SA paramilitary force, leaving glass strewn about the streets. At least ninety-one Jews were murdered and thirty thousand Jewish men were arrested and sent to concentration camps. Although Poland was not part of the Kristallnacht, the event struck fear throughout the Jewish community in Poland. Cass wondered, *Could that happen here?*

One afternoon, while riding home from school, Rajmund said, "Hey, do you want to come to my dad's new jazz club?"

Cass, who loved jazz, sat up. "A jazz club. That would be amazing. Can Zofia and I come too?"

Rajmund laughed. "Actually, kids aren't allowed in the club. Even Thad and I aren't supposed to be there. But since my dad owns it, I think we can probably get you in if you promise to sit at a back table. And you and Zofia will have to stay off the dance floor."

Thaddeus said, "I think that would be a lot of fun."

"I do too," Rachel said.

"When could we come?" Sarah asked.

Rajmund replied, "I can ask my dad if you can come next Saturday night. It will be busy, so no one will notice there are minors in the place."

With a great deal of effort, Cass and Thaddeus persuaded their parents to let them visit the jazz club the following Saturday evening. They knew how much the boys liked jazz and decided it would be beneficial for them to hear it live. It was only because Josef promised to keep an eye on the children that Sigmund was persuaded to allow it. Zofia was permitted to go because her father, Lech, would be there. Sarah and Rachel just told their parents they were going to Mr. Litynski's restaurant and said nothing about the jazz club.

After a week of excited anticipation, Saturday night finally arrived. Following the instructions of Josef, Lech took the children to the alley behind the club and entered through a rear door. At Sigmund's request, the chauffeur promised to stay with the children until they were ready to go home. Rajmund took them to a reserved table at the rear of the club next to the stairway to the wine cellar. Lech found a booth a short distance away, where he could watch the children and was soon joined by Patrycja, his wife, who agreed to meet him there.

Cass looked around the room and saw that it was filled to capacity. The music was loud; the patrons were laughing and dancing. He was amazed at the way they swung around on the dance floor.

After talking for a few hours, when the room was crowded with patrons, Thaddeus asked Rachel, "So do you want to do this?"

"Do what?"

"Do you want to dance?"

"What? I don't know how to dance."

"Do it," shouted Cass. "It will be fun."

"It's easy," Thaddeus said. "All you do is move in time with the music and swing each other around."

"Try it," Sarah said. "We're going to, right, Rajmund?"

"Yeah, let's go." Rajmund took Sarah's hand and led her out onto the dance floor. Rachel and Thaddeus followed them. The band played "In the Mood" by Glenn Miller. Cass and Zofia held hands and swayed in time with the music in their chairs.

"I wish we could dance too," shouted Zofia over the music.

"Me too," Cass agreed. They continued to sway in their chairs, holding hands while Rajmund, Sarah, Rachel, and Thaddeus danced on the floor. Cass looked over at Lech, who smiled at him. *I wonder if they will dance,* thought Cass.

Josef came over to the table and asked, "Are you kids having fun?"

Zofia smiled and nodded.

Cass said, "Yeah, this is great. The band is really good."

"They're music students over at the university," said Josef. "They play here to earn extra money for tuition. Someday you two will be in college. Do you know what you want to do when you grow up?"

"I want to work on airplanes," Cass said. "I want to fly them too."

"I want to be a housewife," Zofia said.

Rajmund, Sarah, Rachel, and Thaddeus finished their dances and returned to the table. "Hey, Papa," Rajmund said to his father. "We had a great time tonight."

Josef laughed. "Okay, well, you kids are going to have to go soon. It is almost ten o'clock. Your parents wanted all of you home by ten, but you can come back again if you would like to."

"We would like to," Cass said as the group got up to leave.

The children accepted Josef's invitation and returned the following Saturday evening and the one after that. Chanukah arrived on December 17, 1938. Ordinarily, the days of Chanukah were the happiest days of the year in the Bieberstein home. This Chanukah season, however, was enveloped in a dark cloud that hung over the festivities. Everyone silently went through the motions of lighting the candles and celebrating the days, but something felt wrong. The normal excitement of the season was not there. As Christmas approached, the staff celebrated in the usual way with a tree on the landing, but even they seemed affected by the atmosphere of impending doom.

On the Saturday before Christmas, which was Christmas Eve that year, they children visited Josef's club and sat at their usual table. The interior was decorated with lights and a large pine tree. Cass looked around the large dance hall and was mesmerized by the beautiful colors. Electric Christmas lights were still a novelty in Poland in 1938. The Biebersteins had electric Christmas lights, as did a few of their neighbors, but only the wealthy could afford this novel invention. The lights excited Cass.

Throughout the night Rajmund, Sarah, Rachel, and Thaddeus danced zealously. They had learned the moves and danced with the skill of many of the older couples. Cass and Zofia sat at the table talking and listening to the music. Cass heard someone behind him say, "Hey, look. It's the Jew kids. What are you Jew kids doing in here?"

Cass turned around to see Rajmund's old friends. One of them asked, "What are you stupid kids doing in here? This is a place for adults."

Cass looked at the booth where Lech had previously been sitting, but the booth was empty. He looked out at the floor and saw Lech dancing with Patrycja.

"What are you going to do now that your big brother isn't here to protect you?"

"Ignore them, Cass," said Zofia. "They aren't worth it."

One of the boys said, "Oh, the little Jew whore finally speaks."

That comment was too much for Cass. He picked up a glass and threw water into the teenager's face, splashing water all over the table next to theirs. A man and a woman at that table had seen what was happening, and the man stood up quickly and left the table.

"Ah!" The older boy bent over, wiping the water from his face with his hand. Just as the other teenager grabbed Cass by the collar to drag him out the back door, Josef ran up to the table. "Stop it! If you boys came to cause trouble, then you need to leave."

"We were joking," one of the teenagers whined. "This punk went crazy."

"I know what you said about this little girl. The man sitting at this table came and told me. I would have done the same thing if I were Cass. If that is how you intend to behave, then you should just go. We don't want troublemakers here. What happened to you boys, anyway? You were always such gentlemen when you were growing up. No more trouble if you want to stay. Understood?"

"We won't cause any trouble," one of them said.

Thaddeus had noticed the commotion and returned to the table with Rajmund and the two girls. Rajmund asked, "Are you guys causing trouble again?"

"It's okay," said Josef holding his hand up for Rajmund to be silent. "I want you boys to meet Thaddeus, Rachel, and Sarah. You already met Cass and Zofia, and you know Rajmund."

The older boys laughed. One of them said, "Yes, we know Cass. He packs a mean kick. Someday he is going to play soccer." He paused for a moment and said, "My name is Ludwik. This is Feliks."

"Why don't you guys try to get along? There is no reason for all this fighting," Josef said, "especially on Christmas Eve."

"Yes, sir. We will," Feliks replied.

"You can take this table. The couple sitting here left because you were too noisy."

The older boys sat at the table next to the one where Cass was sitting. Despite the awkwardness, Ludwik said, "I will say one thing, Cass, you are a brave little fellow." Everyone laughed.

"So what brings you here tonight?" Rajmund asked.

Feliks replied, "We heard that your dad opened a jazz club. We wanted to see it."

"Where were you all summer, Rajmund?" asked Ludwik.

"I went with the Biebersteins to their summer home on the water."

"Where's that?" asked Feliks.

"Sopot."

"I've never been there. Is it nice?" asked Feliks.

"It's beautiful. We went out into the sea in the boat. We fished and swam. It was so much fun."

"Do you go to the yeshiva where Rajmund goes?" Ludwik asked, looking at Thaddeus.

Thaddeus nodded. "We all go there."

Ludwik said, "I think we are going to play a preseason soccer game with your school."

"That's right." Rajmund nodded. "Are you going out for the team at your school?"

"Yeah, we will probably meet up on the soccer field."

Rajmund nodded again. "So what have you guys been doing?"

"Not much," replied Feliks. "We just hung out most of the summer. Now that school started, we have been studying hard."

Rajmund asked, "Who were those guys you were with when we saw you in the street that day?"

"Those are just friends from church. They go to Saint Mary's," Feliks said.

Thaddeus had been silent since Feliks and Ludwik had sat at the next table. "Why don't you join us at this table? We have plenty of room."

Rachel looked at Thaddeus and whispered, "Thad, what are you doing? These guys are Nazis."

Thad kept his voice low. "No one ever gets past their hatred until they get to know the people they hate."

Rachel shook her head. "I don't know, Thad. I think these guys are pretty bad."

Feliks and Ludwik seemed surprised. They slowly stood up, walked over to the table where Thaddeus and his friends were sitting, and then sat down.

Thaddeus looked directly at Ludwik. "Why do you hate Jews?"

"What?" Ludwik's face reddened.

Rajmund spoke before Thaddeus had an opportunity to respond. "Why do you hate Jews?"

"Why do you think I hate Jews?" Ludwik asked.

Rajmund didn't respond verbally. He just tilted his head and looked at Ludwik as if to ask, "Seriously?"

Ludwik continued, "I don't hate Jews. I was just playing around."

"You were playing around when you called this beautiful little child a Jew whore?" Thaddeus asked, holding his hand out toward Zofia.

Cass looked at Zofia. Her beauty was spellbinding as she looked at Ludwik with an angelic expression.

"How can you hate someone as beautiful as this?" Rajmund asked.

Ludwik looked at Zofia, who gazed back at him. "I don't hate you," she said quietly.

Feliks leaned over and whispered to Ludwik, "Let's go. This is getting too strange."

Ludwik continued to look at Zofia. "The smoke is bad in here," he said waving his hand in front of his face. As he got up to leave, he whispered, "I'm sorry, Zofia."

Feliks and Ludwik left the club. Cass wondered why Ludwik said he was sorry to Zofia. He had been insensitive, calling Zofia a little Jew whore repeatedly. Now he suddenly tells her he is sorry. *Why the sudden change in behavior?*

Rajmund, Thaddeus, Sarah, Rachel, Zofia, and Cass stayed at the club for a couple of hours after Feliks and Ludwik left. Zofia and Cass even got up and danced to a few songs. By half past ten they were tired and were out way past the youngsters' bedtime. "We better get you kids home," said Lech.

As the group left the club they noticed a number of swing kids on the street in front of the club. They were talking and smoking cigarettes. As the limousine drove by slowly, some of them held up their hands to say hello.

"I don't understand why Hitler hates swing," Rachel said.

"Swing is improvisation. For Hitler, everything has to be planned and precise," Lech told her.

It was a little surprising to hear Lech speak. He was generally very quiet during conversations in the car. To Cass, it seemed that everything in the world was changing. Lech speaking during conversations of the passengers was just another unexpected event. In his mind, Cass pictured the following morning's newspaper headlines: "Lech speaks." He laughed quietly but out loud.

Zofia asked, "What's funny?"

"Lech speaks."

Rajmund and Thaddeus looked at Cass.

"Lech speaks," Cass repeated.

Lech looked in the rearview mirror then chuckled quietly to himself.

"Oh," Rajmund whispered with a smile. "Lech speaks."

The following Monday morning, Lech drove the children to school as usual. As the children got out of the car, they noticed the students were standing outside the front of the building. "I wonder what happened," said Cass. As he looked at the school, Cass could see that most of the windows had been broken. Swastikas had been painted all over the front of building in red and blue paint.

Zofia said, "Wow, this is bad."

As the children stood looking at the building, Cass heard someone shouting behind him. Turning around he saw approximately eighty teenagers on the other side of the street shouting at the schoolchildren. At first, he could not understand what they were saying, but then he heard it. "Go home, Jew."

Cass did not understand. *Go home? What do they mean? Where is home?*

Lech said, "Don't pay attention to them. Go inside the building."

The children walked through the crowd and into the front door of the schoolhouse. Inside, the halls were painted with swastikas, and the lockers were dented and some of them smashed. When Cass and Zofia reached their classroom, there were large swastikas written on the blackboard. The windows were broken, and the desks were turned over. An aquarium was smashed; water and dead fish were on the floor. The teacher was standing in front of the classroom, crying. Cass asked, "Are we having school today?"

The teacher nodded as she wiped her eyes with a handkerchief. "Would you help me turn the desks over before the other children come in?"

Cass and Zofia began turning the desks over and placing them in straight rows as the teacher erased the blackboard. Soon other children entered the room. Some of them were crying. Others were talking. The teacher instructed the students to finish straightening the desks. A custodian came in and mopped up the water on the floor, then picked up the broken glass from the windows and the aquarium. When all the desks had been placed in neat rows and the water and glass cleaned up, the children took their places.

The headmaster, Rabbi Lieberman, entered the room and stood in front of the class. He cleared his throat. "Children, you have seen something very ugly here today. The world can be a very cruel place. But this is not new for our people. Many years ago, our ancestors in Israel were conquered by King Nebuchadnezzar. The Jews were taken into captivity in Babylon. We have lived in exile since that time. Everywhere we have gone we have been criticized, persecuted, and blamed for all of the world's misfortunes. The symbol you saw on the outside of the school building and on the blackboard is called a swastika. It was put there by people who hate Jews.

Whenever you see that symbol you know that the person who wrote it hates Jews, and it is not safe for you to be around him."

The rabbi sat at the chair behind the teacher's desk. "The Jews were exiled. Then at the beginning of this century, they began to return to their homeland, the land of Israel, then called Palestine. When you hear that chanting 'Jews, go home,' you should proudly hold your head up because they are acknowledging that your real home is in Israel. While they mean it as an insult, it is actually the highest honor they can give you. They are acknowledging your place in history as the chosen people of God. Don't be ashamed when you hear those words. Hold your head up high and be proud that you are one of the children of Jacob. You are a Jew."

The words of the rabbi were intended to console but did little to alleviate the fear of the children. After he left the room the children began talking about what they had seen and heard. Cass turned and looked out the window.

Zofia whispered, "Cass, what are you looking at?"

"I am looking at those people across the street. Everyone knows they did this to our school. Why aren't they being arrested?"

"I don't know," Zofia said. "I don't understand any of this."

"Remember what Rabbi Lieberman said."

Zofia sighed. "It still doesn't make me feel very good, and I don't like hearing it. And when I see that swastika it reminds me of those German soldiers on the boat last summer."

Cass nodded. "Don't be afraid, Zofia. Everything will be okay." But Cass watched as the police arrived at the scene and just told the teenagers to disperse.

After the rabbi left the room, the teacher stood up and instructed the class to take out their history books. Cass opened to the page on the Babylonian invasion of Israel during the reign of Zedekiah. *Are we still paying for his disobedience?* he wondered. *Jeremiah warned of the consequence of disobedience. Is this why the Jews are dispersed throughout the world and enduring persecution today? This is what I have learned in yeshiva.*

Cass sat at his desk throughout the history lesson, half listening and half pondering the unsettling situation between the Jewish schoolchildren and the non-Jewish teenage community. *Why is there so much hatred and anger toward the Jews?* he asked himself. *What created such anger? Are the Jews really so bad?*

Later that evening, Sarah, Rachel, Thaddeus, and Rajmund studied in the dining room, as usual. They were all unusually quiet, still distraught over what they had seen that day at school. At about nine thirty, Cass came downstairs for some cookies and milk. As he walked past the dining room, Sarah said, "Hi, Cass. How are you doing tonight?"

"I'm fine, thank you," Cass replied as he walked into the kitchen. He was not really fine. He had a terrible feeling that things were only going to get worse. It seemed that every day he saw a new alarming event, and each of those events seemed directed toward the Jews. Each day seemed to carry him closer to an unknown object. Now the hidden object seemed so close he could almost reach out and touch it. *What is it?*

One night, Cass overheard the nanny Adelajda and Irena talking with Sigmund at the kitchen table. Sigmund and Irena each had a glass of wine. Cass stood in the hall outside the kitchen door listening. Lech sat in a corner in a chair, but was not participating in the conversation.

Sigmund said, "If we have to leave quickly, you can come with us to the lodge in the forest."

"Wouldn't it just be a matter of time before they found us there?" Adelajda asked.

"Possibly, but it might also be a place we could hide out until the conflict ceases. We don't know that Poland would lose."

Irena ran her index finger along the stem of her wine goblet. "I keep hearing that Poland would not be able to withstand the Germans for more than a few weeks at most. We are outmanned and outgunned. Do you think we could really survive an attack, Sigmund?"

"I don't want to be the bearer of bad news," Sigmund said, "but Papa and my other friends in the military tell me the same thing. If Germany launched a full-scale invasion, we wouldn't stand a chance. I just don't believe the Germans would do something that crazy."

Irena shook her head. "I hope you're right. These are scary times."

Cass turned and walked down the hall to the steps. *Everything is happening so fast*, he thought. *I am growing up fast.* He walked up the steps then down the hall to his bedroom. A fire in the fireplace kept his room warm. He pulled back the clean white sheets, climbed into the bed and under the covers, and soon fell asleep.

CHAPTER

8

CLASSES RESUMED AFTER the winter holidays. Nearly every day the students at the yeshiva would see the local teenagers sitting at the café across the street from the school. When they came out to get into their cars, the locals would often stare at them. Sometimes the teenagers would say something unpleasant, usually with an ethnic overtone. Sometimes the teenagers would shout "Jew, go home," to which the students in the yeshiva would begin chanting, "aliyah." The rabbi had told them that aliyah is the call of every Jew to come home to Israel, and that when the Poles told them to go home, they were unknowingly honoring the sacred call of aliyah.

As the weather became warmer, Cass, Zofia, Sarah, and Rachel would attend the soccer games to watch Thaddeus and Rajmund play. When it was cold they would all huddle together in the bleachers under a thick blanket. Cass enjoyed these times. He liked Sarah and Rachel who always wanted to hug him. He especially liked Zofia, who would snuggle next to him under the blanket. One day at the game, Zofia was unusually quiet. Cass asked, "What's wrong?"

Zofia shook her head slowly. "Do you ever get frightened? Do you ever worry that Germany will invade? It seems like that is all anyone talks about anymore."

Cass nodded as he looked down at the blanket. "Papa says our childhood is being stolen."

Sarah, who overheard the conversation, said, "I think the best thing is to not worry about it, but we need to plan what we're going to do if we're invaded. We must all agree to meet somewhere."

"Where?" Zofia asked.

"Maybe we could meet at the schoolhouse," Cass said.

"I don't know if the school would be a good place to go with the local kids hanging out at the café. They might try to start a fight if they know there is no one to help us," Rachel said.

"Maybe we should meet at my house," Cass said. "Then we can go up to the mountains and get away from the city."

The children continued to watch the game in silence. The excitement was gone. There was too much fear.

Due to the events of the previous year in the Baltic Sea, the family decided not to spend the entire summer of 1939 in Sopot. They visited several times, and stayed for about a week each time, but the memories of the events of the previous summer took the joy out of the place. Most of the summer was spent at the mansion on Pulawska Street. When they stayed at the house they had no encounters with anti-Semitism. Cass and Zofia spent most of the summer studying. Thaddeus and Rajmund spent most of the time practicing with the soccer team.

On Friday, September 1, 1939, the Bieberstein family arrived at Shabaro Resort Hotel, located thirty miles east of Warsaw, for a weekend visit. They had left Warsaw at three o'clock, planning to arrive before Shabbat, which would begin at sunset. As the concierge checked them in, Cass heard roaring outside of the hotel.

Zofia, who was traveling with the family, asked, "What is that?"

Sigmund turned his head slightly to hear better. "I don't know. It sounds like airplanes."

Irena and Sigmund continued to check in as Cass, Thaddeus, and Zofia walked out the front door of the hotel to investigate.

"Cass, why are all those planes in the sky?" asked Zofia. "There must be hundreds of them; what are those little things falling from them? They look like little pieces of rice."

The sky was filled with thousands of German Stuka dive-bombers. Cass recognized them because his grandfather Major Bieberstein had showed him pictures of all of the German warplanes. The planes had a terrifying high-pitched whining sound as they dived before dropping the bomb. Some of them had sirens to increase the sound audible on the ground. Cass knew the pilots didn't need to dive before releasing a bomb, so they must be doing it only to cause the loud whining sound to frighten the people; or maybe they wanted to be closer to the target for accuracy. Whatever the reason, it was terrifying.

Thaddeus put his hand over his eyes to block the sun. "What the heck is going on? What are those things falling from the planes?"

The earth began to shake. Low-pitched explosions could be heard as bright flashes of light appeared ominously on the horizon. As dozens of guests ran out of the hotel, Thaddeus, Cass, and Zofia ran back inside looking for Sigmund and Irena. "What is happening?" Cass screamed.

The concierge frantically turned the dial on the lobby radio seeking a clear signal. After several minutes of finding only static, squealing, and poor reception, he finally found a Warsaw station broadcasting the news. Intermittently between static and high-pitched squeals, the patrons could hear the voice of an announcer clearly reading a script. "Poland has been attacked by Germany. Please stay in your homes. Do not panic. Warsaw is safe. This will be over soon. We have a strong army."

Sigmund, who had given Lech the day off, ran out of the hotel to get the car. The rest of the family stayed by the reception desk. A few minutes later Sigmund came back inside and motioned for everyone to follow him out the door. Cass saw his father opening the right rear door. "Get in," shouted Sigmund. Cass had never heard his father speak with such stress.

"What's happening?" Cass asked.

"Get in, I'll tell you!"

Zofia, Cass, and Thaddeus climbed into the rear seat of the car. Sigmund climbed into the front seat with Irena. "We're being bombed by Germany," Sigmund said. "Bernie was right."

The car sped away from the hotel as Cass gazed out of the window at the skies. He saw thousands of bombers flying overhead in the direction of the city. Bombs fell from the sky, exploding fiercely as they hit the ground.

"Why are we going to Warsaw? Warsaw is being bombed," Cass asked. Bombs exploded all around the car. Dirt and debris showered the automobile. Zofia looked at Cass for comfort. Overwhelmed, he embraced her. "Don't cry, Zofia. Everything will be okay." In truth, he did not believe everything would be okay; he really believed they would die.

"We have to get back to the city," said Sigmund, belatedly responding to Cass. "We'll have the protection of the military. Here we are vulnerable to Germany's ground troops."

"What about our plans to go to the mountain house?" Thaddeus asked.

"If Warsaw is being overrun by the Nazis we'll go to the mountains. Let's get to Warsaw to see what's happening. At least there we'll have protection against the ground troops."

"What ground troops?" asked Thaddeus.

"I'm sure they will be here shortly."

Upon approaching the city, shock and horror filled the passengers of the vehicle. Bodies, and parts of bodies, lined the streets. Buildings had collapsed into crumbles of brick. A once-pretty young woman, her left arm severed from her bloody body, staggered and fell against their car, spilling blood over the window next to Zofia's face. Zofia screamed and put her head in her hands.

"What's happening?" asked Cass frantically.

"Germany has invaded," replied Sigmund a second time.

Irena sat silently peering through the window. Was she in shock, or could she simply not decide what to say? Cass remembered that she was the one who always realized the threat of Germany and encouraged Sigmund and Grandfather to listen to Bernard, who warned repeatedly of the possibility of a German invasion. Irena was not in shock; she was heartbroken that she had allowed this to happen to her family, even though she was helpless to prevent it. Sensing the gaze of Cass, she turned to him lovingly and said, "I didn't want this to happen to you children. I am so sorry I could not prevent this." Her guilt manifested the feelings of hundreds of thousands of mothers in Poland that day, who cried bitterly, "Why couldn't I protect my family from this horrific evil? I have failed as a mother."

The car approached a bridge on the Vistula River. Cass saw a Stuka coming straight at the limousine. The engine made a terrifying screaming sound. The plane got so close Cass could see the pilot in the cockpit; then the pilot pulled up.

Bombs dropped from the sky into the water and exploded. Sigmund put his foot on the brake and hesitated. "Should I cross?"

"Yes," Irena replied. "We have no choice. We need to get back to Warsaw."

Sigmund looked toward the sky to see if any bombs were falling toward the bridge. The dark sky, filled with smoke, blocked the sunlight. Visibility was near zero. He pushed the accelerator to the floor, and the vehicle sped across the bridge with the tires squealing. On the bridge, they had to swerve around several cars that had stopped behind a carriage whose horses had been spooked by the bomb blasts. Sigmund again pushed the accelerator to the floor. Zofia screamed as the right side of the vehicle scraped against the railing of the side of the bridge. Cass was relieved when they reached the other side of the river. On the road, hundreds of people ran in different directions, jumping over bodies and debris strewn everywhere. Unbelievable anguish and shock appeared on the faces of the people running along the side of the road. Some of them reached out to the car as if they could find relief in it.

"Where are we going to go when we get to Warsaw?" asked Thaddeus. He had not spoken much since they'd gotten into the car.

"We'll go home to see what is happening there. Then we'll find out where it's safest in the city," replied Sigmund.

Irena asked, "Do you think our house is still there? It looks like the bombs destroyed most of Warsaw."

"I hope so," said Sigmund as if he thought things would soon return to normal and they could go back home. "If it isn't we can go to the mountain chalet."

Irena said softly, "Sigmund, you need to get out of Warsaw. You've been helping the Jews from Germany. Everyone knows it. They'll come looking for you."

"I can't leave you and the children here alone. Who will take care of you?"

"But Sigmund, they will kill you. You are an enemy of Germany because you helped their Jews. If Poland doesn't win, you'll be sought out for execution."

Cass asked, "What are you talking about, Mama?"

"Nothing. Just adult talk."

Thaddeus looked at his father. "Mama is right, Papa. You can't stay here. When we get back to the house, we need to find a place where it is safe, but you need to leave. Maybe you should join Uncle Bernie in America. When things settle down, we can join you."

"I think I will head toward Lithuania. I believe I can get passage north through Lithuania where I can get to the coast. As soon as I get to America, I'll get a house for us and send for you."

"What if you run into Soviets along the way? Soviets have been brutal to the Jews in Russia too. I don't know that they will be any better than the Germans," Irena said.

"I don't know what else to do."

When they arrived at the Bieberstein mansion, they ran into the house. Relieved to see the home had not been damaged, they assembled in the dining room with the staff to decide what to do.

Irena said, "Papa is going to leave for Lithuania and try to make his way to America where Bernard went. Once he is settled in, he'll send for us."

"Do we need to leave if Poland wins this war?" Thaddeus asked.

Cass noticed that Lech, the chauffeur, seemed preoccupied with the keys to the automobile as the family discussed the plans.

Sigmund said, "Right now we need to act as if Poland has already lost. If Poland wins, then we can come back and take over our house again."

"What are we going to do after you are gone?" Cass asked.

His father said, "I know a businessman who has a Chanel gift factory over on Marszalkowska Street. It is a six-story building and will be far safer than this house during the bombing. It's a much larger brick building, and a bomb won't do as much damage if it gets hit. I will arrange for Lech to take you there. You can stay there until the fighting stops."

Later that day Sigmund and his brothers decided to take the car to the Lithuanian border, intending to get out of Poland and to America so he could send for the family. As he stood at the front door and said good-bye, Irena and the children cried. "It won't be long," Sigmund promised. "You have plenty of money to survive until I send for you. Go to the perfume factory until the bombing stops. Then you can come back home and stay here until I send for you."

After Sigmund left, Irena, the children, the grandparents, and all of the house employees walked with Lech to the factory. It took an hour to get all of them there. When they arrived they went into a large room on the first floor that had served as the boardroom. In the center of the room was a table large enough to seat thirty people. While they stayed at the factory the table would serve as the dining table. They placed blankets out on the floor where they would sleep at night.

Cass and Zofia laid their blankets out next to each other. Adelajda said, "Cass, you and Zofia shouldn't sleep that close. You are a boy and she is a girl."

Irena said softly, "I think it is okay this time, Adelajda. These are very unusual circumstances. They are going to need whatever comfort they can give each other. Besides, we're all in here together. They can't get into trouble in here."

"As you wish, ma'am," Adelajda said.

All afternoon they could hear bombs dropping outside. The ground shook furiously and incessantly, instilling terror in the families hiding out in the factory. Several times Zofia cried to herself. Her mother tried to comfort her, but she seemed to need the comfort of Cass more than that of her mother.

The bombing left the city with no electricity, so they used candles for light. They burned a fire in the fireplace for heat. There was no radio. Toward evening Lech said he was going out, but he would be back shortly. He was going to take his wife with him.

"Where are you going?" Irena asked.

"We're going to find out what we can and get some supplies."

"Why don't you take Thaddeus instead of Patrycja?" asked Irena. "He could help you carry supplies."

"That's okay. I'm sure I will need Thad to help me later." Lech and Patrycja turned and walked out of the room.

Grandpa Szyncer came over to Irena and sat next to her. "How are you holding up?"

"I'm okay, but I'm worried about the children," she said, looking at Cass and Zofia.

"I am too," he replied. "How about you, Adelajda? Are you doing all right?"

Adelajda nodded her head. "I have no family except for my parents, so for me, this is probably much easier than it would be if I had children."

Irena nodded. "Knowing you can't do anything for the children is the hardest part."

Grandpa Szyncer said, "Irena, did it strike you as a little odd that Lech left with Patrycja? Why wouldn't he want to take Thaddeus to help him carry supplies?"

Irena nodded. "Yes, it did seem a little strange. Maybe they just wanted to spend time together in light of all that has happened."

"I don't know," replied Dr. Szyncer. "It makes me a little uncomfortable. You don't think they would abandon us and leave Warsaw without Zofia, do you?"

Irena shook her head. "I don't think so."

Around the room people were cuddling and leaning back against the wall for support. Cass lay down on the blanket, and Zofia lay next to him with her head on his shoulder and his arm around her.

We are just children, thought Cass. Then he said, "Zofia, we are young, and we have had to grow up so fast. I want you to know that whatever happens, I love you too. I always will."

"Do you think we will ever be married?" she asked.

Cass could smell the pleasant fragrance of Zofia's perfume in her hair. "Maybe we will." He paused then said, "That would be nice."

"But what if we die tonight? Then we will never be married."

"I know."

Zofia pulled herself up on her elbows and looked at Cass in the dim light. "We could get married tonight."

Cass looked into her eyes and observed her soft features. "How could we do that? There's no rabbi or priest."

"You don't always have a priest or a rabbi," she said. "Sometimes you just have to do what you need to do."

"Are you saying we should get married tonight by ourselves without a priest or a rabbi? We are way too young. Our parents wouldn't let us."

"You don't always have a priest or a rabbi to marry you, and our parents don't have to know. Think about it. Adam and Eve didn't have a priest or a rabbi. Let's just say our vows to each other."

"That sounds really strange, Zofia," said Cass.

"It isn't as strange as being in a building in the middle of a city with dead people and bombs falling everywhere."

Cass gave Zofia a gentle kiss on the cheek. "We can't be married, but things will always be different now. We both said we want to be."

Irena said, "You children need to be quiet now. We are trying to sleep."

"Okay," replied Cass.

Zofia slept in Cass's arms that night. It was a pleasant, gentle sleep. The sweetness of the moment engulfed them in love and affection. They slept well, notwithstanding the bombs exploding outside. They awakened the following morning to the smell of biscuits and gravy. "That smells so good," said Cass.

"I'll get some biscuits for you," said Irena. "But no gravy for you, Cass—it's bacon gravy. Do you want gravy on your biscuits, Zofia?"

Zofia replied, "No, I'll have what Cass is having."

"Okay." Irena placed a plate of biscuits in front of the children with a small container of jelly and butter. "Here's some jelly." She retrieved a glass of water for each of them. "I'm sorry we don't have milk or orange juice; for now, this is all we have."

"It's good, Mama," Cass said as he picked up a biscuit from the plate, put some jelly on it, and began eating.

Zofia took a biscuit then looked around the room. "Hey, where are Mama and Papa? I don't see them."

Irena looked at Cass then Zofia. "They haven't come back yet. They probably decided to stay somewhere last night."

"But how do we know if they're okay?" Zofia sounded panicky.

Irena replied, "I'm sure they are okay. They're probably at our house picking up food."

"Did they say when they would be back?" Zofia asked.

"No, don't worry, sweetie. They'll be back soon."

A few moments later Zofia's parents returned carrying boxes of food. They set the boxes on the floor next to Irena. Zofia stood up and ran over to them and hugged them. "Mama, Papa. I didn't know what happened to you."

"We had to get supplies," Lech replied. "We have bags of white beans and rice."

Grandpa Szyncer said, "There's no more water. The pipes must have been hit by a bomb. We thought that might happen so we filled up some tanks, but with this many people it won't last for more than a day or two."

"Did you have breakfast?" Irena asked Zofia's parents.

"No, we stayed at the house last night and loaded up the supplies this morning," replied Lech.

"What's it like out there now?" Grandpa asked.

Patrycja replied, "It's terrible. Buildings everywhere are completely destroyed. There are bodies all over the streets. I counted forty-three dead bodies just going from here to the house."

"Is the house damaged at all?" asked Grandpa.

"No, the house is fine," said Lech. "I didn't see any houses bombed on our street. I fed the animals."

"Are the animals scared?" asked Irena.

"Yes, the dogs were looking for places to hide all night." Lech took his hat off and rubbed his head. "Rex was not as frightened as the little one. I think Rex was more concerned with protecting the house than hiding. He was so shook up he didn't even recognize us when we first came in the door."

Patrycja asked, "Did you children sleep okay last night? We were worried about you. Did the bombing keep you awake?"

Zofia looked at Cass and nodded. "We slept fine last night. The bombing didn't keep us awake."

Later in the day, Adelajda began preparing chicken and beans for everyone staying at the factory. She had three pots of beans cooking over the fire in the fireplace and several chickens boiling in a large pot. The pleasant aroma filled the air. After a warm meal, everyone went back to their locations along the wall and tried to relax as they waited for the bombing to stop. Later in the afternoon, there was a large explosion on the roof and everyone realized the building had been bombed. Smoke soon permeated the room. People began coughing from the smoke as they were trying to find the source of the smoke. "Where's the fire?" shouted Cass.

"I don't know," Irena replied. "Maybe—"

Her words were cut short by a deafening crash upstairs. Suddenly the ceiling in the center of the room burst open and a large object crashed through from the floor above. It landed on top of the large table, breaking it into several pieces, then crashed through the floor, and came to rest in the basement below.

The object that crashed through the floor was followed by debris that fell into the basement landing on top of it. Looking down into the basement, they could see a large bomb that had not detonated. They decided among themselves that the factory was going to burn to the ground, so they would go to an apartment building over on Freta Street. One hundred and fifty people ran to the apartment building to hide in the basement. These were people—many of whom worked at the Chanel factory and lived in the neighborhood—who had sought refuge at the factory. Most were strangers to one another, but the war had brought them together in a strange chance at survival.

The basement was damp and musty, but no one seemed to mind. All around people were crying as they tried to find a place to sit. They settled around the walls of the room, where they remained throughout the day. Everything inside became quiet except for people crying, and one could hear the bombs and artillery outside. Cass heard a loud voice of a young man who appeared to be about fifteen years of age. "I'm going outside to see what is going on."

An elderly man said, "You shouldn't go out there. Bombs are still falling."

"None have hit the building so far," the young man said.

"That doesn't mean one won't."

I wonder if that is his father, Cass thought.

The young man stood up and walked out of the room.

Cass looked about the room to see if there was anyone he knew. He saw some children from the yeshiva, but they were in a class younger than his. As they looked around, they heard a loud crash coming from up the stairs. Debris tumbled to the bottom of the steps, and blood was splattered on top of the debris. Lying on top of the debris was the torso of the young man who had just gone outside. He had been struck by a falling bomb that exploded with such force that it had severed his torso from his legs, killing him instantly. Cass looked around for the rest of the boy's body but could not find it. Zofia stood next to him and reached out her hand to take ahold of his arm. They walked upstairs and looked outside to see what happened. Several people followed them. Everyone stood motionless gazing out at the devastated street as bombs fell within a few blocks of their location. No one said a word. There was nothing to say.

CHAPTER

9

CASS, THADDEUS, IRENA, Grandpa Szyncer, Grandma Szyncer, Adelajda, Zofia, and Zofia's parents remained in the basement of the Freta Street apartment for several days along with 150 other people. The blasts of bombs falling on the city precluded any sense of security and comfort. In the midst of it all, Lech and Patrycja said they needed to leave again but would return with more supplies.

"Irena, will you watch over Zofia while we're gone?" Patrycja and Lech prepared to leave.

"Of course."

Adelajda said, "Patrycja, I would like to go to my parents' house to see if they're okay. They're only a few blocks from here. Would you and Lech walk with me? I don't want to be walking around out there by myself."

"Of course," Patrycja said. She put her arm around Adelajda, and they left with Lech. That was the last time Cass ever saw Adelajda.

All of Warsaw was an inferno. Bombs fell without a moment of peace. Knowing that they could all be killed in an instant terrified Cass. He stayed awake at night listening for the sound of an explosion close enough to be the last sound he would ever hear. He wondered if he would actually hear a sound if he died in an explosion. He wondered if he would feel any pain. He stayed next to Zofia day and night, wanting to die with her if they had to die, wanting to live with her if they could live.

After three days, the incessant bombing stopped. Except for the sound of people crying, the only sound to be heard was the sound of silence. Someone said, "The war is over." Hope filled the hearts and minds of everyone. Could it be that Poland had driven back the Germans and won the war? People began to walk outside. When they looked into the sky, they saw German airplanes flying overhead, but very low, and not dropping bombs. The city was devastated. Debris was everywhere, and the buildings were ablaze. Bodies of people and horses were lying along the side of the streets. Everywhere people were crying. Thousands of people had been buried alive in the debris and could be heard crying for help under the collapsed buildings. No one was helping them because there were too many to help. In the chaos and devastation, only Irena seemed calm. Lech and Patrycja had not returned for several days, and Irena feared the worst.

Zofia cried, "Where are Mama and Papa?"

"Don't worry, they'll find us," said Grandpa Szyncer.

Irena tried to soothe them. "Children, everything is going to be all right. We're going to go home now." She took Cass's hand in hers. Cass took Zofia's hand in his, and they all began walking toward Pulawska Street. They looked for transportation, but there were no cars on the street. They saw a horse and buggy driven by a stranger. Irena asked, "Would you take us to Pulawska Street? I can pay you."

The stranger pulled the buggy to a stop. "I don't know if we can get through because of all the debris, but I will try. Where on Pulawska Street are you going?"

"We're going to the Bieberstein house."

"Oh, I know where that is. The Bieberstein mansion. Everyone knows that house. Why are you going there? Do you work there?"

"It's our house," said Cass, wondering why the man would think they worked there.

"You're the Biebersteins?" The stranger sounded amazed.

"Yes," replied Grandma Szyncer as they climbed into the buggy. "You seemed surprised." Like Irena, her daughter, Grandma Szyncer was delicate, refined, and very pretty. She kept her graying hair pulled back under a headscarf. A Chassidic Jew, she had been taught as a child to keep her hair covered whenever in public. Her clothes were always neat and tidy, and she usually wore a white apron over her skirt, which was rounded at the bottom with ruffles. Her native language was Yiddish, but she spoke primarily German, and she taught Cass and Thaddeus to speak German when they were very young.

"I guess it never occurred to me that people as powerful as the Biebersteins were going through this just like the rest of us."

"We are all going through this together. When one of us hurts, we all hurt."

The stranger drove the buggy to Pulawska Street, but after turning onto the street, it was obvious they could not get through. Debris and bodies blocked the way. The Bieberstein family and Zofia climbed out of the buggy. Irena gave the driver several zlotys.

The driver said. "Thank you. I hope you folks can make it all the way to your house. I'm sorry I can't drive you farther, but I can't get through all that debris."

"That's okay. We'll be fine," Irena said. "Thank you for helping us."

They walked up the street toward the house. When they arrived, it became immediately apparent that there was no damage to the structure though the gardens and the yard were destroyed. The iron gates in front of the house and driveway had been knocked down. They walked through the collapsed gates. Broken wine bottles were strewn on the porch steps leading to the front door. They opened the door and walked slowly inside. The interior of the house had been trashed. Furniture was turned upside down and stained with wine and food. A German soldier's helmet was lying on the living room floor.

"It looks like German soldiers were here. I didn't know that they had gotten this far into the city," said Grandpa Szyncer.

Stepping around the furniture, Cass and Zofia walked through the house, looking for Rex, the German Shepherd. They searched from room to room. Cass wanted Rex for protection. As they walked through the house, he noticed that the birdcage that held his parakeets was missing, as were the birds. They walked up the steps to Cass's bedroom and saw that the bedding had been pulled off the bed and the furniture was broken into pieces. Even the mattress was turned upside down on the floor. "I wonder what they were doing in here," Cass said.

"Why would they do this?" Zofia asked.

"I don't know. This is strange."

"Who did this?"

"Well, there was a German soldier's helmet on the floor downstairs, so they must have been German soldiers."

"But why did they make such a mess?"

"I don't know. Who do they think they are to come into someone's house and destroy everything?"

Cass and Zofia continued to search the house for Rex—they did not find him and went outside to look in the yard. After searching for nearly twenty minutes, they went into the garage where they found a note left by a German soldier. The note said that the dog was a brave dog, but he had to be shot because he was protecting the house, and the soldiers couldn't get in. Looking around the yard, Cass found a grave mound where Rex was buried. A marker on the grave said, "Here lies a brave dog." Looking further Cass also found graves where the parakeets were buried. He could not understand why the parakeets were killed. They would not have been trying to protect the house. The only animal left alive was Tiny, the family dachshund, who was so scared he hid under the bed even after he recognized Cass.

Cass and Zofia went back to his bedroom and saw that most of his toys were gone. The soldiers had destroyed the bedding, the beautiful furniture, and the works of art. They went downstairs into the basement and saw that the soldiers had gotten into the wine cellar, where they drank and smashed hundreds of bottles of expensive wine. This was a sad day for Cass. He felt violated. He kept wondering why these people thought they had the right to invade his family's property.

Within days aunts, uncles, and cousins had arrived at the Bieberstein mansion looking for a place to stay until they were sure it was safe to go back out onto the streets. Zofia's parents did not come to the house, and everyone became resigned to the probability that they had been killed during the bombing. For several days, Zofia seemed traumatized and cried with frequency. After a time, she stopped crying and just held her pain inside.

After a few days, it appeared that the Biebersteins would be able to remain in the house, but the soldiers had destroyed the furnace, and the temperatures were beginning to drop. There was a fireplace in Sigmund and Irena's master bedroom, so everyone stayed in there to be warm. The city water supply had been destroyed in the bombing, so they had no running water in the house. They gathered snow and brought it inside for water. The entire family remained in the master bedroom under blankets trying to stay warm with the single fireplace. They survived on food supplies that had not been found by the Nazis while they occupied the house. After several weeks, they began to run out of coal. When they looked out the windows, they saw Nazi soldiers walking up and down the street. They were afraid to go out looking for firewood because they had seen the soldiers behave cruelly toward people on the streets. Often soldiers would stop them for no apparent reason and shout at them or hit them.

On a Wednesday afternoon in the first week of October, bulldozers appeared in the street to clear away debris. Work crews of skinny men and women, wearing yellow armbands with a star, were throwing broken pieces of concrete, wood, and metal into buckets and then dumping the buckets into large dump trucks. The work crew slowly worked their way down the street, continuing to remove debris.

"Where did those people come from? Who are they?" Thaddeus asked.

Grandpa replied, "I don't know, but they don't look very happy. Maybe they are prisoners being forced to work."

As they looked out the window, they heard the front door open. Since the door was locked, they realized someone had a key. Irena and Grandpa walked slowly out into the hall and to the stairs where they could see down to the front door.

"Patrycja," Irena said.

Zofia ran out of the room and shouted, "Mama." She ran down the steps and into her mother's arms. "Mama, where were you? Why didn't you come back?"

"I couldn't come. Your father and I had to help find housing for the soldiers."

"What soldiers?" asked Zofia.

Patrycja replied, "The ones who won the war."

"Why were you helping them?" Grandpa asked.

"We didn't have a choice," Patrycja replied. Irena looked at her with a puzzled expression.

"Don't worry Zofia. I will be here now," said Patrycja. "Papa will join us in a few days."

Patrycja and Zofia walked up the steps. "Why are all the rooms empty? Who took out the furniture?"

"This is what we found when we got home after the bombing," Irena said.

They went into the master bedroom. "Is this where you all have been staying?"

"Yes," replied Zofia.

"Okay, I will have someone bring in firewood and coal in a few days. Then we can get the furnace working, and we'll be warm."

It puzzled Cass that Patrycja spoke so openly, and he wondered how she would find someone to bring firewood; more important, he wondered why she was helping Nazi soldiers find housing. In the past she had always been quiet and reserved, but now she seemed assertive and unafraid. *Something must be wrong with Patrycja.* Patrycja and Zofia stayed in the master bedroom with the other family members and household employees.

On a cold Friday afternoon there was a loud pounding on the front door. They were all huddled in the bedroom trying to keep warm. "Should I answer it?" Irena asked.

"I'll answer it," said Grandpa Szyncer. He got up and walked down the steps to the front door. Cass followed him and peered around the corner of the steps. Grandpa Szyncer opened the door. "May I help you?"

A German officer stood outside the front door. "We're looking for Sigmund Bieberstein."

"He isn't here," said Grandpa Szyncer.

"When will he be back?"

"He left before the bombing started. We haven't seen him in weeks. Why are you looking for him?"

Cass wondered why Grandpa said he left before the bombing started. That wasn't true, he left when the bombing started.

"I'm not at liberty to say," replied the officer. "Do you mind if we look around?"

Knowing that refusing would accomplish nothing, Grandpa Szyncer decided to be compliant. "Not at all."

The officer pushed the door open and walked inside, followed by two German soldiers and a Polish police officer. Grandpa Szyncer looked at the Polish officer with a puzzled expression. *Why is there a Polish police officer with Nazi officers?* The police officer glanced at him then quickly looked away.

The German soldiers walked through the first floor of the house and looked into rooms and closets. After satisfying themselves that there was no one on the first floor, they started up the steps to the second floor. Cass, who was still watching from behind the door, noticed that they acted as if they knew their way around the house. He followed them up the steps to see where they were going. One of them noticed him following and turned to look directly at him before walking on. They looked in each of the bedrooms and found them empty until they came to Sigmund and Irena's bedroom. They opened the door and saw the family lying around the room with blankets pulled up to their chins.

"Who of you can tell me where Sigmund Bieberstein can be found?" the officer asked.

"He's not here," Irena said.

"Where is he?"

Irena replied, "He left Poland before the bombing started."

Again Cass wondered why Grandpa Szyncer—and now Mama—said he left before the bombing started.

"Where did he go?"

"We don't know. We thought we would have heard from him by now."

"Did he say where he was going?"

"He said he was going to America on business," Irena replied.

The officer looked at her with an expression of doubt. "We'll be back to look for him again. If he shows up, tell him not to go anywhere. We need to talk to him."

"Is he in trouble?" Grandpa Szyncer asked.

"Not unless he leaves again." The officer turned and walked downstairs and out the front door with his entourage. Cass and Grandpa Szyncer followed them down to the front door and watched as they left. After they were gone, Cass and Grandpa Szyncer went back upstairs to the bedroom.

"What was that all about?" Irena asked. "Why do they want Sigmund?"

"I think it's because he was helping Jews escape from Germany before the invasion," Grandma Szyncer said.

Irena nodded.

Thaddeus asked, "What's going to happen now?" Thaddeus had not said much since the bombing started. Cass wondered if he was okay.

"We'll have to wait and see," Irena replied.

In his parents' room, Cass saw, everyone looked depressed. He felt a deep sadness inside. Zofia was crying. "Where's my papa? Mama won't tell me. She just says he will join us later."

Cass shook his head. "I don't know."

A few hours later they heard another knock at the door. "Don't answer it," said Zofia fearfully.

"No matter who it is, we have to answer it," said Grandpa Szyncer. "If it's Nazi soldiers they will just knock the door down and come in angry. If it's someone who needs our help we need to help them." He went downstairs, with Cass following behind him.

When Grandpa Szyncer opened the front door, Cass saw Rajmund with Sarah and Rachel. He ran over to Rachel and hugged her then Sarah. "Is it okay if they stay here?" asked Rajmund.

"Yes, they can stay here," said Grandpa Szyncer. "Where are your families?"

"Mine is staying down at the restaurant," said Rajmund.

Sarah said, "Ours were—" she stopped and burst into tears.

Rajmund whispered softy to Grandpa Szyncer, "They were killed the first day of the bombings."

Grandpa Szyncer shook his head. "Come on upstairs. You will stay here with us."

They walked up the steps into the bedroom where everyone was trying to keep warm. Sarah and Rachel sat by the fire. Thaddeus walked over and sat down next to Rachel. They hugged each other, and Rachel began to cry. "They killed Mama and Papa," she whispered.

Thaddeus shook his head. "It finally happened. Everything we talked about. We'll take care of you. You'll be safe here with us."

When evening drew close, the family and visitors began to doze off as they huddled together for warmth. At approximately ten o'clock they were awakened by bright lights and shouting outside. They gathered around the window to see what was happening. In the street below were a dozen Nazi soldiers knocking on doors of houses up and down the street, shouting orders in German. They watched as people were taken from the houses and told to line up in the streets. Zofia said, "Look, isn't that Papa down there by that car?"

"No, you are mistaken," Patrycja said. "Papa is in Krakow."

"What are they doing?" asked Thaddeus. No one responded.

As they watched, the people taken from the houses were forced to line up side by side along the sidewalk. Some of them had not even had time to put on a coat and some were in their nightclothes. Several of them were barefoot. They were all cold.

"Why didn't the soldiers come to our house?" asked Irena.

Grandpa replied, "I don't know, they passed right by our place."

Within forty-five minutes, fifty people were lined up on the sidewalk of Pulawska Street. An officer exited one of the vehicles and began shouting in German. "All of you who are Jews, cross the street to the other side."

"Oh no," Irena whispered as they watched from the bedroom window.

The German officer continued. "All you on this side of the street, since you are not Jews, you may go back into your houses. The rest of you, since you are Jews you have been selected to go to a special work camp. You will be fed and clothed. You will be given work to do. Now, before you get on the truck, let's play a game. How many of you saw the Olympics in Berlin last year?" No one raised his hand.

"Since none of you saw it, you missed the footraces. Tonight we are going to have footraces." The officer pointed at a young man and said, "Can you run?"

"Yes," replied the man.

"Step forward."

The man did as requested.

"I am going to give you to the count of ten to try to get to the end of the street. If you can get to the end of the street before I reach ten, or before I can shoot you, then you can go free. I won't shoot until I reach ten."

The young man faced the officer and said, "Please, sir. I have a family—"

Before the young man could finish his sentence the officer pulled his pistol and shot him in the head.

Rachel let out a faint scream.

"Shh, we need to be quiet," said Grandma. "We don't want them to know we are in here."

The officer then pointed at a pretty young girl barely in her teens. She was barefoot, wearing only a nightgown, and she was shivering from the cold. "It's your turn. *Eins, zwei…*"

The young woman looked at the officer in terror and disbelief. An older woman who had been standing next to her said, "Please don't make her run. I will run for her."

"Aw, that's touching," said the officer. "Are you her mother?"

"Yes, I am."

"Then stand there and shut up, or I will shoot your daughter where she stands." He looked at the young girl. "Start running."

The young girl began running down the street away from the officer as fast as she could. As the counting neared ten, she was approaching the intersection. The officer lifted his pistol, pointed it at the young woman and fired. The bullet hit her in the middle of the back, and she fell to the ground. As the blood began to cover the back of her nightgown, her arms moved about, and she writhed on the pavement in pain. The soldiers cheered and laughed. "Good shot," one of them shouted. "That's how you take down a pretty kike."

The officer holstered his pistol then looked at the young girl's mother, who by now was crying bitterly. "Now it's your turn," he said. She ran down the street toward her daughter as the officer counted loudly. When she reached her daughter, the officer shot her in the back, and she fell next to her daughter. The soldiers cheered and laughed again. The officer shouted, "The rest of you, in the truck."

The Jews began climbing into the truck. Suddenly, a man jumped from the truck and tried to run. He was shot by one of the soldiers before he traveled fifteen feet.

Soon all of the people had been loaded into the truck. The driver started the truck and drove away with his passengers in the back. The soldiers got back into their cars and trucks and left.

The Biebersteins closed the curtain and moved away from the window. They were so overcome with the trauma of the event that they could not speak. Finally Irena said, "I just can't believe that happened. How can anyone be so evil and so cruel? And I still can't understand why they left our house alone."

Zofia asked, "Mama, why was Papa down there? What was he doing?"

Cass noticed that Patrycja was gazing into the fire, ignoring her daughter's question. "Mama, I know that was Papa down there with the soldiers. He looked right at me when I was looking out the window."

Zofia stood up and came over to sit by Cass. "Cass, that was Papa down there. I would recognize him anywhere. He was standing next to the car with the German who shot the people. He had a swastika armband on his arm. He was wearing the long coat my mom bought for him last year. Why was he down there?"

Cass knew she was right. He recognized Lech too. His mother was looking at Zofia, whom she overheard. She looked at Cass and nodded. She recognized him too.

"I don't know," replied Cass.

That night the temperature outside dropped well below freezing. The wooden leg of a chair burned in the fireplace in the master bedroom of the Bieberstein mansion. In order to keep warm, the family had begun burning furniture along with the coal. It was necessary to preserve the remaining flammable materials as long as possible. They felt it was too dangerous to venture out into the city to find coal. The Nazis were shooting Jews just for sport. This was the coldest night of the year so far, and the room was frigid. The following morning when Cass awakened he could not feel his legs or feet. He took off his shoes and socks. His feet were dark blue and his toes were black. Zofia asked, "Cass, what's wrong with your feet?"

Grandpa Szyncer and Irena came over to Cass to look at his feet. Grandpa said, "Let's get him over to the fire. Quick."

Grandpa and Irena picked up Cass and carried him over to the fire. They put his feet up on the stone hearth of the fireplace just inches from the fire. Everyone gathered around to see if they could help. They began putting blankets on Cass. "Why didn't you say something if you were that cold?" asked Thaddeus.

"I didn't know I was that cold."

"What? Didn't your feet hurt?" asked Grandpa.

"I couldn't feel anything at all. Why are my feet so blue and black?"

"You have severe frostbite," Grandpa said.

"What does that mean? Are my feet going to come off?"

"We have to get them warm but not too fast. Otherwise it will be very painful."

Cass overheard Irena ask Grandpa quietly, "Are we going to have to amputate? They look dead."

"I don't know yet," whispered Grandpa. "It doesn't look good. Even next to the fire there isn't enough heat to warm his feet. We need more firewood."

Grandpa walked out of the room and into the next bedroom. There he found a small table. He stomped on one of the legs and then another, breaking them off. He took both table legs back into the master bedroom and put them on the fire. Eventually, the fire grew and began to warm the room. Grandpa stood up and said, "Everyone take off your shoes so I can see your feet. We need to make sure no one else has frostbite."

After everyone had removed their shoes, Grandpa Szyncer walked around the room and examined their feet. When he had finished, he said, "Okay, everyone put your shoes back on. Everyone is okay, but we are going to have to do something to get more firewood or coal. We need to keep the temperature higher in here. If anyone notices that they can't feel their feet, let me know right away. Frostbite is serious."

Thaddeus said, "But if we burn too much wood or coal, they'll see the smoke from our fire and will know we are in here."

Grandpa looked at Patrycja. "I think they already know we are here." He took some blankets and wrapped Cass's feet. He told Cass to keep them by the fire. Cass was lying on his back on the floor in front of the fireplace. His feet were elevated onto the stone hearth. Grandpa motioned for Thaddeus and Irena to follow him out of the room. "I'm going to have to get some firewood or coal. We can't keep burning the furniture."

"It's too dangerous to go out," said Irena. "We'll buy more furniture when this is over."

Grandpa replied, "We can't keep burning the furniture. Soon we will run out. Not only will there be no furniture to burn, but we will have burned up thousands of dollars of irreplaceable chairs, tables, and artwork."

"I don't care about the furniture now," Irena insisted. "I don't want you to go out there."

"I'll go with you," Thaddeus said.

"No, neither one of you can go. It's too dangerous. They're killing people out there."

Grandpa replied, "We have to. We'll go when it starts to get dark. That way no one will see us."

"I don't think it's worth the risk. You have seen what's going on out there."

Thaddeus replied, "It's okay, Mama. I know where there is a big stack of firewood at a neighbor's house just down the street. We'll take straps. Each of us can carry a big load. I think if we make a couple of trips we can get enough wood to last a few days or a week."

Finally Irena said, "Okay, but go the back way down the alley."

"That's what we'll do," Grandpa agreed.

In the late afternoon when it began to get dark, Thaddeus and Grandpa put on their boots and warm coats. They each took a long leather strap and placed it in a coat pocket. They went out the back door toward the garage and walked beside the garage through the back gate into the alley that ran behind the houses. They knelt down beside the garage for several minutes to make sure there was no one in the alleyway. Once they were certain, they ran alongside the back fences behind the houses until they came to a house three doors down. They opened the back gate to that property. Next to the fence was a large stack of firewood. Each laid his strap on the ground and placed pieces of firewood on the strap and wrapped the straps around the firewood. They hoisted them on their backs and headed back to the Bieberstein house. They entered the back gate of the Bieberstein property, carried the wood in through the back door, and set it on the floor in the rear entryway. After repeating the trip several times, they had a large stack of wood, enough to last for a few weeks.

They went back into master bedroom where Grandpa put a log in the fireplace. Then he examined Cass's feet. They appeared to have no change.

Irena drew him into the hall. "How are his feet?"

"I don't see any change. The circulation was cut off when his toes froze."

"Are they going to have to be amputated?"

Grandpa shook his head. "I sure hope not. We don't even have any anesthesia. I might be able to get to my office to get some."

"Oh no, your office is over a mile from here." Irena shook her head and looked at the floor. "That is too far to go with Nazis everywhere."

"It's time to pray for him," Grandpa said.

Back in the master bedroom, they sat next to Cass. They prayed for his feet to heal. Zofia came over and prayed for him too. Patrycja watched them with a distant expression in her eyes. She was not really looking at them; she was looking at something behind them.

The following morning Sarah and Rachel went downstairs to get some firewood. Thaddeus awakened in time to see them leaving the bedroom. He decided to let Rajmund sleep so he stood up quietly to follow the girls downstairs.

As they walked down the steps, the girls heard Thaddeus behind them. Sarah turned and asked, "Thad, what's happening? What are they going to do to us when they find out we're here?"

"I don't know. All we can do is wait and see."

His words provided little comfort to the girls, who were in fear for their lives.

They went into the back room and picked up several pieces of wood. Then they went back upstairs. They put a piece of wood on the fire and sat in front of the fireplace. Thaddeus put some oatmeal in a pan full of water and set it on the iron rack above the fire.

"I think you're supposed to boil the water first then put in the oatmeal," Sarah said.

"You are?"

"Yeah, that's generally how we do it," Rachel said. "But we can warm the water and take the pan off the fire before it boils. The oatmeal will have time to cook slowly. You have to keep stirring it, but it will be okay that way."

Slowly people in the room began to awaken to the smell of oatmeal in the pan. Grandma Szyncer brought in some yogurt she had made the night before and mixed the cooked oatmeal into the yogurt. She sprinkled walnuts on top of the mixture then stirred it again. She took a large spoon and a stack of bowls and began putting two spoons of the oatmeal-yogurt mixture into each bowl. Thaddeus and Sarah passed the bowls around to everyone in the room. They all ate quietly as they waited for another day of isolation inside the master bedroom of the Bieberstein mansion.

"I just want this nightmare to be over," Sarah said softly. "I want this horrible time to stop. I wish someone would make it stop. I want to wake up and find out this is all just a bad dream." She sat with Thaddeus, Rajmund, and Rachel, eating their oatmeal by the fireplace.

"No one can make it stop," Rajmund said. "A terrible time has fallen on our people. Don't you remember when we used to sit downstairs in the kitchen and talk about what might be coming?"

Sarah put her spoon in her bowl and set the bowl on the floor. "I never believed it would really happen. It was just a faraway idea that I didn't believe was possible."

Rachel said, "I can't stop thinking about Mama and Papa. They didn't have a chance. The bomb landed right on our house. It destroyed the whole building and everyone in it."

"Where were you when it happened?" Thaddeus asked.

Rachel replied, "We were trying to get home during the bombing. We thought it would be safer there, and we wanted to be with Mama and Papa. We were at Rabbi Levi's house studying the Torah with his family when the bombs started falling. Rabbi Levi told us not to go out, but we didn't listen. By the time we got home, the house was destroyed. It was still burning. They never found the bodies because the damage was so bad, but since they haven't showed up anywhere, we know they were still in the house. I keep thinking that we are being punished for not following the instruction of the rabbi not to go there."

"You know that isn't right," Thaddeus said. "The rabbi wasn't commanding you to do something, he was only recommending it. That is a big difference in obedience. You don't have to obey a suggestion, and you aren't punished for disobeying one. You are just blaming yourself. That is what people do after something bad happens."

"I know what you're saying is true, but I can't help but wonder about it."

Rajmund said, "Do you remember how we used to play table games? Maybe if we could find one of the games, it would help take our minds off this."

Sarah shook her head. "This is too hard. I wouldn't be able to concentrate to play a game. I don't even want to try."

"Where's your family, Rajmund?" Thaddeus asked.

"They're staying down at the restaurant. Now most of our customers are Nazi soldiers instead of swing kids, so we don't play swing music anymore."

"What does your father say about all of this? Is he upset that you aren't at the restaurant?"

"He's very upset about the Nazis being here. He's just serving customers who come into his business like he always did. It's just that now they are Nazis. Since the whole family is staying down there, they can get by without me for a few days. He was worried when I told him I was coming over to your house to bring the girls because it's dangerous to go into a Jew's house. I told him I was just bringing Rachel and Sarah over and that I would be back within a day. I should go back over today so they don't worry."

"Aren't you worried that the soldiers will stop you on the way?" Thaddeus asked.

"No, I have papers...and this." Rajmund took a Nazi armband from his pocket and handed it to Thaddeus. "I put it on when I'm outside."

"Doesn't it feel weird to wear that?" Rachel asked.

"Yeah, really weird. I hate it, but it is the only way I can go across town without being stopped."

Later that morning Rajmund slipped out the back door, walked down the alleyway to the next street, and went to his father's restaurant. Rachel and Sarah stayed with the Biebersteins because they now had nowhere else to go. The yeshiva and most of the synagogues in the neighborhood had closed their doors out of concern for safety, so the Bieberstein home presented the only option for them, other than living on the streets. Rachel and Sarah were grateful.

CHAPTER

10

WITHIN A FEW days Cass's feet began to recover from the frostbite. The blackness in his toes lightened, and eventually they became their normal pink color. Soon he was able to walk again.

One afternoon they were sitting around the fireplace to keep warm. "I thought we were going to have to amputate your feet," Grandpa said.

"I did too," Irena said. "I think it's a miracle that we didn't have to."

Cass tried to think of what it would be like to have no feet. He remembered a story he heard in yeshiva from the book of Daniel, in the Tanahk, about a statue with feet of clay. He had looked at his feet while they were black with frostbite and wondered if they had turned to clay. "Thank you, Grandpa and Mama, for taking care of me while my feet were bad."

Irena hugged Cass. "You know we wouldn't do anything else."

"I know, Mama." Cass loved the kindness his mother and grandfather showed him. Even in the worst situations they seemed to focus attention away from the problem and on to something pleasant. Irena always said that thinking about a problem solves nothing once the best solution is identified. Thereafter, dwelling on the negative only leads to negative results and depression.

The winter of 1939–1940 was exceptionally cold. On a Sunday morning in mid-November, the Bieberstein household was suddenly visited by a familiar face. They heard the front door open. Knowing that it was locked meant someone with a key was entering. Cass wondered if it might be Sigmund. The children jumped to their feet and ran toward the door. Irena shouted for them to wait, but the children were already out the door and running down the steps.

The children reached the bottom of the steps only to see Lech standing just inside the front door. Everyone, including Zofia, was shocked to see that he was wearing a bright-orange armband with a black swastika on his left arm. Zofia stood looking at her father in shock. She did not run to him. Patrycja walked over to him and gave him a hollow, emotionless hug.

"Is this all I get?" Lech said with a loud laugh. "Zofia, is this how you greet your father?"

Zofia slowly walked over to Lech and gave him a hug as empty as her mother's.

"Celebrate the Deutschland," Lech shouted. He held his hand up in the air. "Heil Hitler."

Everyone just stared at Lech in disbelief. Finally Irena said, "Lech, what are you doing?"

Lech looked at Irena sadly. "I'm just doing what has to be done to save us, Mrs. Bieberstein. I hope you understand."

"I don't understand," said Irena softly. "How can you wear that vile symbol of the Nazis on your arm and shout *Heil Hitler* in our Jewish home? Haven't we always been good to you? You are like family to us. Patrycja is like a sister, and Zofia is like a niece."

Lech looked sadly toward the floor. "Yes, ma'am, you have been very good to us, and we will never ever forget that, but that isn't what this is about. I'm doing this so we can all survive. They're killing Jews like flies out there. Why do you think they didn't raid this house the evening of the roundup? It was because of me. I was the one who told them to leave this house alone. I said you were loyal to the Reich."

"And you are the one who watched while they killed innocent Jews in the streets that night," said Irena.

"And you also watched, didn't you? I saw you in the window. I couldn't do anything more to stop it than you could."

The words of Lech caught the attention of Cass. *Was Lech right? What could he have done?* He was in no more position to prevent what happened than the Biebersteins were as they watched from the bedroom window. Lech was also a victim of the ugly Nazi regime. So it was with what would later become known as the Nuremberg defense.

Lech said, "I have some food in the car, but I will need help to carry it in. I also have several bags of coal."

Thaddeus and Rajmund went down to help carry the food into the house. Lech moved into the house and immediately repaired the furnace so the family could have heat. He soon asserted himself in the household and began giving orders. He assigned bedrooms for everyone. Then he moved into the master bedroom with Patrycja and Zofia. Lech was not cruel to the Biebersteins, but now the roles were reversed. Now the Biebersteins were the servants, and they served Lech's family. However, the relationship between Cass and Zofia did not change.

One day in late November, Lech called everyone together on the landing to give the new directives. Cass and Zofia stood next to each other beside Lech. Though Cass despised the authority Lech represented, he was mesmerized by the authority Lech now asserted in the house. Zofia held her father's hand, and Cass held Zofia's hand. Cass thought of the day they left the apartment basement on Freta Street—he held his mother's hand, and Zofia held his. *Holding hands is comforting*, he thought.

Lech stood at the same location Irena used to stand when she gave the daily assignments to the household staff. Irena now stood where Lech used to stand. Lech said loudly, "From now on, no one is to leave the house without wearing an armband. The Biebersteins, who are Jews, will have to wear the Star of David." Lech took a dozen yellow armbands with the Star of David from his satchel and gave them to Irena.

He continued, "Zofia, you, Mama, and I will wear this armband instead, because we are not Jews."

Zofia whispered to Cass, "But I *am* a Jew."

Lech leaned against the banister as he spoke. "It's very important that you don't go outside of the house without the proper armband. If you do, you might be arrested or even killed." Lech gave Cass a yellow armband with a black star, and he gave Zofia a red armband with a black swastika.

Cass held up his armband and looked at it. Zofia held up her armband next to Cass's armband. She looked at them side by side then dropped the Nazi armband on the floor. Her father looked at her for a moment. Finally she said, "Our armbands are different. Why can't they be the same?"

Lech continued, "If you Jews are walking on the street and you see a German soldier approaching, you must step off the sidewalk and into the street. You are not permitted to walk on the sidewalk with a German. Cass, you don't actually have to wear one until you are twelve, but I think you should wear it anyway, in case anyone thinks you are over twelve. Those of us who are not Jews are not required to wear the swastika armband, but it is better if we do. That way no one will accuse us of being Jews."

He paused for a moment, and he looked directly at Irena. His voice softened. "I want you to understand. The German soldiers are permitted to kill the Jews for any reason they wish and even for no reason at all. I have seen Jews beaten or shot simply because they weren't wearing the armband. You have to follow the rules. The best thing to do is not go outside unless you absolutely have to."

Irena nodded while looking at Lech, though her expression was empty.

Later that evening Cass and Zofia sat at the top of the steps above the landing where they had often sat before. Zofia said, "I don't understand what's happening. I feel like everything is coming apart."

Cass replied, "Nothing is normal now. We need to just accept what we can't change and fight to change what we can."

"I like that," she said. "Where did you learn it?"

"I learned it from Grandpa Szyncer," Cass replied. "If it wasn't for Grandpa, Grandma, and Mama, I don't think our family could survive this. Mama always seems to be able to get past bad things. She says that the Jewish children in Europe today are true Israelites."

Lech would come and go from the house frequently. Sometimes he would be gone for several days at a time. It was uncomfortable having Lech take control of the household, but it was a relief to have the central heating system working again and to have enough food to eat.

The Biebersteins did not celebrate Chanukah in 1939. Zofia's family celebrated Christmas in a limited way, with a very small tree. One day in February of 1940, the Bieberstein family was sitting around the table in the dining room. They heard a car pull into the driveway. They looked out the window and saw a limousine with German flags and swastikas on the side. To everyone's surprise, Lech was driving. He got out with several military officers and a balding man who walked with a limp. He wore a trench coat and a swastika armband, but no uniform. The men walked quickly into the house without knocking.

The balding man with a limp was called Herr Schindler by the others. Cass could tell that he was important because even the officers showed respect to him. Cass learned that his first name was Oskar. Schindler began shouting orders at the Bieberstein family, and even the officers followed his instructions. There were numerous Nazi officers and a Polish police officer in a blue uniform. Lech explained that Herr Schindler was going to take over the Bieberstein house for business operations, and he was going to live there when he was in Warsaw. Lech explained that Schindler had a business of confiscating property from Jewish homes in the affluent district and selling it to German officers. Schindler and Lech talked to Cass's mother in private in a bedroom upstairs. Irena came out of the bedroom with a distressed appearance and said, "Children, we have to leave the house tomorrow."

"Where are we going?" asked Cass.

Irena replied, "We're going to live in an apartment not far from here. We'll come back to the house later."

Irena walked back into the bedroom with Lech and Schindler. Cass could hear them talking about taking some coal from the basement.

Cass was told that they could not take anything. No toys, no art, only the clothes on their backs. They were given twenty-four hours to get ready to go. The following day as the family was leaving, Zofia went to Cass and said, "I will find out where you are going, and I will come to see you. I won't forget about you, Cass." Zofia took Cass in her arms and held him while she cried.

Cass cried too. "I won't forget about you either."

Lech said, "Zofia, come over here now. Cass has to leave with his family."

Zofia cried bitterly as she walked over to her father, who put his hand on her shoulder.

Cass had his dachshund on a leash and asked as they were leaving, "Can I take my dog?"

One of the officers replied that he could not.

Cass protested, "But he is my only dog now. The soldiers killed my other dog." Cass led the dog out into the front yard.

The officer said again, "The dog is staying here."

Schindler heard the commotion in the front yard and walked out the front door. "What's going on?"

"He wants to take his dog," replied the officer. Schindler took his pistol from his holster and shot the dog in the head. "Let him take the dog."

Through Lech's persuasion, Irena was allowed to take some jewelry and a small amount of cash. After further discussion, Cass was permitted to take his favorite brown teddy bear, Misha, and a little bit of clothing.

Lech assured the family that he would take care of the house for them and that they would get it back when the war was over. He said he was going to live in the house and serve as Schindler's chauffeur; Patrycja would be Schindler's maid. He also said that an apartment had been prepared for them. They would have a nice place to live, but there was no room for the aunts and uncles, so they would have to go with the soldiers in the back of a truck, though Lech said he did not know where they were going. The aunts and uncles put on their Star of David armbands and climbed into the back of the truck as instructed. The truck drove away. They were never seen again.

The Biebersteins, the Szyncers, and Sarah and Rachel put on their Star of David armbands and walked down Pulawska Street until they came to the streetcar station. There they waited for a streetcar that would take them to their new home in the apartment building they owned. When the streetcar arrived, they climbed on. They were instructed by the operator to sit in the rear. Cass looked back toward Pulawska Street and wondered if he would ever see his home again.

CHAPTER
11

T HE STREETCAR DROVE for several miles then slowed to turn at Aleja Wilanowska. The area was clean but old. Known as an affluent part of town characterized by opulent apartments in the 1800s, now the elegant apartments housed middle-class families. The tall apartment buildings loomed high above the Warsaw skyline. They traveled several more blocks to Wilanow Street.

As the car came to the intersection of Aleja Wilanowska and Wilanow, Irena said, "This is where we get off."

"Where are we, Mama?" asked Cass.

"This is where we are going to live," she replied. "There is an apartment for us. It is just down the street."

"Who arranged for us to live here?" Thaddeus asked.

"Lech arranged it. He gave me the address where we're supposed to go," replied Irena. "It's one of the apartments your father owns. I have never seen it, so I don't know what it's like."

As they got off the streetcar, Sarah asked, "Will there be enough room for all of us? Where will Rachel and I go?"

"You have a place. We have a three-room flat on the fifth floor, but there is a one-room flat right next to ours. You and Rachel can stay there.

It was going to be for Grandma and Grandpa, but they decided to stay in our flat so they can be with us. You and Rachel can have that one."

Rachel looked at Grandma and Grandpa Szyncer. "Thank you so much. We didn't think we had a place to go."

"We can never repay you for this," Sarah said. "Let us know how we can help you with whatever you need."

"It's okay. We would rather stay with the family anyway. It works out fine, because now you have a place too."

Cass knew things would be different now. He knew by the way people looked at them and the way they were required to ride at the rear of the streetcar. The Jews were no longer respected and revered in the community. They were now considered undesirables, those who should be avoided at all cost. They were seen as vile and despicable, much like rodents or disease. The Jews were being separated from everyone else and concentrated in a single area of Warsaw. Not far away he could see a fence under construction around an area of the city that the neighbors were already calling the Jewish ghetto.

"I'm glad they aren't making us go into the ghetto," Thaddeus said.

"Me too," Sarah replied. "Rajmund said that he will come and see us and that his father is going to take care of us."

Thaddeus nodded. "I believe him. Rajmund is a good friend."

After walking for several blocks, Irena said, "This is it." She turned and walked up the sidewalk to a tall apartment building. The yard was well kept, and the building was a brick multistory structure. The new apartment was on the fifth floor. Walking up the steps was an exercise in stamina. They dragged their few belongings behind them. Thaddeus tried to relieve the tension with a little humor, but to little avail. "I think if I walk up one more step, I might reach heaven."

When they reached the fifth floor, Irena said, "This is our flat, the first door on the right at the top of the stairs." She walked to the door and inserted a key into the lock. The door opened easily. She pushed the door open then said, "This is our new home."

The apartment was empty except for a few pieces of furniture: a red Victorian couch, a matching love seat, two end tables, two blue wingback chairs, and a coffee table in front of the couch. They walked down the hall into the first bedroom. On each wall was a twin bed, and in between them was a chair. "Thaddeus, this is where you and Cass will sleep," said Irena. Cass put his teddy bear and his bag on the chair and sat on one of the beds. He looked out the window at the street below.

Thaddeus threw his clothes on the floor and sat on the other bed. Everyone else walked on to the next room. Thaddeus said, "You know, this really isn't that bad. It isn't like our house on Pulawska Street, but it's nice."

"Why are they building that fence over there?" asked Cass.

"I don't know. They call it the ghetto. Maybe they're planning to separate the city for some reason. Maybe that part of the city will be Poland, and this part will be Germany."

"Do you mean Germany is getting bigger and taking part of Poland?"

"Maybe. That is what happens when one nation is conquered by another."

"But if that's true, shouldn't we be on that side of the fence? Germans don't like Jews."

"I'm sure if we are supposed to be over there, Mama will take us there."

Cass and Thaddeus walked out into the living room. The front door was open, and everyone was gone, so they went into the hall. The door was open at the apartment next door, so they looked inside. Sarah was sitting on the couch, crying, and Irena was sitting next to her with her arm around her. Rachel was looking out the window. Grandma and Grandpa were dusting the furniture and arranging the room partly to create a pleasant atmosphere for the girls, but mostly to appear busy in the awkward situation.

Cass and Thaddeus entered the girls' apartment. Thaddeus sat on a chair, and Cass moved to the window and stood next to Rachel. She put her arm around him. Her touch was comforting but also overwhelming, and he began to cry. His stomach was tied in knots; he thought he would throw up his breakfast. He knew that his pain was caused by Zofia's absence. *So this is what love is. This really hurts.* He didn't know if he would ever see Zofia again, and the pain was more than he could endure. *I don't know if I want to live without Zofia.*

That evening, after the family had settled in, they all went to the Bieberstein flat for dinner. Irena had gone down to the street and bought potatoes, bread, and a slab of beef. As she cooked the evening meal, everyone was silent. While the food was cooking, Irene took a box from a bag. "This is a game I bought from a vender on the street. It is a game from America called Sorry." Everyone laughed. She laid the board out on the coffee table.

"That is what the Germans should be saying to us," Thaddeus remarked.

"That's definitely true," Grandma said. "They have made a mess of our lives."

Irena continued, "The instructions are in English, but the vender gave me a set of instructions in Polish. Papa, could you read the instructions and get everyone started while I stir the potatoes?"

"Parker Brothers."

"I think you can skip that part, Papa," said Irena. Everyone laughed again.

Grandpa continued, "Okay, it looks like these little pieces go around the board. You roll the dice and move the number of spaces on the dice. You can pass someone else's piece…"

Cass could no longer hear what was being said. He was thinking about Zofia again. In his mind he pictured her beautiful blues eyes, her soft blond hair, and her smile. "I love you, Zofia," he whispered.

"Did you say something, Cass?" asked Sarah.

"No, I didn't say anything. I was just thinking out loud."

Sarah sensed his pain. "Come and sit by me," she said as reached for him. Cass sat next to her as she put her arm around him. "Are you okay, Cass?"

Cass nodded but didn't speak.

Sarah said, "I know this is hard for you. It's hard for all of us, but it won't last forever. In a little while this will be over."

Her words were kind but not really comforting. No one could know how much he missed Zofia because no one knew how close they really were to each other. "How is it ever going to be over?" he asked. "The Germans won, and Germans hate Jews. We are Jews. How can it ever get better?"

"I don't know, Cass, but I trust God. He will never give us more than we can handle. Do you remember the story of Esther and King Ahasuerus of Babylon? By deception the wicked Haman had persuaded King Ahasuerus to allow the Babylonians to kill all the Jews. But God didn't allow that to happen. Esther told the king what had happened. Although Ahasuerus could not reverse his command under Babylonian law, he did command the Jews to fight back. This was a warning to the Babylonians not to attack them. Haman was hanged, and all of his belongings were given to Esther's uncle Mordecai, who had exposed the plot. Mordecai was made the prime minister of Babylon. That is how it will be for us. Hitler is like Haman. He wants to kill all of us, but God won't allow that to happen. Someone bigger than Hitler will come and save us, someone like King Ahasuerus."

Cass listened, and though her words provided some comfort, he was far from convinced that what she was saying was going to happen in Poland. The story of Esther seemed so far away to Cass. *Maybe this story will play out in a different way*, he thought. *Maybe it won't be so good in the end.*

Thaddeus tossed the dice on the board. "Seven." He moved his piece forward seven spaces. "It's your turn, Cass." he said.

"Okay, everyone save your places. Dinner is ready," Irena called.

They all gathered around the dining table. They hadn't eaten since early morning, so the food seemed exceptionally good. They ate dinner in silence and returned to finish the game. After that game they played several more, but there was little communication. That night Cass lay awake until the early hours of the morning, wondering what was going to happen. Before, things were bad, but at least they were in the house on Pulawska. Now they were in a strange place. An apartment like the common people lived in. It occurred to Cass that the life of luxury and opulence that he had known since birth had come to an end. *Whose fault was it? Was it Papa's fault for not listening to Uncle Bernie and taking the family away before the war? Even Mama had said they should go, but Papa wouldn't listen. Then when the war started, Papa disappeared. Where did he go? How could he leave the family like that and not come back to get us? Maybe this was Papa's fault.*

It finally occurred to Cass that it wasn't his parents' fault. It was the fault of the Nazis. He remembered the decision he had made years earlier that he would kill Nazis if they ever attacked Poland. Now they had attacked. But how could he kill Nazis? He was just a little boy. The Nazis were big men. Cass felt helpless. *This is like a terrible dream that will never end. Maybe God is making us go through this so we will know how hard it is for the common people. Maybe we are being punished for having so much wealth and not sharing it.* Cass did not really believe that. He knew that his father gave substantial amounts of money to charity, but he desperately wanted to understand why God would allow this to happen. He could find no answer. No reason explained it well enough to satisfy him. It was a question that would haunt him for the rest of his life: Why did God allow this to happen?

CHAPTER
12

OVER THE NEXT few days the Biebersteins settled into their new home. It was difficult to move from a thirty-two-room mansion on Pulawska Street to a four-room flat in the Jewish sector. From their fifth-floor window, Thaddeus and Cass could watch activities on the street below. Several times each day they saw Nazi soldiers walk three abreast on the sidewalk in front of their flat. When they approached, they saw Jews immediately jump to the curb to avoid their wrath. They quickly learned that the soldiers came by at exactly the same times every day: six o'clock in the morning and six o'clock at night. All the neighbors realized this too, and they soon learned to stay off the streets at those times. When they did go out, the Jews always wore their armbands.

"These Nazis are really stupid," Cass said one day. They were all sitting in the living room of the Bieberstein flat. Sarah and Rachel were with them.

"What do you mean?" Sarah asked.

"They do everything like clockwork. The soldiers come by at exactly the same time every day. If someone wanted to commit a crime or worse, kill one of the Nazis, they would know exactly when to do it because they always come at exactly the same time."

"Cass, don't say anything about killing Nazis. If someone overheard you they might arrest you," Irena said.

"But it's true," Cass protested. "All a person would have to do is wait behind a building on the corner, and after the Nazis walked by, he could run up behind them and kill them with a knife before the Nazis even knew what happened."

The room grew silent for a moment. Then Cass said, "Look—it's almost six o'clock. The Nazis will be coming by."

Everyone went over to the living-room window to watch for the Nazis on the street below. As they waited they saw an elderly woman walking on the sidewalk in front of the building. Irena said, "Hey, there's that old woman who lives in the corner apartment building. I wonder what she is doing. I've talked to her a few times. She doesn't have her senses. I think she has Alzheimer's. It won't be good if the soldiers run into her. She isn't even wearing her armband. I better go down and get her inside before they come." Irena started toward the door.

Thaddeus said, "It's too late, Mama. Look, the soldiers are already coming from the other direction. She is walking straight toward them on the sidewalk."

Irena came back to look out the window. "Oh no! I need to go down and help her." She started toward the door again when they heard a yell from outside. Irena came back to the window a second time and looked out.

"Get off the sidewalk, you old Jew witch. Where is your armband?" shouted one of the three soldiers.

The old woman started laughing and began dancing in front of the young soldiers, who also started laughing. One of them said, "Crazy old woman. You aren't supposed to be on the sidewalk with us, and you're supposed to be wearing your armband." He gave her a hard shove. She fell into the street and hit her forehead on the pavement. She slowly stood up and started singing and dancing in the street in a mocking way. The three soldiers walked over to her. One of them took his nightstick and began beating her. Another kicked her. They knocked her to the ground, and all three were kicking and hitting her.

"We have to do something," Irena said.

"What are we going to do?" Grandma said.

"I don't know but we have to do something." Irena opened the window and shouted, "Stop!"

Suddenly they saw someone running from a building on the opposite side of the street. He appeared to be in his fifties, wearing loose-fitting trousers and a baggy shirt. He appeared physically fit. One of soldiers turned and saw him just as he executed a flying kick, planting his foot squarely in the face of the soldier, knocking him across the sidewalk into a yard. The man then turned his focus on the other two. His moves were perfectly executed. Within seconds he easily disarmed both of them using hand-to-hand techniques. The Biebersteins had never seen someone fight like this before.

"Look at that," Thaddeus said. "That guy is beating the crap out of those Nazis. Who is he?"

"I don't know. I've never seen him before," Sarah said. "He can really fight. Look."

Other people were running into the street. They started beating the Nazis with their fists. Soon there were two dozen people. They stripped the uniforms off the Nazis and forced them to sit in the middle of the street in their undergarments. "Let's get them inside before someone comes along," shouted the man who had first attacked the Nazis. As the others dragged the soldiers into a building, the man who'd fought so fiercely helped the elderly woman to her own flat. She laughed as he walked with her across the street. She attempted to emulate the moves of the man who had so easily disabled the Nazis. Then she laughed and pointed at him. "Are you the moshiach?" she asked repeatedly.

He laughed and shook his head. "No, I don't believe in that stuff."

In the apartment Cass turned to Thaddeus. "How did he learn to fight like that? He pulverized those Nazis."

"That's a good question. I have never seen someone fight like that before. We need to find out who that guy is. I think he can help us. Maybe he can teach us how to fight."

"They took those Nazis somewhere. What do you think they did with them?" Irena asked.

"I don't know, but it can't be good," Thaddeus said.

Although the Biebersteins watched the streets daily and talked to neighbors, no one seemed to know what happened to the Nazi soldiers.

When they asked, they were told it was better not to ask questions. "But no Nazis have been on patrol for several days. Where did they go?" Grandpa asked a neighbor one day.

Yitzhak, a neighbor on the second floor, asked Grandpa, "You have two young boys in your flat. Who are they?"

"They are my grandsons, Thaddeus and Cass."

"Do they hate Nazis?"

Grandpa laughed. "I think it would be fair to say they do not like Nazis. Why do you ask?"

Yitzhak stroked his beard and gave Grandpa a bottle of German beer. "Did you see the man who beat up the Nazis?"

"Yes, I did. They didn't have a chance. Who was he?"

"His name is Ari Levine."

"Where did he learn to fight like that?"

"He studied with Imi Lichtenfeld."

Grandpa frowned and looked out the window as he reflected. "Imi Lichtenfeld...isn't he the Jewish Hungarian boxer and wrestler?"

"That's him," Yitzhak replied. "He has a martial arts training program that he only teaches to those he calls Israelites."

"What is an Israelite to Levine?"

"Right now it's anyone who hates Nazis," Yitzhak said with a laugh.

"I think it might be good for Cass and Thaddeus to meet Ari. How can they meet him?"

"He teaches classes every Tuesday and Thursday evening at seven. Admission is only by permission. But if you can assure me that they will attend this coming Tuesday, I will make arrangements for their admission."

"Where should they go?"

"They meet in the basement of the building directly across from yours. The important thing is that they can't be late, or he won't let them in. Once class starts no one gets in or out until class is over. That is the only way they can be safe."

"I will tell them about it. Thanks."

The following Tuesday, Thaddeus and Cass walked across the street to the apartment building. They went around back to the basement door. They pounded on the heavy metal door.

A view door slid open and a gruff male voice asked, "Who is it?"

"It's Thaddeus and Cass Bieberstein. We want to study fighting."

"Are you Israelites?" asked the voice from the other side of the door.

"Yes," Thaddeus said. "We hate Nazis." This was the code they were told to use.

The door opened and Cass and Thaddeus entered and walked down the basement steps. The entrance was dimly lit. There were candles burning on the walls of a hallway that led to a large room. They walked down the hall to the room at the end. They entered and saw approximately thirty young men and women seated on a large mat on the floor facing the same man they had seen beat the Nazis a few days earlier.

"Shalom," said the man in front of the class. "I'm Ari."

"Shalom," Cass and Thaddeus said simultaneously. "I am Thaddeus, and this is my brother, Cass."

"Why are you here?" asked Ari.

"We want to learn to fight like you. We saw you fight in the street against the Nazis. We want to fight like that too."

"I know of your family, and I have met your grandfather. You're welcome here. Please take a seat on the end." Ari pointed toward the end of the front row of people seated in front of him. "When you sit, sit on your knees and cross your feet under your buttocks like this. That way if you have to get up quickly, you can."

Cass and Thaddeus looked at the other students who were all seated as the instructor described. They sat down accordingly.

Ari continued, "For those of you who are new to our class, we are studying the art of close-quarter combat. We have another class in weapons, but in this class we are studying hand-to-hand fighting. Although it does not have an official name yet, some of us call it Krav Maga, which is Hebrew for *contact combat*."

"Krav Maga," whispered Cass. He repeated the words in his head so he would not forget.

"What do you do if someone attacks you with a knife?" asked Ari. "Shlomo, come up here."

A student stood up and walked to the front of the room. Ari tossed him a piece of wood cut like a knife. "Attack with the knife."

Shlomo ran forward, holding the knife in an underhand position. Ari sidestepped the upward thrust while simultaneously intercepting the knife arm and simulating a punch to Shlomo's jaw. He then used a cavalier wrist lock along with a semicircle step to take Shlomo down while mimicking a thrust of the knife into Shlomo's throat.

"Try an overhand attack," said Ari.

Shlomo raised the practice knife above his head and thrust it downward in a stabbing motion. Ari stepped slightly to the side while intercepting the incoming knife by rotating his forearm outward in a mini-chop while simultaneously punching Shlomo in the throat. Ari used his blocking to immediately grab Shlomo's knife arm by the wrist and to then execute another cavalier wrist lock to control the knife. Ari immediately dislodged the knife from Sholomo's hand and demonstrated how it could be used offensively against a disarmed attacker.

"Wow," Cass said. "That's amazing."

"We are going to work on both of these techniques tonight," said Ari. "Work on them with each arm attacking, until it becomes your instinct. Now, everyone, to your feet. Line up and practice."

Cass was paired with a young man about Thaddeus's age. He practiced the moves repeatedly until he had committed them to memory. His partner already knew the moves, so he let Cass practice them while giving him pointers. Ari showed them several more moves, and Cass committed them to memory as well. After practicing for twenty minutes, Ari required them to engage in cardiovascular exercises.

When the class was over, Cass and Thaddeus walked back across the street. Cass's arms and legs were sore. They walked up the steps to the fifth floor and into the apartment, where they lay down on the floor of the living room. Sarah and Rachel were visiting.

"How was the workout?" Grandpa asked.

"It was good," Cass said.

Sarah asked, "Can you show us some of the moves you learned?"

The boys stood up and showed them the knife defenses. "We're supposed to practice every day so that it becomes second nature," Cass said.

"We'll practice with you," said Sarah. "That would be fun."

"Why don't you kids practice in Sarah and Rachel's flat? That way you won't be bothering Grandpa and Grandma in here," Irena suggested.

"Oh, they won't bother us," Grandma said.

"That's okay, we don't mind practicing in our flat," said Rachel. Rachel, Sarah, Thaddeus, and Cass went next door and practiced the new moves for a half hour. Then the boys returned home.

The following morning Cass and Thaddeus were awakened by a knock on their bedroom door. They didn't go out to the living room initially. Irena knocked again and said, "Cass, Thad, we have a surprise. There's someone here to see you."

Cass and Thaddeus got up and went into the living room. Much to their amazement, Rajmund and Zofia were standing there. Cass walked over to Zofia. She hugged him and said, "I missed you so much."

Thaddeus embraced Rajmund. "Why are you here? Isn't it dangerous for you to come down in the Jewish district?"

"No, we drove down in my dad's truck," replied Rajmund. "I asked Patrycja if Zofia could come to see you. She agreed as long as we came straight here and straight back."

"Where do you live now, Zofia?" Cass asked.

"We live in the house on Pulawska."

"Our house?"

"Yes. Papa is the driver for Oskar Schindler now. The house is empty most of the time. Mr. Schindler is almost never there, and Papa is usually driving him somewhere. It is just Mama, me, and Schindler's cook and gardener most of the time. I wish it were like it used to be, Cass, when we were all living in the house."

"Your papa says that someday it will go back like it was, and we will come back to the house," Cass said.

"I don't know, Cass, but I hope that's true. I really miss you."

"What did they do with Tiny, the dog that Schindler shot?"

"Papa buried him in the backyard by Rex." Cass and Zofia were silent for a moment. Then Zofia said, "Have you heard anything about what they are doing to the Jews?"

"No, we don't hear much about it down here. No one knows what is going to happen."

"Cass, they are building a fence around the Jewish ghetto."

"Oh, I know that. You can see them working from the window."

"They're planning to make all the Jews move into that fenced-in ghetto."

"They can't do that; the area isn't big enough. I think they're making a prison," Cass said.

"Cass, you don't understand. There's a rumor that Hitler is planning to start killing the Jews. You have to find a way to get out of here."

"Killing the Jews? Why would they start killing the Jews?"

"It isn't official yet, but they're talking about it. And they're already doing it in Germany."

"Do you mean killing the Jews who break the law?"

"No, I mean killing all the Jews. Papa told Mama about it. Mama is very upset. Papa says he doesn't want it to happen, but there's nothing he can do to stop it. It's what is coming."

"But we're okay down here. We have plenty of food. The Jews here have jobs. They just concentrated us into this area so we are separated from the other people."

Zofia didn't respond.

"Zofia, what is that suit you are wearing? It looks like a uniform."

"This is what I have to wear now," she said. She reached in her purse and took out her armband with the swastika on it and put it on her arm. When she did, everyone in the room suddenly looked at her. Irena said, "Zofia."

Zofia said, "I was just showing Cass what I have to wear. We took off the armbands when we came into the Jewish quarters. Papa made me join the Hitler Youth Girls. After school is out in May, I have to go away to camp for education." She removed the armband.

The room was deathly silent. Finally Irena asked, "How do you feel about it? Do you want to do it?"

"No, I hate it. I hate the Nazis."

"Zofia says that the Nazis want to start killing the Jews, and they're already doing it," Cass said.

Grandma asked, "Is that true, Zofia?"

Zofia nodded. "That's what Papa told Mama. Papa told her it's coming and is already happening. He said when they pick them up in trucks and take them away they take them out into the woods and shoot them and bury the bodies in mass graves."

Irena gasped. "That can't be true, can it?"

Rajmund replied, "Yes, it's true. Some of the Nazi officers told Papa the same thing at the restaurant. You know Papa also owns an auto repair shop where his mechanics work on the German trucks. The soldiers tell the mechanics the same thing when they bring the trucks in. The officers don't say much, but the soldiers go into detail. They said they make the Jews dig a deep trench then they make the Jews take off all their clothes. Men, women, and children all standing together naked in front of the huge trench in the middle of winter. Then they take their guns and shoot them so they fall all backward into the trench. When the trench is full of bodies, they bulldoze dirt over them. Some of the soldiers are very upset about it, but others think it is funny. They're told that the Jews deserve it because they killed Jesus."

"How do they decide who they are going to kill?" Grandma asked.

"They go into neighborhoods and round up all the Jews. Then someone decides who can work and who can't, according to their appearance. If they look strong, then they're spared. Then once they decide who can't work—like little children and older people—they go into the line to be killed. They're taken away in the trucks and killed."

Zofia reached over and squeezed Cass's hand. Cass wondered if that was what happened to his aunts and uncles. He dismissed that thought. Lech would never have allowed that.

Cass asked softly, "What do you have to do at the camp you are going to?"

"I have to learn about the Aryan race, and I have to study Hitler's books."

"Will you be the same after that?"

"They won't change what I believe, Cass, and they won't change how I feel about you. I will always love you."

Cass was worried that Zofia might change once she went to the camp. He looked at her beautiful blue eyes and her blond hair. "I don't want to lose you."

"You won't lose me, Cass. No matter what happens, you won't lose me."

After their visit, Rajmund and Zofia got up to leave. Zofia hugged Cass. "I'll come back to visit as often as I can. I love you, Cass."

"I love you too, Zofia."

Zofia and Rajmund left the apartment and walked down to the street. From the window of their apartment Cass watched them climb into Mr. Litynski's truck. He saw the name Litynski written on the side of it. He watched as Zofia climbed into the passenger side. He felt as though the wind would be knocked out of him when he saw her put her Nazi armband on. She looked up and realized that he had seen her put on the armband and quickly put her hand over it so he couldn't see it. She waved good-bye with the other hand. Cass waved good-bye. Rajmund and Zofia drove away.

The following morning Grandpa and Grandma Szyncer began operating a dental office on the first floor. The neighbors had been asking for days that they do this since there were no other dentists in the community. The first day they had so many patients that they had to stay open until eight o'clock in the evening. People paid with whatever small amount of money they had. Some paid with food. Grandpa and Grandma earned more money in that first day than most of the Jews would earn in a month, and they did not overcharge.

The Biebersteins stayed up late that evening talking about how well the dental office had done on its first day of operation. "If it stays like this, it won't be too bad," said Grandpa.

Irena replied, "Yes, let's just hope and pray that what Zofia and Rajmund said isn't true. We would be okay if it did not get any worse than this. It isn't our home on Pulawska, but we're comfortable here."

"It would be nice to visit our house in Sopot," Cass said.

"We have no way to get there. Besides, we can only assume the Nazis have taken control of that as well," Thaddeus replied.

"I wonder if they found our mountain house," Grandpa said.

Irena shrugged. "I think Lech told Schindler about all of our properties, and I'm sure he made himself right at home."

The family went to bed after midnight. The following morning, Cass and Thaddeus awakened to the sound of men's voices in the apartment. They crawled out of bed and put their clothes on then went into the living room to investigate. They saw two German officers standing by the front door talking to Irena. "Are these your sons?"

"Yes," said Irena. "Thaddeus, these gentlemen are asking about some soldiers who apparently deserted the army. About a week ago they failed to show up after their patrol. They were last seen coming to this street for their morning patrol but have not been heard from since. Do either of you remember seeing three soldiers in uniform on Wednesday of last week?"

Cass realized that his mother had spoken before the officers so that she could warn them before they said something that would reveal that the soldiers had been attacked.

Thaddeus said, "No, I used to see them, but I haven't seen them for about a week. I haven't seen a patrol at all in about a week."

"When did you see them last?" asked one of the officers, looking at Cass.

"I haven't seen them for about a week either."

"You know, it's a serious crime to help a German soldier desert. Tonight you're going to have new patrol officers. If you see the three who deserted, you should tell the new patrol about it," said the officer.

"We will," said Irena.

The officers left the Biebersteins with some relief, but they wondered what really had happened to the German soldiers. "If they didn't report in that evening, and still have not reported in, what happened to them?" Irena asked. "Is Ari holding them captive somewhere? Did somebody kill them?"

After several moments of silence, Grandpa said, "I really don't know. I assumed they were released somewhere, but when there was no patrol, I thought that the mob must have killed them."

Irena looked at Cass and then at Thaddeus. "What have we become? Are we now killing people?"

Cass jumped to his feet. "I hope so! If Ari had not stopped them, those Nazis would have killed that old woman. Are we killing Nazis? I hope so."

Cass stormed to his bedroom. He lay down on the bed with his face in the pillow. He felt a deep sadness. He did not know why he was sad; he was just sad. Then he became angry. Irena came in and rubbed his shoulders until he fell asleep. Then she went to her own room and slept.

The summer of 1940 was only too welcome after one of the coldest winters in the recorded history of Poland. The dental office proved to be very profitable for the Biebersteins. The extra income made living much more comfortable. They always had plenty of food and clothing. Yet the summer was a difficult time. They missed their mansion on Pulawska Street. Life was comfortable, but they could not escape the glaring contradiction.

After enjoying a life of opulence and luxury, they were now living simply. Cass and Thaddeus continued to practice Krav Maga with Ari. Since they were not in school, they decided to spend every waking moment studying the art of contact combat. They soon discovered that Ari worked out a minimum of five hours per day and sometimes as much as twelve hours per day. He invited them to work out with him every day and they accepted his invitation. Soon they were working out as often and as intensely as Ari. At this accelerated pace, it did not take long before Cass and Thaddeus were among the best fighters in the Jewish sector—and quite possibly the best fighters in Warsaw—notwithstanding their youth and small size.

Cass did not see Zofia all summer since she was away at the Hitler Youth camp. *I wonder what they are teaching her.* He thought about the rigorous Nazi training she was enduring. Cass, now nine years old, thought about Zofia day and night. *I hope she is okay, and I hope they have not perverted her to their evil way of thinking.*

The summer passed quickly. The Szyncer dental practice flourished. Cass and Thaddeus worked diligently at Krav Maga and physical endurance. By September, Cass had decided that given the evil influence upon Zofia, especially with the influence of her father, Zofia could not possibly have resisted the Nazi ideology. She must be a hard-core Nazi by now. Not having heard from her for four months reinforced his belief. *If she really wanted to see me, she would have found a way. She probably has a tall, handsome Nazi Youth boyfriend, and she probably thinks I am a stupid Jew joke.* He tried to put her out of his thoughts and forget her, but it was impossible. The more he tried, the more painful the memories became. He even tried to picture her as a Nazi Youth who died, so he could forget her, but that was more painful than just thinking about her. *I love that evil Nazi girl, and she does not even come to see me, though she knows I can't come to see her.* Cass tried and tried to forget her, but he could not.

Irena knew how much he was suffering, and she introduced him to Jewish girls in the neighborhood. Some of them were quite stunning in appearance, but seeing them only made Cass think more about Zofia. It made things worse, so Irena ceased this effort. *Maybe God does not want me to put her out of my mind,* he thought. *But why would God want me to think about someone whose very existence causes me pain?*

At 6:30 p.m. on September 13, 1940, Cass was sitting on a tree stump in the yard behind the apartment building. He had heard on the news that morning that Italy had invaded Egypt. *Idiots,* he thought. *This whole war thing is just plain stupid. What did Egypt ever do to Italy?* The leaves on the trees were beginning to turn brown, and the cold season was approaching. Cass began to cry softly as he thought about Zofia. *I will never see her again,* he thought. *I love her so much I would die for her, but I will never see her again. I am a Jew, and she is a Nazi. She hates me. Now she has been to the Nazi indoctrination camp. Now she has learned everything Hitler teaches.* He whispered, "Zofia, wherever you are, please know that I love you with all of my heart."

As the sun set on the horizon and the cool wind began to blow, Cass pulled his sweater up over his neck. His tears were beginning to dry. Suddenly, he was startled by a gentle touch on his shoulder. It was a touch he remembered. It was a touch of energy and spirit that only one person in his entire life had ever sparked. Zofia had touched him exactly like that so many times before. But it wasn't possible. It couldn't be Zofia. He turned and looked up and saw the stunning face of the girl he loved. Her beautiful blue eyes were glossed with tears. The sun setting behind her gave her the appearance of an angel with a glowing halo. Immediately they both burst into uncontrollable sobs. He jumped to his feet and held her in his arms. "I am so sorry I couldn't come to you earlier," she said. "I couldn't get away from camp, and then Papa wouldn't let me come. I finally slipped away with Rajmund."

They embraced so tightly as they cried that Cass thought he might be hurting her. "I'm so sorry I doubted you, Zofia. It has been so long that I thought you no longer loved me."

"I gave you my promise, Cass. I will never stop loving you. It doesn't matter what the Nazis tell me. I will always love you and no one else. You are the only one I will ever love."

After they had overcome the immediate emotion of their reunion they walked to a bench in the yard, where they rested. "What was the camp like?" Cass asked.

"It was awful. I passed so I won't have to go back, but I don't believe one word of the garbage they taught us. They made us walk around in really short white dresses. They were so short that our bums were showing, and Hitler came to see us. He smiled and nodded approvingly. I thought he was a despicable pig. Every night when he was at the camp they would make four or five girls go to his room. They would stay with him all night. They weren't supposed to talk about it later, but one of the girls told me that he made them do really bad things. She said they were so bad that she doesn't believe she can go to heaven when she dies now. I wanted him dead, Cass. I really wanted him dead. I hope that doesn't make me a bad person, but I really wanted him dead. I wanted to vomit. I hate Hitler. I want him to die a very painful, slow, and horrible death. He is a horrible, horrible, man. I pretended to believe what they were telling us at the camp only so I could get out of there and never go back."

"But you graduated, so now you won't have to go back, right?"

"That's right. I'm finished with the camps. Now I just have to go back to school."

Cass and Zofia sat on the bench holding each other for over an hour. He had his right arm around her shoulder. Eventually, he pulled his right arm down so it was by his side. She leaned her body against his, and he rested his head on her head. She reached her right hand over and took ahold of his right bicep. Startled, she reached across his chest and felt the bicep of his left arm. She stroked his chest gently. "Cass, are you doing exercises? Your muscles are huge."

Cass laughed. "Yes, I work out five to ten hours every day. We don't go to school anymore, so I decided to work out all the time."

"You're really strong. What are you going to do with all of these muscles?"

Cass laughed. "I am going to protect you from the Nazis."

"Cass, I'm going to have to leave in a few minutes. Papa said I can't come to see you. Mama lets me come when Papa isn't home, but he doesn't know I have ever been here. He says it is too dangerous to go into the Jewish sector. I have to go back before he figures out where I am because then he will really try to prevent me from coming here, but I figured out a way I can come and see you every day."

"Are you serious? How can you come and see me every day?"

"I'm back in school now. I told Papa I want to walk home from school every day. It takes about an hour to walk home. But I found out that there's a streetcar that comes to the school every day, five minutes after school gets out. That streetcar comes to a stop right at the intersection of Aleja Wilanowska and Wilanow Street. If you can meet me there every day we can visit for forty minutes. At exactly three fifty, another streetcar comes by that stop that goes straight to the stop on Pulawska that's a half block from your old house. That means I can visit with you every day for forty minutes and still be home as soon as I would be if I walked all the way."

"But how will you pay the streetcar fare?" asked Cass.

"I get an allowance. I choose to spend my allowance on a streetcar so I can come and see you."

"That would be wonderful to see you every day, and I will be there every day; but I don't want you to get into trouble."

"Don't worry, Cass, I won't get into trouble. Monday is my next school day. If you meet me at the streetcar stop at three o'clock, I can spend forty minutes with you."

"Okay, I will be there."

The following Monday, Cass waited for Zofia at the streetcar stop, and she came to see him just as she promised. They began meeting that way every day except on weekends when there was no school. When Schindler went back to Krakow, Lech went with him since he was Schindler's driver. So Lech was gone for several months at a time. Zofia and her mother talked often about what was happening to the Jews. Patrycja said that it was a horrible thing that was happening and that she was very sad that Lech was helping the Nazis. Eventually, Zofia confessed to her mother that she was really spending time with Cass every day. Her mother told her that it would be okay for her to go with Rajmund when he went to visit Sarah, but that she could not tell her father about it. He would be very angry. Also, she did not want her to go alone on the streetcar as she had been. She could only go with Rajmund.

Patrycja understood that even though they were very young, the love between Cass and Zofia was strong, and as the days passed, it only grew deeper. Cass eventually introduced her to Ari and Ari's wife, Leah, but Ari would not allow Zofia to study Krav Maga with them or attend their workout sessions because he was concerned that she might inadvertently tell her father, which could be dangerous for them. Sometimes when she came to visit with Rajmund, Rachel, Cass, Zofia, Ari, Leah, Thaddeus, and Sarah would have lunch together at a small deli operated by a Jewish family near the apartment where they lived. Ari had grown fond of Cass and Thaddeus and was pleased with their diligence in studying Krav Maga. The days passed and soon the red and brown leaves on the trees began falling to the ground. Poland had entered the fall of 1940.

CHAPTER

13

C ASS AND THADDEUS exercised and studied Krav Maga all day, six days per week. Cass had been employed to work at a local gun manufacturing factory but generally worked about three days per week. It was slave labor that his mother had arranged to keep him from being exterminated with the other Jewish children. When he wasn't working, he was exercising. On Shabbat they rested. Ari was pleased with their hard work and the speed at which they learned. If the situation did not get worse, it would be tolerable. Several times per month the family would receive an anonymous package in the mail with food and money enclosed. Unbeknownst to the Biebersteins, the packages were sent by Sigmund, who had managed to reach America and was arranging for the family to come.

The family discussed the possibility of leaving Poland, but they learned that Jews were no longer permitted to travel. They had to stay within their own neighborhood and could not travel on streetcars without disclosing the details of their travel plans to the streetcar operator. Still believing the situation was temporary and soon they would return to their home on Pulawska Street, the Biebersteins were generally not troubled that they were living in an apartment. Grandpa, however, often expressed concern about the wall that was being constructed around the ghetto. Every day he would walk in the direction of the ghetto to see what was happening with the construction. Sometimes Cass would walk with him. Jews living in the ghetto appeared to be emaciated.

"It looks like those people aren't getting any food," said Grandpa one day.

"Where does their food come from?"

"I heard that they get food rations. Those who work get about half of what a person needs to eat and those who do not work only receive only one third of what the people who work get."

Cass frowned as he looked at an elderly man who seemed to be staggering from weakness. "Why don't they give them more food?"

"I don't know. That's what concerns me. I'm also concerned that we might also be forced to move into the ghetto someday."

"In there? That would be awful. Why would we have to move into the ghetto?"

"Because we are Jews," Grandpa said. "I just have a concern. But don't worry about it. For now, we are safe."

Grandpa's dental practice was able to generate enough income that, combined with the money Irena had been able to keep when they left Pulawska Street, and the food and money that always arrived in packages, they all had enough to eat. Periodically, they would see people walking with all of their belongings toward the ghetto. One day when Cass, Thaddeus, and Irena were walking back from a trip to the market, they saw a group of about a dozen men, women, and children approaching. They were all wearing Star of David armbands, and they were carrying clothing.

"Good morning," Irena said. "Do you mind if I ask where you are going?"

An older man looked up sadly and replied, "They're moving us into the ghetto."

"Who is moving you?" Cass asked.

"The Germans."

"Why?" Thaddeus asked. "I thought they moved us into the Jewish Quarter to separate us from the non-Jews."

"That's what we thought. We thought when they moved us here that this is where we would remain. About a half hour ago, some German officers came to our apartment and said that they now need this area for non-Jews. I asked where we were moving and was told we were moving into the ghetto and that we had fifteen minutes to gather one article of clothing for each person. Fifteen minutes later they were yelling at us to get out."

Irena asked, "Did they arrange for a place for you to stay in the ghetto? What if there are no vacant apartments?"

The old man shook his head. "I asked that question. They said it's our problem, and we have to figure that out on our own."

"Do you have any money for food?" Irena asked.

"No, we don't have anything."

Irena took a loaf of bread and some cheese from the bag she was carrying and gave it to the elderly man. "Here, this will help you while you are looking for a place." She also gave him some money.

"Thank you," the old man said. "This means a lot to us."

Cass thought about the starving people he had seen when he looked through the fence into the ghetto. *They are going to wind up like the other people in the ghetto.*

As the days passed, they began to see a larger number of people walking to the ghetto. More and more non-Jews began moving into the neighborhood. Twice per week, every Tuesday and Thursday afternoon, Zofia and Rajmund would drive into the Jewish Quarter to visit Sarah and Cass. When Lech was in town, he believed that Zofia was at school, participating in a girls' soccer team. Patrycja and Zofia said nothing to cause him to believe otherwise.

The Jews soon learned that a ruthless German officer named Colonel Unger was responsible for ordering the Jews into the ghetto. Unger took exceptional pleasure in harassing the Jews. He would often order them to strip naked in the street and then order non-Jews to beat them, before killing them or sending them to the ghetto or the work camp. He enjoyed causing them pain.

Colonel Unger lived in a mansion about a half mile from the apartment where the Biebersteins were living. The mansion, which served as the base of operations, was well fortified; German soldiers walked the sidewalk at every corner of the property. The area was considered undesirable since it was in the Jewish Quarter, and it was Unger's responsibility to move the Jews into the ghetto so non-Jews could move into the neighborhood. His job was to clean up an area of approximately five square miles and make the neighborhood suitable for Aryans.

Unger's family lived in Germany, and the Jews were told to stay off the streets the week of Christmas 1940 because the Unger family was coming for a visit over the Christmas holidays. He did not want his family seeing the Jews. Ari and his team of fighters decided to take advantage of the opportunity to send a message to the Germans that the Jews would not go without a fight. They carefully studied the mansion from all angles and discovered that every evening Unger would sit in the den on the first floor, drinking alone until he passed out. He would go to bed when he awoke at approximately four o'clock in the morning. They could see him every night through the window of the den. Because of the curfew, it was particularly difficult to watch the house, but by Christmas they knew where they could find him on any given evening.

The house was surrounded by a wrought-iron fence. Each night Ari and a team of five fighters hid across the street from the house and watched the movement of the soldiers guarding the property. The four soldiers would walk back and forth on each side of the property and meet the soldier from the next side of the house when they came to the corner of the yard. It was timed perfectly so that each side of the house was seen at all times.

Back at Ari's gym they discussed the plans. "We are going to have to take out all four of them simultaneously. Otherwise, they will know something is wrong when they reach the corner of the lot and the other soldier isn't there to meet them," said Ari. "That's the only way we can do this."

"What are you going to do?" Cass asked.

"We are going to assassinate Colonel Unger," Ari replied.

"I would like to come along."

"No, Cass, you are too young for this one. It is going to be brutal."

"How are you going to do it? I have trained hard for a long time. I really want to come."

Ari shook his head. "Sorry, Cass. We can't let you come."

Disappointed, Cass accepted the decision.

As anticipated, Unger's family arrived for the visit several days before Christmas. On the first and second evening of the visit, Unger did not sit in the den. Instead he went to bed with his wife. He did the same for the next two nights. Finally, on Christmas Eve, the family went to bed early, and Unger went into his den. He took out his brandy and poured a drink and then another. Soon he had passed out.

Four Jewish fighters, equipped with bows and arrows, sat across the street, one on each side of the house. It was imperative that they not be heard. Ari gave the signal, which was the sound of a garbage can striking the pavement. Immediately, each of the archers fired an arrow into the German soldier, that was guarding his side of the house. The fighters then ran across the street and using their knives, made sure that each of four guards was dead.

Ari and one of the Jewish fighters, Walter, immediately ran across the street. They quietly scaled the wrought-iron fence and jumped into the yard. They ran up to the window and with a crowbar quietly pried the window open. Unger never moved. Raising the window high enough to crawl through, they quietly entered the den through the window. Ari ran up behind the colonel, held his hand over his mouth, and slit his throat with his knife before the colonel knew what was happening. As they stood there looking at the dead German in his leather swivel desk chair, Walter took his finger, dipped it into the blood on his neck, and with it, drew a star on his forehead. They then crawled back through the window, closed it, and ran back to the gym with the other fighters. On Christmas morning the family awakened to find Colonel Unger still sitting in the leather desk chair, in his uniform, with a bloody Star of David on his forehead, his shirt drenched with blood.

The following morning the Nazis rounded up forty Jews from the neighborhood, forced them to climb into a truck, and drove them over to the ghetto. There they were lined up against a wall and executed by firing squad. The Germans told the Jews in the neighborhood that this was the punishment for breaking into the colonel's house and killing him; any such acts in the future would result in similar retaliation. Word quickly spread through the Jewish community of the consequence of attacking an officer of the Reich.

Lech had come home to the Bieberstein mansion for the holidays, which made it difficult for Zofia to get away to see Cass. The Wagners put the Christmas tree on the landing as they had when the Biebersteins were in the house. Being in the house without the Biebersteins was devastating for Zofia. She spent Christmas Day in her bedroom, crying on her bed. Lech, who had bought her many expensive gifts for Christmas, knocked on the door to her bedroom. She did not respond, so he entered cautiously and sat on the bed next to her. "Zofia, I don't understand. Don't you like the gifts I bought for you?"

"Yes, I like them a lot, Papa."

"But why are you crying?"

Zofia did not respond.

Lech took ahold of her shoulder. "Zofia, if you don't tell me what is wrong, I can't help you."

Finally Zofia said, "I just want things to be like they used to be. I liked it when you were here all the time and when the Biebersteins were living here. I was so happy then. I used to play with Cass in the garden. We would explore in the attic even though we weren't supposed to go up there. I really miss those days, Papa, and I miss Cass. Now Cass lives in a different place. He is a prisoner there."

"The world is changing, Zofia. The changes are for the better, and there isn't really anything we can do about it anyway."

"But they didn't have to move out, Papa. They could have stayed here."

"Zofia, they had to give up the house because Herr Schindler needed a place to stay when he is in Warsaw working. The Jews have been strangling Europe financially for centuries. Now that is coming to an end."

"You forget, Papa, I went to school at the yeshiva. I know the truth."

"They just taught you what they wanted you to hear. They brainwashed you, Zofia. I never should have let you go to that Jewish school."

Zofia sat up on the bed and looked at her father. "Am I really the one who is brainwashed, Papa?"

Lech looked at her in silence for a moment. Then he said, "There really wasn't anything we could have done about it. Like I said, Herr Schindler needed a place to stay when he is here in Warsaw."

"Papa, I remember what happened. You brought Schindler here. You told Mama and me that you had been spying for Germany all those years you lived here. You pretended to be loyal to the Biebersteins. You were really spying for the Nazis. I don't like the Nazis, Papa. If you hadn't told the Nazis and Schindler about this house, they never would have come and taken it away from the Biebersteins."

"That isn't true, Zofia. All the Jews are being moved into the Jewish Quarter. It was just a matter of time before the Biebersteins would have been moved. I actually helped them because I arranged it so they would have a nice place to go, and so that they could take some money with them."

Zofia cried as she talked. "But you helped the Nazis, Papa. You made me become a Nazi, and you made Mama become a Nazi. Mama doesn't like being a Nazi either. She hates the Nazis."

"I know it is hard for you to understand, Zofia, but someday you will. Think of it like this. When a person has a bad infection in his leg, the leg has to be cut off to keep the rest of the body from being poisoned by the infection. It hurts when the leg is cut off, but it is better for the rest of the body. In the same way, it hurts when we have to get rid of the Jews, but it's necessary to keep the rest of society from being poisoned by their infection. Someday you will see that I did the right thing."

"No, Papa, hurting people is never the right thing. Hitler is wrong."

Lech motioned for his daughter to be quiet. "Zofia, you need to talk quieter. Someone in the house will hear you. They will report this."

"That's exactly what I'm talking about, Papa. We can't even say what we think, or Hitler will throw us in jail. It was never like that before the Germans invaded. We could say whatever we wanted to say about the government, and no one cared. Now we can't even question the government, or we will be thrown in jail or whatever else those monsters do. Papa, you saw them shoot that girl right in front of this house. I saw you standing next to the car that night. You were there. Do you think this is good? Do you think we are better now that the Nazis have taken over?"

Realizing that trying to reason with Zofia on these issues would only worsen the situation, Lech exhibited a little sternness. "Zofia, you are a child. You don't understand many things. Someday you will understand, and you will be proud of what I have done for the Reich. We aren't Polish, we are German. Your mother and I both grew up in Germany, and I know what is best for Europe. Now, I don't want to hear you talk this way anymore. The old days are gone, and we need to move on. I want you to dry your eyes and come downstairs and spend time with your mother and me. This is Christmas Day."

"I'll come downstairs because you told me to, but not because I want to. I'm ashamed of what you have done, Papa, and I'm never going to change my thinking about that. I would rather be dead than live under this evil government."

Zofia's words sent a cold chill down Lech's spine. Somehow they seemed prophetic. "Zofia, don't say that. Your mother and I would be devastated if something ever happened to you."

Zofia slowly climbed off the bed and went downstairs with her father. She entered the living room and sat on the couch next to her mother. They both remained silent the rest of the afternoon while Lech drank rum and laughed and joked with one of Schindler's bodyguards. In his intoxicated state, Lech did not even notice that both Patrycja and Zofia were silently crying.

After listening to her father hide his guilt behind a bottle of rum, Zofia grew tired. "Papa, I would like to go to bed."

"Of course, my dear," replied her father as he fought to conceal his inebriation. It seemed Papa was intoxicated most of the time now. Zofia had never seen him drink until after the invasion, but now it seemed there was never a time when he wasn't drunk.

Sleep eluded Zofia the evening of Christmas. She remained awake most of the night, dozing off for only minutes at a time. She awakened at approximately three thirty on December 26, 1940. As she reflected on the events of that day, she began crying. About an hour later she got out of bed and walked over to her vanity. She lit the candles on each side of the vanity mirror then went into the bathroom and lit two candles and an incense stick. She filled the tub with warm water. When the tub was full, she whispered the word "mikvah" several times. Then she dropped her robe to the floor and climbed into the bath. The incense soothed as she slid down in the tub, leaving only her face exposed to the cool air. She knew that the tub did not meet the design requirements of a true mikvah bath with two pools, but the pools in the house had been drained when the Biebersteins moved out.

Zofia finished her bath. She wrapped a towel around herself, went to her closet, and put on the ankle-length skirt she always wore at the yeshiva.

She selected the flowing white blouse that Cass said was his favorite. She reached into her schoolbag and pulled out a Nazi armband. She threw it on the floor. She then reached into her schoolbag a second time and this time pulled out a Star of David armband. "I'm a Jew," she whispered.

Zofia packed some of her favorite clothes into a travel bag. She took her prayer book from the vanity, the one she had been given by Rabbi Lieberman as a reward for academic excellence, and she opened it to her favorite passage. She read from Psalm 23.

> The Lord is my shepherd, I shall not want,
> He makes me to lie down in green pastures, He leads me
> beside the still waters,
> He restores my soul; He leads me in paths of righteousness
> for His name's sake.
> Even when I walk in the valley of darkness, I will fear no
> evil, for You are with me.
> Your rod and Your staff they comfort me,
> You prepare a table before me, In the presence of my
> enemies,
> You anoint my head with oil; my cup overflows.
> Surely goodness and mercy will follow me all the days of
> my life.
>
> Amen.

She then took out a pad of paper and a pen and wrote these words:

Dear Mama and Papa,

Please know that I love both of you very much. You have always taken good care of me, and I know that you would always do anything you could to help me. I love you for this.

I have decided that I am a Jew. I attended yeshiva, and I believe that what I learned there was true. For this reason, I've decided to run away and go to live with the Jews in

the Jewish Quarter. I would rather die with the Jews than
live as a Nazi. Don't be afraid and don't worry about me.
I will be fine.
I love both of you,

Zofia

Zofia left the note on her vanity so it would be easily found. She put
on her winter coat and the armband with the Star of David on her right
arm. She picked up her bag of clothes and quietly opened her bedroom
door. Not hearing anyone in the house, she walked into the hall and down
the steps to the front door, opened it, and left.

The short walk to the streetcar stop took only a few minutes. Zofia
already knew that there would be a streetcar at five thirty. She knew the
schedule. As anticipated, the streetcar was on time. Zofia walked to the
back of the streetcar and sat on one of the seats. There were no other
passengers on the streetcar. The operator looked back at her. "Are you okay,
miss? I think I recognize you from other rides. Are you okay? Why are
you wearing the Star of David armband? You usually wear the swastika.
It's really dangerous to play like that. Someone might think you really are
a Jew."

Zofia nodded. "I'm okay. Thank you."

As the streetcar traveled down Aleja Wilanowska Street, Zofia looked
at the houses. Few of them had their lights on. *It's too early for people to be
up*, she thought.

The streetcar stopped at the corner of Aleja Wilanowska and Wilanow,
and Zofia got off. She thought she would walk to the Bieberstein flat,
not knowing about the German patrol that would pass down the street
at exactly six o'clock. She got off the streetcar and began walking toward
Cass's house. After she had walked about a hundred feet, she heard a man
behind her say, "Hey, little girl, what are you doing out this early in the
morning?"

Zofia stopped and turned around. She saw two German soldiers who
were patrolling the street.

"I'm going to my friend's house."

"Who is your friend?"

"Cass Bieberstein," she replied.

"Does he live on this street?"

"Yes."

"How old are you?" asked the other soldier.

"I'm eight."

"Don't you know that Jews aren't supposed to be on the street this time of morning?"

"I didn't know."

"Where is your Mama?"

"She is over on Pulawska Street."

"And your Papa?"

"He is there too."

"Do they know you are here?"

"No, I am running away."

The two soldiers turned their backs to her then whispered something in German. Zofia wondered what they were saying. Finally, they turned back to her, and one of them said, "So you are all by yourself, and no one knows you're here?"

Zofia nodded.

The two soldiers looked at each other and laughed. Suddenly one of them grabbed her and put his gloved hand over her mouth. He picked her up and carried her, keeping his hand over her mouth so she could not scream. They ran behind a warehouse on the other side of the street. The one with his hands free took a ring of keys from his belt and looked for the key to the warehouse door. After trying several keys, he found the right one and opened the door. They ran inside to a little room and over to a couch. Zofia said, "Please let me go. I don't want any trouble. I didn't know I wasn't supposed to be out." The soldiers looked at each other and laughed.

Unbeknownst to the soldiers, the crazy old woman who had danced in the street with the former guards had watched from the window as the men grabbed Zofia. She recognized Zofia because she had seen her with Cass and Thaddeus. She put on her winter coat and ran down the street to the Bieberstein apartment. She ran up the five flights of stairs. When she reached the top of the stairs she pounded on the door, waking Cass, Thaddeus, and Irena.

Cass opened the door and asked, "What's wrong?"

"The soldiers took your friend, Zofia."

"What do you mean?" asked Cass. By now Irena had come to the door and was standing next to Cass and Thaddeus.

"Zofia came here on a streetcar early this morning. She was walking toward your apartment building when she ran into the six o'clock street patrol. There were two of them. They talked to her for a minute, and then one of them grabbed her and took her into the warehouse on my end of the street—the one right across from my flat. I saw it all from my window. I could see because they were under a streetlight."

"Come on in and warm up." Irena led the old woman into the living room and placed a warm blanket on her. She then went into the kitchen with Cass and Thaddeus.

"I have to go see what is going on," Cass said.

"Yes, we need to check, but remember, Cass, this old woman isn't right in her mind. It is hard telling what she saw, if anything."

"I know, but I have to check."

"Yes, we need to check, but you don't want to be seen by the six o'clock patrol. They will get mad if they see Jews out this early."

Before Irena had finished her sentence, Cass was out the door and running down the steps. Thaddeus was right behind him. When they got to the bottom floor, Cass and Thaddeus ran out the door and down the street toward the building across from the old woman's flat. Irena followed them out the door then ran across the street to Ari's flat in the basement. She pounded on the door, and Ari opened it. Ari put on his jacket as Irena told him what had happened.

Cass and Thaddeus ran to the warehouse across the street from the old woman's apartment. They started looking around for an open door. They found one on the back side of the building. They quietly slipped through. It was still dark outside and in the building. They saw a light in a small room on the opposite side of the warehouse.

Cass and Thaddeus ran through the warehouse. They heard voices speaking German from down the hall in the opposite direction. Cass opened the door to the small room. At first they saw nothing. Then Cass saw a bare foot extending from behind a couch. He approached and saw Zofia, lying naked on the floor. Her eyes were opened as she stared at the ceiling, and her neck was cut. There were cuts all over her body. Blood had poured from her wounds. Even at his young age, Cass knew she was dead. He fell to the floor and put her head in his lap. He began rocking her as he cried and whispered *Zofia* over and over again. Thaddeus stood looking at them in disbelief.

Ari ran over and looked at Zofia. He bent down and took her pulse. "Who did this?"

"The Nazi soldiers," Cass said, sobbing.

Thaddeus whispered, "We heard voices speaking German down that hall." He pointed down a hallway that led to the offices of the warehouse. "The old woman told us they grabbed her and brought her in here. That's why we came and looked."

Ari turned and ran quietly down the hall. Thaddeus followed close behind him. They got closer to the voices and found a light on in a room at the end of the hall. The door was opened a crack. Two German soldiers were putting on their uniforms as they laughed and joked about the little Jewish girl who kept saying, "Please let me go." One of them was washing blood off his knife. When they had put their uniforms on they walked toward the door. Thaddeus and Ari stood next to the door so they could not be seen.

As the first soldier walked through the door, Ari grabbed him from behind and thrust his knife into his throat then pulled it across his neck with a clean motion, cutting his throat from ear to ear. The other soldier jumped back in shock. As he tried to unholster his gun, Thaddeus ran toward him. Using the Krav Maga techniques he had learned, he grabbed the hand of the soldier and used a cavalier wrist-lock to take the soldier to the ground. As the soldier yelled in agony, Ari ran in and thrust his knife into the neck of the prone soldier. Ari and Thaddeus checked to make sure both soldiers were dead. Then they ran back down the hall to the room where Cass was holding Zofia and crying bitterly. Ari knelt down on one side of Cass and put his arm around him. Thaddeus sat on Cass's other side and put a jacket over Zofia. Irena came into the room and knelt behind Cass. They stayed in the room with Zofia's body for twenty minutes. Finally Ari said, "We need to hide the bodies of the Nazis. We can put them in the sewer like we did the other three soldiers who attacked that old woman last summer."

Irena asked, "That's what happened to the other soldiers?"

Ari nodded.

Thaddeus and Ari went back down the hall to the room where the German soldiers' bodies were lying. They stripped off their clothes, picked up their bodies, and carried them one at a time to a covered sewer behind the warehouse. Ari opened the lid, and they threw the bodies down inside. Ari then retrieved a can of petrol from the warehouse, climbed down into the sewer, poured the petrol on the bodies, and set them on fire. He climbed out of the sewer and replaced the lid. "The burned bodies won't give off an odor while they decay," he told Thaddeus.

Ari and Thaddeus went back inside the warehouse. Ari took the uniforms and rolled them into a bundle with the soldiers' sidearms inside. "These uniforms and weapons might come in handy," said Ari. He mopped the blood off the floor. Then they went to the room where Cass was still holding Zofia's body. Irena pulled Cass away from her.

Ari picked her up and carried her down the street to the Bieberstein flat. Ari gently placed Zofia on the floor in the kitchen so blood would not get on the couch. Cass sat on the floor and held her as he had held her at the warehouse. Ari went back to the warehouse and mopped up Zofia's blood from behind the couch, pushed the couch back against the wall, turned off the light, and left.

Zofia's parents got up at eight o'clock that morning. Patrycja went to Zofia's room to awaken her and saw that she was not in the room. Assuming she had already gone downstairs, she went to the kitchen, where she started preparing breakfast. A few moments later Lech came in and asked, "Where's Zofia? Isn't she up yet?"

"She's up, but I don't see her. Maybe she is in the backyard."

Lech went outside to look for Zofia. He came in a few moments later and said, "I don't see Zofia anywhere. Patrycja moved the frying pan with eggs off the burner and walked upstairs with Lech to look for Zofia. In her room they noticed that her bathtub was wet. "She must have had a bath this morning," Lech said. Then they saw the Nazi armband lying on the floor.

Patrycja found the note on the vanity. She read it. "Lech, look at this."

Lech took the note. As he read it his face grew into a frown. "There is only one place in the Jewish section where she would go. She would only go to see the Biebersteins. But how would she know where they are?"

149

Patrycja put her hand on her head. "She knows where they live. She has been there a few times."

"Why was she over there? That's dangerous."

"She wanted to see Cass."

"Well, let's go pick her up. Hopefully she didn't run into any trouble on the way."

Lech and Patrycja went downstairs and out to Schindler's limousine. Patrycja had a piece of paper with the address of the flat written on it. Lech drove to the Bieberstein apartment. The neighbors noticed the swastikas on the side of the car and the Nazi flags on both sides of the hood. As they got out of the car, Lech said, "She is going to have to be punished for this. She can't come over here. It's too dangerous."

Lech and Patrycja walked up the five flights of stairs to the Bieberstein apartment. Patrycja looked at the number on the piece of paper in her pocket. "This is it." She stood next to Lech as he knocked on the door.

The door opened, and there stood Irena, still crying. Patrycja gasped. "What's wrong?"

Irena hugged Patrycja. "I am so sorry."

Cass was sitting on the floor in the kitchen next to Zofia, who was covered with a sheet. Ari, Grandpa, Grandma, Rachel, Sarah, and Thaddeus were all seated at the kitchen table. Not yet realizing that it was Zofia on the kitchen floor covered with a sheet, Lech asked, "What happened?"

Irena said, "I am so sorry to tell you this. Zofia was attacked by Nazi guards. A neighbor saw them grab her and drag her into the warehouse at the end of the street." Patrycja started toward the body in the kitchen, but she collapsed.

"Oh God, what have I done?" Lech went into the kitchen and pulled the sheet from her face, fell on his knees next to her, then burst into tears. He lifted her up into his arms and held her repeating, "My baby. My little baby."

After a few moments, he laid her back down on the floor. He saw the Star of David armband on the floor next to her. "Was she wearing that when they took her?"

Cass said, "It was next to her when we found her."

Thaddeus and Irena helped Patrycja to the couch. She lay staring at the ceiling as if in a coma.

Lech began repeating, "It's my fault."

No one responded.

Then Lech said, "We had an argument yesterday, but I never thought she would run away. She said she would rather die as a Jew than live as a Nazi. She saw me standing by the car when the Jewish girl was shot in the back in front of the house on Pulawska Street. She was wearing the armband, so they would have believed she was a Jew. She would not have denied it."

Lech stood up. In the living room, he sat next to Patrycja and cried. Finally he said, "Whether they thought she was a Jew or not, I am going to find the men who did this, and I am going to take care of them."

"No need," Ari said. "They have already been dealt with."

"What do you mean?"

"They will never bother anyone again."

"Are they dead?"

Ari nodded.

After about an hour Lech picked up her body and walked into the hall and down the steps. Irena and Grandpa helped Patrycja down to the car. Cass followed them down with Zofia's clothes and the Star of David armband. He placed them in the car. As they put Zofia's body in the back seat of the limousine, Cass was sickened by the swastikas on the car. By now the entire neighborhood had heard what happened, and everyone was watching from their windows. Some came out to the street. As they drove away in the limousine, Cass could not help but realize that this was the last time he would ever see Zofia. He wanted to die.

Lech and Patrycja stopped at a local mortuary on the way home and left the body with a mortician. Then they drove home. The rest of the day Lech and Patrycja sat in the living room staring at the walls without speaking. Later in the day, when it was getting dark outside, Patrycja said she was going to take a bath and slowly climbed the steps to the master bathroom. After about an hour, Lech noticed that she was extremely quiet. He went upstairs to see if she had gone to bed.

The bed was empty. In the bathroom, he found Patrycja lying facedown in a tub full of water, wearing only the Star of David armband that Zofia was wearing when she was killed. Patrycja had drowned herself. Lech called the mortician. Now he would be burying two bodies.

CHAPTER

14

AFTER ZOFIA'S DEATH, Cass retreated into his room. He did not emerge for several weeks except to bathe and use the facilities. He thought about Zofia constantly. He could see her beautiful long blond hair and large blue eyes. He thought of the last time he saw her and how much he had not wanted her to leave. He cried day and night until no more tears would flow. Irena brought food to him. Sometimes she would sit with him and gently rub his shoulders, though neither spoke. Finally, after several weeks, Cass emerged from the room. He was not the same. Though not yet a teenager, he had become mentally conditioned to do only one thing: kill Nazis.

On a January morning in 1941, the family was awakened by the sound of someone pounding on the door. Grandpa opened the door revealing two German officers who walked briskly into the apartment. They were followed by several German soldiers armed with Karabiner 98k rifles. The men began walking through the apartment opening bedroom doors, looking in closets, and instructing everyone to go into the living room. Cass and Thaddeus emerged from the bedroom and stood next to Grandpa, Grandma, and Irena.

One of the officers said, "We had two German soldiers disappear from this area while on patrol, and an officer was murdered in his house a few blocks from here at the same time. This is the second time soldiers have disappeared from this street within six months. If it happens once in a specific neighborhood, desertion seems like the most likely explanation. However, when it happens twice within six months, in the same neighborhood, the same night an officer is murdered a few blocks away, then it looks like foul play. Do you know anything about the two soldiers who disappeared on Christmas or the officer who was killed on Christmas Eve?"

They shook their heads. "No, we haven't heard anything," Irena said.

The officer continued, "We intend to search every home until we find some information about what happened to them. If you hear anything notify the authorities immediately."

"We will," said Grandpa.

Later that morning, the stillness was broken again, this time by shouting in the streets below. Cass looked out of the bedroom window. In the street, German soldiers, SS officers, and Warsaw police officers were shouting commands at neighbors they were corralling in the street. Both ends of the street were blocked by large military trucks and armed guards with machine guns. Suddenly, the sound of fists shook the door of the apartment. A man shouted in German, "Open the door. Open the door now."

Thaddeus opened the front door as Grandpa and Grandma came into the room. A German officer stormed into the room and shouted, "Everyone be down in the street in fifteen minutes. Wear all the clothes you can, because you can't take anything but the clothes on your back."

After he left, the Biebersteins looked at one another with blank expressions. "I think they are moving us," said Irena.

Grandpa nodded. "Put on several layers of clothing and your winter coats. It's cold out there. Irena, I think you should take some of the money, give some to Mama, some to Thad, and some to me, in case we get split up."

Irena quickly complied. The family walked down to the street. Rachel and Sarah walked down with them. Cass walked behind Rachel and Sarah. The ominous sound of their winter boots on each step shook Cass to his soul. He thought of the morning they left the house on Pulawska Street. Stuffed into the rear of his pants, under his coat, was his teddy bear, Misha. Cass was still reeling from the death of Zofia. He felt numb. This was just another distraction from his grieving, but somehow, he did not seem to care anymore.

On the street the family stood by the curb in line with the neighbors, everyone facing the center of the street except for non-Jews, who were told to remain in their houses. When all of the houses and apartments were emptied, an SS officer stood in front of the line and shouted, "Someone in this neighborhood has been very bad. Last summer three guards disappeared while patrolling on this street. At the time we thought maybe they deserted. That didn't seem right because Germans are not fearful people, but we could think of no other logical explanation. Then last week, two more guards disappeared while patrolling in this area, and an officer was killed in his home along with four other soldiers. We know the soldiers didn't desert. That would be too much of a coincidence. So now we know someone here did something to them, and probably to the guards last summer."

The German officer pointed at an old woman and said, "You, come and stand here in the middle of the street."

The old woman complied fearfully.

The officer continued, "Now who is going to tell me what happened to them?" He took his sidearm from his holster. "I am going to count to ten. If no one tells me what happened to these soldiers before I reach ten, I am going to shoot this old woman."

The officer started counting. When he reached ten, no one stepped forward. He pointed his pistol at the old woman and shot her in the head. She fell to the ground. "You're all going to stand here in the street, in the cold, while we search every house. Every hour I am going shoot another person until either we find the missing soldiers, or someone tells me what happened to them."

As the Jews stood in the street, the soldiers went door-to-door, searching every house and apartment, looking for the missing soldiers. When an hour had passed, the soldiers were still searching, and the Jews were still standing in the street. The officer motioned to a young boy to walk to the middle of the street. His parents, standing next to him, pleaded with the officer not to shoot their son. The boy began to cry but walked to the middle of the street as instructed. The officer took his sidearm from its holster and pointed it at the boy.

Someone shouted, "Stop. I know what happened to them."

Everyone turned to see who had yelled. The voice seemed familiar to Cass. It sounded like Ari. In fact, it was Ari.

The officer lowered his sidearm. "Come over here," he said.

Ari walked to the center of the street and motioned for the boy to get back in line. The young boy looked at the officer, who nodded. The officer approached Ari and circled him slowly, examining him. He then stood with his face inches from Ari's face. "Tell us what happened to the soldiers."

Ari replied, "I killed them."

The officer stepped back and burst into laughter. "This is what I like—a funny Jew. So you killed them, did you? Where are the bodies?"

Ari looked directly into the eyes of the officer. "I threw them into the sewer where they belong. And now you are going to join them."

Perhaps it was the intensity of Ari's gaze and the firmness of his words, but it seemed as if the officer suddenly realized Ari was not joking. His face revealed terror as he tripped backward and pointed his pistol at Ari. Before the officer could shoot, Ari stepped forward and used his hands to ensnare the officer's outstretched wrist and pistol. Ari immediately twisted the officer's hand around, pointed the officer's own gun into the surprised man's stomach, and forced him to pull the trigger. As the officer began to fall, Ari quickly jerked the gun from his hand and shot two soldiers who were standing nearest the officer. Ari bolted and ran between two apartment buildings. German soldiers came running from both ends of the street following in the direction Ari was running. Cass looked at the dead officer lying on the ground. He then looked to see how far the soldiers were behind Ari. *They will never catch Ari*, he thought. Cass chuckled quietly to himself as he thought of the look on the officer's face when he realized Ari was not joking. He looked at Thaddeus, who was smiling slightly. Thaddeus nodded at Cass.

Several minutes later the soldiers who had chased Ari returned to the line. Another SS officer stepped forward to the location where the dead officer had been standing. He pointed toward the ghetto and shouted, "Start walking toward the intersection of Chlodna and Zelazna. When you get there you will receive further instructions."

Everyone turned and began walking in the direction of the ghetto. Cass asked, "Where are we going to stay?"

"We'll have to wait until we get there to find out," Irena said.

Cass and Thaddeus walked side by side. Sarah and Rachel walked next to Cass. "Do you think they will catch Ari?" Sarah asked.

"No, I don't," replied Thaddeus. "Ari knows this area like the back of his hand. He was born and raised here. Plus, he could run twice as fast as those Nazis. Did you see how fast he was going?"

Rachel replied, "I did. He ran like a gazelle. And those soldiers ran like monkeys. And they call us monkey Jews." Cass and Thaddeus laughed.

Sarah looked at Cass. "That's the first time I've seen you smile in weeks."

"I've been thinking about Zofia all the time. Today I'm laughing at the stupid Nazis. Did you see the look on that officer's face when Ari said he threw the soldiers in the sewer?"

"I did," replied Thaddeus. "Then when he said, 'You're going to join them,' I thought that Nazi was going to have a heart attack."

"Ari is really something," said Irena, who was walking behind Cass with Grandma and Grandpa. "I sure hope he is okay."

Grandpa replied, "I think if any soldier is unlucky enough to catch Ari, it will be a sad day for that soldier. God's hand is on Ari, but I don't think Ari even knows it. He is a blessed man. I think he will be out here fighting Nazis for years to come. He is a true freedom fighter."

"A what?" Rachel asked.

Grandpa replied, "A freedom fighter. That's someone who resists an evil government that is oppressing our people. There were a lot of them in Israel during the Roman occupation two thousand years ago. They have been around since the Babylonian invasion of Israel during the reign of Zedekiah and in Europe for centuries."

"Who are they?" Sarah asked.

Grandpa replied, "They are Jewish people who live off the grid. They are an underground network of Jews who fight for Jews when they're living in an occupied territory. They usually attack at night when they can't be seen. When a Jew gets killed, they strike back. An eye for an eye. It's probably because of the freedom fighters, and the grace of God, that we weren't wiped out years ago. We are a hated people."

"Why are we so hated?" Sarah asked. "What did we ever do to anyone?"

"The prophet Jeremiah said this would happen," Grandpa went on. "He said that because Israel turned away from God, they would be driven into exile and persecuted until there would come a day when the Jewish people would be almost destroyed, but a few would survive. Then those few would be gathered up in Israel, and Israel would be a reborn nation. Jews started migrating back to Palestine in large numbers at the end of the nineteenth century. If that's the beginning of the gathering Jeremiah talked about, then that means we are now at the time of the greatest persecution of Jews in history."

"Do you believe all of that?" Rachel asked.

Irena said, "Yes, he does. Papa is Orthodox."

Grandpa continued, "Cass and Thaddeus are freedom fighters. They just haven't been called up yet. They have trained with Ari, and they already fought the Nazis who killed Zofia."

After Grandpa mentioned Zofia, everyone became quiet. They walked in silence the rest of way to the intersection of Chlodna and Zelazna. When they arrived they saw that gates had been constructed at the entrance to the ghetto. There was one gate to the northern ghetto and one gate to the southern ghetto. They stood between the gates for several hours.

Later that afternoon, an SS officer walked through the crowd. "Bieberstein. Are there Biebersteins here?"

With apprehension, Irena held up her hand. "I am a Bieberstein."

The officer walked over to her and said, "Come with me."

Irena followed the officer into a guard shack that had been erected next to the gate. They emerged about ten minutes later and walked back to the group. "Which ones are Biebersteins?" the officer asked.

Irena replied, "These are my sons, and these are my parents." Then she pointed at Rachel and Sarah and said, "They are with us too."

The officer looked at his paperwork and said, "There are only supposed to be five of you. They have to go into the gated area."

"But they are family too. This is Rachel, and this is Sarah."

The officer shook his head, "They have to go in. My records say only five of you are going to your apartment."

Thaddeus looked at Irena then the officer. "If they have to go into the ghetto, then I want to go with them."

The officer returned his gaze. He took a pencil and wrote something on his paper, then looked at Rachel and Sarah. "This is your lucky day. You can go with the Biebersteins. This young man just saved your lives. At least for now."

"Let's go." Irena began walking toward the Bieberstein apartment building on Chlodna Street. The family began walking with her. Rachel and Sarah followed. The officer instructed a soldier to escort them. As they walked toward the apartment building, Thaddeus asked quietly, "What's going on?"

Irena said, "Someone arranged for us to move into another of our apartment buildings outside of the ghetto."

"Who do you think did that?" Cass asked.

Grandpa replied, "It had to have been someone who knew we were going to be evicted from the other apartment today."

Unaware that Patrycja had died the same day as Zofia, Cass asked, "Do you think it was Lech and Patrycja?"

Irena shook her head. "I don't think Lech has that much influence. He might have been behind the idea, but someone very influential actually made the arrangements."

Grandpa wore a puzzled expression. "Schindler?"

Cass noticed that the soldier glanced at Grandpa when he said the name Schindler. This confused Cass. *Schindler is the man who forced us out of our house on Pulawska with Lech's help. He is the man who shot my dog. Why would he now do something to help us? Maybe he feels guilty.* "Maybe it was Papa. Maybe that's who has been sending us the food and money."

Grandpa replied, "I don't think Sigmund could do this. The food and money that was shipped to us, possibly, but to arrange a place for us to live when everyone else is going into the ghetto? I don't think he could do that from wherever he is. I think this was done by someone here who knew we were going to be evicted today. I think Schindler did it at Lech's request."

As they walked, they heard shouting behind them. They stopped, turned and looked back at the intersection of Chlodna and Zelazna. They waited for a moment to see what was happening. The soldiers had sectioned off twenty-five of the Jews and were telling them to line up against the brick wall of the ghetto. The Jews complied. The soldiers formed a line in front of the Jews and stood at attention with their rifles at their side. The officer shouted a command. They lifted their rifles. The officer shouted another command. They aimed the rifles at the Jews. Upon hearing another command, the soldiers fired, hitting the Jews lined up against the wall.

The soldier escorting the Biebersteins looked at the ground. "What happened?" Irena asked. "Why did they shoot those people?" They started walking again toward the apartment building.

The soldier replied, "They found the burned bodies of the guards a little while ago, right where that fighter said they would be. They were in the sewer. For every German killed, they intend to kill five Jews."

"What happened to Ari?" Cass asked.

"Who's Ari?"

"Ari was the guy who said he killed the guards and then shot the officer and ran."

"So that's his name?" said the soldier.

Cass wondered if he should not have said Ari's name, but then he realized that Ari would have wanted them to know his name. "Yes, his name is Ari. Have they caught him yet?"

"No, they haven't found him."

"Were you there when he ran?" Thaddeus asked.

"Yes, I ran after him. He doesn't run; he flies."

"What's your name?" Cass asked.

"I'm Arnold Shultz," said the soldier. "Okay, this is your building. I would recommend that you stay inside as much as possible. It's getting very bad for Jews."

"Why is this happening?" Rachel asked.

The young soldier looked at Rachel and was obviously taken by her beauty. "I don't know." He shook his head. "The people believe that Jews have been corrupting our society and holding us back."

"Holding you back from what?" Grandpa asked.

"From becoming a pure and superior race."

"Do you believe that you are becoming a superior race?" Irena asked.

"I have serious doubts about everything we are doing. I was at the Olympic Games in Berlin in 1936. I saw Jesse Owens, a black man, win four gold medals. The führer was telling everyone that the Germans were going to win all of the medals because we are superior. We didn't do well

159

at all. And the führer was very angry that Jesse Owens performed so much better than any of our team members."

"Thank you for being kind to us," Irena said.

The young man nodded. "I don't know how much I can do for you, but I will look in on you when I can."

"Thank you so much," Irena said.

Schultz nodded again, turning to walk back toward the intersection of Chlodna and Zelazna. He paused for a moment, then said, "Please don't tell anyone what we talked about. I could get into a lot of trouble."

"We won't tell anyone," Grandpa said.

After Schultz left, the Biebersteins trudged up the steps to a sixth-floor apartment. As they walked down the hall the elegance of the building was apparent. Although old, the expensive lamps and chandeliers revealed a better time in history, when the apartments housed some of Poland's most elite members of society. "This doesn't look so bad," said Cass. "Actually, it's pretty nice."

Irena went to a door on the right side of the hall, put in a key, and opened it. The apartment had a musty smell.

"Has this apartment been empty for a long time?" Sarah asked.

Irena looked around the kitchen. "Yes, it hasn't had a tenant since the war started. Now non-Jews are filling up most of the apartments in the building, but this one has remained empty."

The family took a seat around the dining table. Sarah opened the curtains to let in more light. "Where are Sarah and Rachel going to sleep?" Cass asked. "It looks like this place only has three bedrooms."

"They can take our room," Thaddeus said. "Cass and I can sleep out here."

"Yes, that will be fine," Cass agreed. "The girls should have the bedroom."

"We don't want to take your room," Sarah said.

"It's okay," Irena said. "The boys want you to have it."

"No, no," Rachel said. "You have done too much for us already. We can't take your rooms. Sarah and I will sleep out here. We would feel terrible if we took Cass and Thad's room."

Cass and Thaddeus walked into the bedroom that Irene indicated would be theirs. They sat on the bed. "I don't think this will be so bad," said Thaddeus. Then he pointed at the wall. "What is that red stuff on the wall?"

The wall was covered with something red that appeared to be moving. "What is that?" Cass asked.

Thaddeus got very close to the wall. He touched the red substance with his finger and looked at it. Finally he said, "These are bedbugs. We have bedbugs."

CHAPTER
15

T HE BIEBERSTEINS WERE fortunate to be living outside of the ghetto. Most of the Jews were now in either the small ghetto, which was the area south of Chlodna, or the large ghetto, which was the area north of Chlodna. The situation seemed precarious, but at least for the time being they were safe and secure, though they did not know how long the security would last. With the exception of the bedbugs, the new apartment seemed a reasonably safe place to live. Cass and Thaddeus could no longer train with Ari, but they continued to train on their own in the apartment. They had learned enough that they simply needed to practice. Ari always stressed cardiovascular activities, but Irena told the boys not to run outside because it would draw dangerous attention to them, especially since they would be wearing their Star of David armbands. In order to get their cardiovascular exercise, they would run up and down the six flights of steps several times per day and then do exercises in the apartment. They remembered the techniques Ari had taught them and wrote them down by name. They practiced every move every day. For weight lifting they used buckets of sand filled to various levels to achieve the weights they needed.

One evening after working out, Cass and Thaddeus were resting in the living room, talking to Sarah, Rachel, and Grandma. Grandpa came in the front entrance after working in the dental office all day. He quietly closed the door behind him and said softly, "It sounds like Ari is out there doing some serious damage," he said.

"Did you hear something?" asked Cass.

Grandpa replied, "Yes, I heard that there have been quite a few attacks on SS officers over by the river. There were twenty-seven of them killed last week in six different attacks. Some involved bombing vehicles, some involved shootings, and some close-quarter fighting."

"Why do you think it's Ari?" Thaddeus asked.

"Do you remember the soldier who escorted us here the day we first came to this apartment?" asked Grandpa. "His name was Arnold Schultz."

Thaddeus replied, "Yes, I remember."

"He came into the office this morning and asked how we're doing."

Irena looked up from a book she was reading. "Seriously? He actually came in to ask how we're doing?"

"Yes, he did."

"Did Arnold say something about Ari?"

"Yes."

"What?" Sarah asked.

"He said the SS is convinced Ari is the one behind the attacks. Arnold didn't ever tell them Ari's name, and they don't know it, but they believe it is the same guy who killed the guards and threw their bodies in the sewer. The SS believe he has formed a small army of terrorists who are killing the Nazis."

"Where do you suppose Ari is now?" Sarah asked.

"Ari is probably out there somewhere killing Nazis," Thaddeus replied with a laugh.

Sarah nodded. "He must be the terror of the SS. He threatens their strength and their claim to superiority."

Grandpa replied, "That's what Arnold is concerned about. He says whenever there is an attack on the SS, it creates a risk that the SS will think Jews are behind it, and then they will kill Jews."

"So what can we do? Are Jews supposed to not fight back?" asked Cass.

"That's the reason many of them don't want anyone to fight back," said Grandpa. "I don't buy that argument. They are starving Jews to death and killing them whenever it suits their fancy. This isn't living, this is being part of the living dead."

The room became silent as everyone reflected on Grandpa's comment. Finally Grandpa said, "I don't want to see Jews walking to the slaughter like sheep. I want them to be strong and fight back the best they can."

Thaddeus asked, "I wonder why Jews have never built a huge secret army. I know there's a Jewish underground that fights like Ari is fighting, but I mean, why did they not ever build an army that was big and powerful enough to take on the Germans and other people who want to destroy us? I think Jews have had enough money that they could have done that."

"Probably because the Jews don't really want to fight anyone. They are just forced into it." Grandpa laughed. "Then, of course, there were the Templars."

"The what?" asked Cass.

"The Israelite knights, who served under a grand master named Jacques de Molay." Grandpa winked at Thaddeus.

Cass looked at Thaddeus and shrugged, which he often did when Grandpa spoke in a strange and peculiar way.

Sarah stood looking through the front window at the street below. She asked, "Has anyone ever noticed the SS officers who walk into the restaurant in the building across the street? They go in every Thursday night at eight. I have noticed it since we moved in five weeks ago. It looks like some kind of meeting place. They're going in now."

Thaddeus nodded. "Actually, I have noticed it. Some of them are high-ranking officers. I have even seen generals go in."

"Generals?" Cass stood up and walked to the window, then looked at the street below.

"Yes, it's a meeting place," Grandpa said. "Those meetings are where they discuss the strategic operations of the city and the concentration of the Jews."

"What's the concentration of the Jews?" asked Rachel, who was sitting on the sofa.

Grandpa stood up and walked over to Rachel, then sat on a chair directly in front of her. He was silent for a moment and then said, "Hitler has a plan to concentrate and exterminate all Jews. It hasn't been approved yet, but that's what he is promoting." The room became silent. Finally

Thaddeus asked, "What does it mean to concentrate and exterminate all Jews?"

Grandpa's answer was neither unexpected nor surprising. "Concentration means to herd them into one location much like a shepherd herds his sheep into a particular pen. This is what they're doing when they force the Jews to move into the ghetto. They are concentrating us in one location."

"Then what is extermination?"

Grandpa fell silent. Cass asked again, "Grandpa, what does it mean to exterminate the Jews?"

Grandpa leaned forward in his chair and looked at the floor. Moments passed. Then Sarah stood up and walked over to Grandpa and sat on the floor next to him. Thaddeus walked over to Rachel and sat next to her. He put his arm around her. Then Irena and Grandma walked over and sat on the floor in front of Grandpa. Finally Cass walked over and sat on the floor in front of Grandpa, who said, "The Jews suffered terribly in slavery in Egypt. God chose Moses to lead them out of Egypt to freedom. Moses encountered God at the burning bush and then returned to lead the people out of Egypt. He said to Pharaoh, 'Let the Jewish people go.' That part of our Passover story occurred nearly four thousand years ago, and it is still our Passover story today."

Sarah began to cry. "These are the hard times like they knew in Egypt, aren't they, Grandpa?"

Grandpa nodded.

"Will we die?" Rachel asked.

Grandpa did not reply. He just looked at her with sad eyes and a slight smile.

"I'm not ready to die," she said. "I want to grow up and marry and have babies." She looked at Thaddeus as the tears rolled gently down her cheeks.

"All we can do is trust God to see us through," said Grandpa.

Rachel stood up. "If God is good and God is loving, why would he allow this to happen to us? This makes me angry. Am I bad to be angry?"

Grandpa shook his head. "No, there is no sin in being angry about what has happened to us, as long as you listen to God. It isn't that God allowed this to happen. God only set the rules in place. Man was given a choice of either allowing God to control our lives or controlling our lives ourselves. Mankind chose to be in control. That means we will face the good and the bad. It is not until mankind realizes that our way is inferior to God's way that our suffering will stop. It isn't that God allows our suffering, it's that God allows us to face the consequences of our decisions."

The room again grew silent. Finally Cass said, "I'm ready to face whatever God gives us."

Sarah nodded. "Me too."

"I am too," said Rachel. Softly, one at a time, everyone in the room said he or she was ready to face whatever God gave them. They remained in the living room for the rest of the evening. As they sat in the room, they took turns softly saying prayers. At two o'clock they noticed that the SS officers were finally coming out of the restaurant. They walked to their respective vehicles, climbed in, and drove away.

The following Thursday, the family was again gathered in the living room after dinner. At approximately eight o'clock, Cass walked over to the window to watch the SS officers go into the restaurant across the street. They arrived in expensive vehicles and walked in one or two at a time. Cass watched them go in. Then he sat by the window, looking at the street. Every twenty minutes or so someone would walk by. The street had a yellow hue created by the gas lamps that lined the curbs on ten-foot poles. As they did every evening, the family talked about what was happening in Warsaw and how the Jews were being persecuted. And as they did every evening, Grandpa read aloud from the Torah in Hebrew.

Cass sat on the chair next to the window resting his chin on his hands on the windowsill. The window was open. He watched as a cat walked across the street to search in a garbage can behind the restaurant for food. Suddenly, there was movement across the street in the shadows by the buildings. Cass looked more closely. He saw a man. The man was wearing the clothes the students of Krav Maga wore when practicing a nighttime mission: black slacks and a black sweatshirt. "Thad, come here. Quick!"

Thaddeus jumped to his feet followed by Rachel, Grandpa, Sarah, Grandma, and Irena. They all gathered around the large window. "What is it?" asked Thaddeus.

Cass pointed. "Watch the alley under the streetlight."

"Hey, there's someone down there," Rachel said.

Grandpa said, "Yeah, I see him. I wonder who that is and what he's doing."

They watched quietly as the man carried an object to a basement window of the building. Then he set it on the sidewalk in front of the window. Soon another man in an SS officer uniform ran up behind him. The first man cut the glass, reached in and opened the window, and climbed inside. Once he was inside, the second man picked up the package, handed it to the man inside, and stood guard for the first man. The Bieberstein family continued to watch for about twenty minutes. Eventually, the man in the SS uniform lit a cigarette. When he did, his face was visible.

"Hey, I recognize that guy," Thaddeus said. "That's one of the guys who used to work out with us. His name is Pawel Frenkiel. Why is he wearing an SS officer uniform?"

Cass replied, "Yeah, that's Pawel, all right. I wonder what they're doing. And who is the other guy?"

Eventually, the first man emerged from the window without the package. As he climbed out of the window and walked under a streetlight, he looked up at the Bieberstein family. For a moment, his face could be seen clearly. He smiled and nodded then ran down the street with the man in the uniform. "Hey, that's Ari," said Cass.

Thaddeus replied, "It is. That was Ari. What's he doing here with Pawel?"

Sarah asked, "I wonder why Ari and Pawel would be here. What do you think Ari took into the building?"

Irena said, "That window is right under the restaurant where the SS officers are meeting."

Suddenly Grandpa said, "Everyone come away from the window. Quickly."

Before they could react, there was an explosion and a flash of light. Flames burst from the basement window and the windows of the restaurant above it. Glass and debris flew into the street. The force of the blast was so strong the heat could be felt on the sixth floor where the Biebersteins sat looking through the window. In a short time, fire trucks and police cars arrived at the scene with sirens blaring. The Biebersteins moved away from the window and pulled the curtains closed. They sat silently in the room. They could hear the shouts of the people in the street below.

"Now we know for sure who has been attacking the SS officers," Thaddeus said.

Grandpa replied, "Now we know. Don't tell anyone that we saw anything tonight. If anyone asks, just say that we heard the explosion." Everyone nodded. Grandpa got up and turned off the lights. The commotion in the street lasted throughout the night as charred bodies were pulled from the building on stretchers. The question concerning Ari's whereabouts and activities had been answered.

CHAPTER
16

PERHAPS IT WAS the image of Ari crawling from the basement window across the street minutes before the explosion, or the memory of Ari attacking the three German soldiers who were beating the elderly woman, but just knowing he was out there resisting the Nazis gave Cass a sense of hope. Desperation does not seem so severe when one actually sees another victim stand up to the tyrants. Cass and Thaddeus began working out even more vigorously after seeing Ari and Pawel bomb the Nazi meeting place. Cass wondered, *How can they move about so freely with Nazis everywhere? It is almost as if they are invisible. The image of Pawel disguised as a SS officer was brilliant, but where did he get the uniform? Did he take it off an officer they had killed?*

Cass and Thaddeus continued to work out all day, every day. They were not in school, and there were no jobs to be found other than the work Cass had at the gun factory, which did not pay. The family was surviving on the money Grandpa brought in from his dental practice along with the money that would arrive in packages in the mail. They still did not know who was sending the packages but in time concluded that it must be Sigmund. The combination of these sources of money allowed the family to eat well. Sarah and Rachel cleaned the apartment for Irena in exchange for the food, though she told them it was unnecessary. Because Irena believed it was unsafe, the boys were not allowed to go outside except to pick up groceries from the little store down the street.

Summer passed, and soon it was fall. The Biebersteins stayed indoors as much as possible and were cut off from the outside world, except for Grandpa, who maintained his dental practice on the first floor, and Cass and Thaddeus, who occasionally made the trip to the grocery store. They were fortunate to have running water in the apartment so they did not have to go out to fetch water. Food was becoming scarce. They wanted to stretch it as far as possible to avoid running out. They celebrated Chanukah to the best of their ability with the limited supply of food. As 1942 approached, there was a hope that everything would get better, but it was a hope filled with doubt. The truth was that everything seemed to be getting worse. Why should they expect a change in the New Year?

On January 23, 1942, Rachel and Sarah decided to walk to the grocery store. "I have to get out of this place, even if only for a just a few minutes," said Sarah. "I feel like I am going crazy." The grocery store was only two blocks up the street from the apartment.

"I don't think that's a good idea," said Irena. Cass and Thaddeus were in their bedroom exercising and were unaware of the discussion.

"We'll be okay," Rachel said. "We will be back in a few minutes."

"Well, then"—Irena reached into her purse, took out some change, and handed it to Sarah—"would you mind bringing back some milk?"

Rachel and Sarah left the apartment. At the street, they turned in the direction of the grocery store. They were wearing the dresses and the long overcoats they had brought with them when they were forced to leave the previous apartment so quickly. That is all they had to wear. Each was wearing her Star of David armband. They arrived at the grocery store, entered, and began to look around. It was a small store with only basic food items such as bread, corn, beans, onions, potatoes, and meat. Using the money Irena had given to them, they bought a bottle of milk. "I haven't seen you in here before," said the proprietor as they paid for the milk. Sarah and Rachel both noticed that he was not wearing an armband.

"We live just up the street," Rachel said.

"I didn't know there were any Jews around here except Cass and Thaddeus," replied the proprietor.

"That's who we're living with," Sarah said.

"Oh, you're living with the Biebersteins?"

"Yes."

Rachel asked, "Where are all the Jews?"

"They moved them all into the ghettos."

"You mean there is no one left outside the ghettos except us?" asked Rachel.

The proprietor nodded. "I haven't seen any Jews around here for several weeks now. I think you probably shouldn't be on the street. The officers all know Cass and Thaddeus, but they don't know you. They might round you up and take you into the ghetto too. God knows what happens in there."

"Why are they rounding them up and taking them to the ghetto?" Sarah asked.

The proprietor paused and leaned against the counter. "There was some meeting a couple of days ago among top Nazi officials at a place called Wannsee. That's a small town just outside of Berlin. I don't know all the details yet, but they decided to round up all Jews."

"What are they going to do with them after they round them up?" asked Sarah.

The proprietor shook his head and looked down at the floor. "The best advice I can give you is to stay off the streets as much as possible." His troubled expression disturbed Rachel and Sarah. Rachel picked up the bottle of milk that the proprietor had placed on the counter. "Good-bye." The proprietor just nodded his head again as he picked up a broom and started sweeping the floor.

As the girls walked back toward the Bieberstein apartment they came to an intersection. They looked up the street to the right and saw a staff car with SS officers inside, not more than ten feet away. On each side of the hood of the car were Nazi flags. As they began to cross the street, the officer on the passenger side of the vehicle got out and said, "Girls, come over here."

Rachel and Sarah stopped and looked at the officer. His long green coat was decorated with pins and medals and seemed ominous. "Come on over," he repeated with a smile.

The girls walked toward the car.

"What are you doing here?" he asked.

"We're just coming back from the grocery store," replied Rachel.

"There aren't supposed to be any Jews in this part of the city now. How long have you been here and where do you live?"

Rachel replied, "We live just up the street at the Biebersteins' apartment. We have been here since last summer."

The officer opened the rear door of the car and said, "Get in."

Rachel and Sarah stood looking at the officer with blank expressions. The officer stepped away from the car and pointed at the door with a smile. Again he said, "Get in."

Rachel and Sarah climbed into the rear of the car as they were told.

The officer shut the door, then walked around the car and into a nearby building. The building had large Nazi flags on each side of the door, and the girls knew it was a government building of some kind. The driver remained in the car but said nothing to the girls. Finally Rachel asked, "What are we doing here?"

The driver looked at Rachel in the rearview mirror but said nothing. The officer came back out of the building and got into the front seat of the car. He then said, in German, "To the railroad yard."

The driver nodded his head and began driving. He turned right on Chlodna. They traveled for a few blocks then stopped on the north side of Chlodna, near the railroad yard. Next to the train were hundreds of Jews lined up in rows, wearing their armbands and holding suitcases. The officer on the passenger side of the vehicle got out, walked over to a Nazi soldier, and began talking to him. Rachel and Sarah could not hear what he was saying. They talked for several minutes; then they both looked at the back seat of the car. They laughed, and the officer came back to the car and opened the rear door, motioning for the girls to get out.

When they got out of the car, the officer said, "Go stand in that line next to the building on the south side of the street. Someone will instruct you."

"But we have to go home. Irena is waiting for us," Sarah protested.

"Who is Irena?"

"Irena Bieberstein. That's who we live with," Sarah said.

"Bieberstein? They're Jews too, aren't they?"

"Yes," replied Rachel.

"Don't worry, I will let them know. You have to go over there in the line now."

Rachel and Sarah walked across the street to the line next to the building. They wanted to ask the officer why he was telling them to stand in line, but they were afraid to ask. They had nothing with them but the clothes they were wearing and the milk they had bought at the grocery store.

"What's this line for?" Rachel asked a woman who was standing next to her.

The woman replied, "They're taking us to a work camp. We'll have plenty of food there, but we will have to work."

"I'm Rachel, and this is Sarah. Do you know the name of the camp?"

"Treblinka. We've been living here in the ghetto. We've been so hungry. At least there we'll have food. My name is Olga."

Neither Rachel nor Sarah had heard of Treblinka. Somehow the information about work seemed questionable. "We have to get back home," said Sarah. "Maybe we can make a break for it. Irena will know what to do."

"Those soldiers have guns. We wouldn't get ten feet," Rachel replied.

"Don't even think about it," said Olga, who overheard Sarah's comment. "They would shoot you. They shoot people all the time here in the ghetto. You girls aren't from the ghetto, are you?"

"No, we live on Chlodna Street just a few blocks that way," said Rachel as she pointed to the west. "Are we in the ghetto now?"

"Yes, this is called the little ghetto. You have never seen anything like the ghetto. We see people die every day in here. Often the soldiers grab girls and take them somewhere then we later find the girls dead in a back alley or in a trash can."

"What do they do to them?" Sarah asked.

Olga glanced at Sarah. "You are young and innocent. You really don't know, do you?"

Sarah shook her head.

"Did you go to yeshiva? Do you remember learning about the story of Amnon and Tamar?"

Sarah nodded.

"Do you remember what Amnon, son of King David, did to Tamar?"

Sarah nodded. "Rabbi Lieberman told us what it meant. Absalom killed Amnon because he did that."

"There is something about the way some men are made that makes them want to hurt women that way. German soldiers are forbidden by Rassenschande to touch Jewish girls, because if the Jewish girl becomes pregnant, the child will be impure, so they rape them in secret. After the rape, the Jewish girl has to be killed to prevent her from having an impure child."

"What is Rassenschande?" asked Rachel.

"That's what Germans call the laws against racial defilement."

"Where did you learn all these things?" asked Sarah.

"I once knew a German soldier. He told me."

Cass, Thaddeus, Grandma, and Irena were seated at the dining room table in the Bieberstein apartment when Grandpa came in with the German soldier Arnold Schultz. "Gather everything quickly," said Grandpa. "They're moving us into the ghetto. Where are Rachel and Sarah?"

Irena replied, "They went to the grocery store about an hour ago. We were just talking about it. They should have been back by now. Thad and Cass were going to go look for them."

Grandpa shook his head. "No, it's too dangerous. Two days ago there was a conference of high-ranking officers at a place called Wannsee. They decided to exterminate all Jews."

"What?" Irena asked.

Grandpa replied, "They are rounding up all Jews and shipping them to death camps for extermination. Arnold was sent to pick us up and take us into the ghetto. They are rounding up Jews in the ghetto, in sections. He is going to put us in the last section scheduled for roundup. He said it will probably take a year to get to that section, which will give us more time to decide what to do."

Arnold said, "That's right. Grab everything you can carry. There is a truck downstairs. When did Rachel and Sarah go to the grocery?"

Thad replied, "It was about an hour ago. They should have been back a long time ago. The grocery is only two blocks away."

"Okay, I am going to go see if I can find them while you get ready. Be ready in ten minutes. I won't be able to stall much longer."

Arnold ran down the stairs and out the front door. He walked briskly to the grocery store and asked the proprietor, "Have you seen two young Jewish girls in here this afternoon?"

The proprietor replied, "Yes, they came in to buy some milk. After they left I heard someone call out to them. I went outside to investigate and saw them sitting in the back seat of a staff car. I turned around and came back in because I didn't want to get into trouble. Later I saw them drive away with the girls in the car."

"Okay, thanks." Arnold turned and walked out the door and back to the Bieberstein flat. The Biebersteins were waiting by the front door of the apartment building.

Arnold said, "They picked up Rachel and Sarah at the grocery store this morning. They probably took them to the ghetto. Maybe you can find them there. Everyone climb into the back of that truck, quickly." The Biebersteins complied. Arnold jumped into the passenger seat, and the truck drove toward the ghetto.

Rachel, Sarah, and Olga stood quietly for a time. About an hour later a train came to a stop on the other side of the street. A soldier came over to them and told them to cross the street and climb into a cattle car. Sarah, Rachel, and Olga, along with the others, complied, sadly and reluctantly. The car was almost full, and there was no room to sit on the floor, so they were forced to stand. Even when the car completely filled with people, the guards continued to force more people inside. Rachel and Sarah were both crying. They were cold. Sarah was still holding onto the bottle of milk. Soon the train started moving, slowly at first, then increasing in speed. The sound of the metal wheels rolling on the metal tracks clanged in a hypnotizing rhythm. With each clang, Sarah thought she heard the words "Jews are bad. Jews are bad."

After traveling for slightly more than an hour, the train came to a stop. A few minutes later the doors to the cattle car opened. The passengers were told to get out. They jumped to the ground and found themselves in a heavily wooded area. They were told to walk into an area enclosed by a barbed-wire fence. As they entered the fenced area the men were told to go to a building on the right and the women to a building on the left. A third group was told to go and stand by a barn. When the girls got inside the building they were instructed to put their belongings in a pile by the door and take off all their clothes. "There are men soldiers in here," Sarah said. "We can't take off our clothes."

"You better do what they say. You don't want to make them angry," Olga said.

As the women began to remove their clothing a guard came and took the bottle of milk from Sarah. Once they were disrobed, the women were herded into a shower area. They showered and then were directed into an area where their heads were shaved. Then a white powder was thrown on their heads. As they left the room where their heads had been shaved, they were taken into another room where they saw piles of dresses lying on the floor. "Find clothes that fit," said a guard. Sarah and Rachel rummaged through the pile of dresses until they each found one that fit. The clothes were old and worn and not even clean. They were then directed to a pile of mismatched shoes and told to find two shoes that fit. "Don't worry about finding two shoes that match. In here it won't matter," said one of the guards.

"Where did these clothes come from?" Rachel asked.

Olga shrugged. "I don't know. Somebody wore them before."

Suddenly, they heard a guard shouting at one of the girls. "Who told you to take two dresses?" His voice was husky and sharp.

"I just thought I would take an extra one for when this one is dirty or wears out."

The guard took a leather strap and began striking the naked girl with it. "From now on you do exactly as you are told—nothing more and nothing less."

The young girl put the dress back on the pile and walked quickly away from the guard.

After they had found clothing, the women were shuffled outside into the cold air and told to line up. They stood shivering, waiting for further instruction. Finally, when everyone was outside standing in line, a guard came to the front of the women. "Welcome to Treblinka I. You are here to work, and you will work hard. You will be given food rations once per day. If you miss your food rations, you will not have food until the following day. You will receive your daily work assignment every morning. You will follow every instruction you are given. If you refuse to follow any instruction, you will be shot. If you get sick and can't work, you will be executed. Do you smell the diesel fuel burning? That is how we exterminate those who can no longer work. So if you cannot work, you will be exterminated in that building over there. Then your body will be burned or buried in a grave with the others who can't work." The guard pointed to his left. "Over there they are building Treblinka II. Treblinka I is a work camp. Treblinka II, when it is finished, will be an extermination camp. When Treblinka II is finished this summer, that is where you will be taken if you can't work. No one will come out of Treblinka II alive. Now go into that building over there for your rations for today. Then you will be assigned your sleeping quarters." The guard pointed at a building behind the women.

The women turned around and walked into the building, where they received their rations, which consisted of a boiled potato in a cup of hot water. They were given ten minutes to eat then were directed to their sleeping barracks. The barracks consisted of wooden bunk beds lined up in rows. Sarah, Rachel, and Olga selected bunks next to one another. Folded at the foot of each bunk bed was a wool blanket. In the center of the room was a wood-burning stove, but the heat generated by the stove was less than adequate to heat the room. Sarah noticed a woman sitting on the bed in the far corner of the room. She was already there when the other women arrived.

"Does anyone know what kind of work they are going to have us do?" asked a woman who appeared to be in her thirties.

Another woman replied, "When I was waiting by the shower, I was next to a woman who has been here for about a year. She said that they will take some of us out in trucks, and we will have to work on the road or in the town. Others will have to stay here and work in the camp. She said that they are building the new camp to kill Jews. She said that if we can work, they will let us live longer, and maybe by then we will be liberated. Both Britain and the United States have been sending troops to defeat Hitler."

"Where does this woman get her information?"

"She works in the dining room where the officers are fed. She overhears them talking all the time. They talk openly in front of her. She said some of the officers were angry because last year Hitler and Mussolini declared war on the United States. Some of them said Hitler was a dummkopf."

"Are we going to have women guards in here?" Olga asked.

The woman who was sitting on the bunk when the other women came in said, "All the guards here are men. There aren't any female guards, so you will have to get used to it."

Sitting on their beds in silence, the women noticed a sound they had been hearing since they arrived at Treblinka. It was the sound of men cheering in the distance as if someone was playing a game. Listening more carefully, they noticed that there seemed to be a pattern. First, there was the sound of men cheering and getting louder and more excited. Then there was a sound of someone shooting a gun. Sometimes there was more than one shot. Then the cheering would suddenly become very loud and combined with laughter. "What is that sound?" asked Olga. "It sounds like someone playing a game."

"They call that 'target practice,'" said the woman in the corner. "The soldiers take turns. They keep about a hundred women, a hundred men, and about twenty children in barns by the front gate. Every day they select about ten of them, men, women, and children. They take them to an area just outside of the camp. They then tell the prisoners to take off all their clothes. One at a time, the prisoners are required to run naked into a large fenced-in area. The commander shouts either 'maim' or 'kill.' One of the soldiers takes his pistol and shoots at the person running. If the order is to maim, he is only supposed to shoot the prisoner in the leg so they can't run. If the order is 'kill,' then the soldier shoots to kill. The prisoners are left lying on the ground until the next day when they are thrown into a pit and covered with dirt."

The room was deathly silent.

The woman continued. "If you notice, the sound of the cheering gets louder and louder before you hear the gunshot. That means a prisoner is running in the field before being shot. Then after the shot you hear a sudden burst of laughing and cheering. That means the prisoner has been hit."

Another woman asked, "Why do they make them take off their clothes?"

"Because they don't want to waste the clothes, and the guards think it's more fun if the prisoner is naked."

Again the room was deathly silent. Finally Olga asked, "How do they decide who they are going to choose for target practice?"

The first woman replied, "Remember when you first got off the train and the men and women were sent to different groups?"

"Yes."

"You might have noticed that there was a third group of people who were told to go stand by a barn?"

"I did notice that," said Olga.

"Those are the ones who were selected for target practice today. They usually like to select young pretty girls because the guards enjoy shooting them the most. The younger and prettier you are, the more likely you will be chosen. Sometimes they also come in here and select some for target practice."

Rachel looked at Sarah. They were both told often how pretty they were, and they knew it as well. They suddenly realized that they had just walked through the valley of the shadow of death. That night they hardly slept. They were worried. They wondered if they would get sick and be exterminated. They wondered if a guard might decide they were pretty enough for target practice. Only time would tell their fate. For now, they would work as hard as they could, try not to get sick, and try to remain as dirty and unattractive as they could. Hopefully, then they would survive.

CHAPTER

17

T HE TRUCK CARRYING the Biebersteins and the Szyncers drove into the ghetto. As they traveled down a main street they saw bodies lying next to the curb. Some were naked, and some were covered with newspaper. The truck came to a stop at an intersection. Cass saw an elderly, thin-framed man stagger and collapse on the sidewalk. Within seconds, several people ran over to him. At first, it appeared they were going to help him. Then reality set in. The people began stripping off his clothes as quickly as they could, and before the traffic light changed the man was lying naked on the curb, still alive. The thieves ran away with everything he owned. The truck continued down the street. The buildings were dilapidated, with broken windows and trash strewn about. On every corner were several guards with Karabiner 98k rifles. The image sent chills down Cass's spine. *This is a dead place*, he thought.

Eventually, the truck came to a very old area of the ghetto where there were fewer officers on the streets. They stopped in front of an apartment building. The area seemed less populated in comparison to the areas they had previously passed through. As they climbed down from the bed of the truck, Grandpa asked, "Where is everyone? This place seems deserted."

"Because this is an older area, there aren't as many people here," replied Schultz. "There's no way I can keep you out of the ghetto, but this is probably the safest place in the ghetto. Eventually, people are going to figure it out, and they will be moving in here, but for now, it's fairly quiet. You can probably find an abandoned flat. But the buildings have no plumbing. You have to go to the pump house for water, and the toilets are outdoors."

"Thank you for everything you've done for us," Grandma said.

"I wish I could do more. I'll be back to check on you in a few days. There is a general store one block over. You can probably set up a dental practice in this building here. There's an orchestra that practices in that building across the street, and they're operating a Jewish school in that building on the corner."

The Biebersteins stood in the street as the truck drove away and then walked into the building where they had been dropped off. There was no heat. They saw a vacant flat on the first floor. Thaddeus and Cass started to go inside. Grandpa said, "I think we would be safer if we go up a few floors. If the Nazis come looking for people, they might not want to walk up steps."

They walked up three flights of stairs. Grandpa knocked on one of the doors. There was no answer. He attempted to open the door, but it was locked. They turned to walk to the next apartment, but they heard the deadbolt slide on the door. Slowly the door opened, and an elderly man put his head out. He looked at the Star of David armbands. "Who are you looking for?"

"We're looking for a vacant apartment where we can stay," replied Irena.

The old man came out and walked down the hall. "Come with me," he said. "One is vacant." They walked to apartment 301 and opened the door. It was furnished but obviously vacant. They walked in and put their belongings on the floor in front of a couch. The elderly man said, "I am Shmuel."

"I'm Irena. This is my father, Dr. Szyncer. And my mother, we call her Grandma. This is Cass and Thaddeus. Do you live alone?"

"No, my wife, Liba, lives with me. She isn't well. We have lived in this building since we were children. About half the apartments here are vacant."

"Where did everyone go?" asked Cass.

Shmuel looked at the floor and shook his head. "Most of them have died. Some were taken away to the work camps."

"How did they die?" asked Thaddeus.

"We're starving down here. We're lucky to have any food at all. About the only thing we can get are potatoes and bread and that's not very often."

"What do you do with the bodies when the people pass?" Grandpa asked.

"We carry them down to the street and lay them on the curb. In a few days a truck comes by and picks up the bodies along with the garbage."

"Do you have any contact with people outside of the ghetto?" asked Grandpa.

Shmuel replied, "Our only contact with the outside world is the mail."

"You get mail deliveries here?" Irena asked.

Shmuel nodded. "We have a mail deliveryman who rides a bike. He comes once each week. We have to pay him, or he wouldn't come at all."

"Where does the mail come from?"

"We used to be able to get mail from just about everywhere. But after Britain and the United States entered the war, we have only been getting mail from Poland and Germany. It would probably come in from Italy and France, but I don't know of anyone getting mail from those countries. You aren't permitted to have any radios in the ghetto, so if you have one you should hide it somewhere where they can't find it."

"We don't have a radio," Grandpa said. "We had one, but when they made us leave our house, we weren't permitted to take it with us. Who is the mail deliveryman?"

"His name is Arturo. He is Polish Catholic, but he is sympathetic to the Jews. He brings us things we could not ordinarily obtain."

Grandpa sat on the couch. "Like what?"

"He brings us books and other things that are banned by the Reich. Sometimes he is able to get plum brandy for us." Shmuel started toward the door. "I will let you folks get settled in, then you can come by later if you like. I don't have much food to offer you, but we can give you friendship and a glass of water."

"Thank you," Irena replied.

After Shmuel left, Grandpa asked, "How are we going to find Rachel and Sarah?"

"We can ask if anyone has seen them but the ghetto is big. I don't think we will be able to find them," Grandma said. "I just hope they are okay."

The Biebersteins settled into their new flat. They had been told by Lech that they would be able to move back into the mansion after the war was over and that this was only temporary, but the war seemed to drag on forever. Although Poland was now a defeated and occupied territory, everyone knew the war was continuing elsewhere as Germany vied for world domination. "Do you think we will ever be able to go back to Pulawska Street?" Cass asked one day.

"I sure hope so," replied Thaddeus. "I really miss the house."

"What if we can't? Are we going to live like this for the rest of our lives?"

Thaddeus just shook his head.

After several days in the new apartment the family grew accustomed to the lack of amenities. Every morning Cass and Thaddeus would walk to the pump house to fetch water. Soon they had gotten to know their neighbors. Unlike their last apartment, in a location where Jews were not supposed to be living, here they were in a location specifically set aside for the Jews. They could walk up and down the streets without fear as long as they stepped into the street when they passed the soldiers. People spoke of the plan to exterminate the Jews, but most did not believe it was true. When the soldiers rounded up people to take them away on trains, they told them that they were going to work camps. This made more sense than killing an entire race of people. What would be the purpose of killing an entire race? No one, not even Hitler, could be that cruel, they said. Grandpa set up a dental practice as he had at the previous locations.

One afternoon in late February, Grandpa came home acting strangely. He was not in his usual jovial mood. He walked into the apartment and sat down at the dining room table. "What's wrong?" asked Grandma.

Grandpa looked at her but remained silent.

"What happened? You seem really upset."

"Some German soldiers came into my office today. They were not friendly like Arnold. They told me that I have to start removing the gold from people's teeth if I want to keep my dental practice."

"Why do they want the gold?" asked Irena. "A little bit of gold in a person's tooth isn't worth that much."

"It is when you collect a little bit from hundreds of people and melt it down into gold bricks. Then it's worth a lot."

"What did you say? You can't do that to people."

"I didn't have to say anything. They told me that this is what I am going to do. They didn't bother to ask me if I intended to comply. I think they just assumed that I would do what they said."

"But if you take out the gold fillings, the nerve endings will be exposed to open air. That would be very painful for them," Irena protested.

Grandpa replied, "If I don't take it out the Germans are going to. They have set up little stations on the street corners, and they are inspecting people for jewelry and gold fillings. If they see jewelry they take it. If they see gold fillings, they use a pair of pliers and pull the tooth out, then throw it in a bag. They take the bag of teeth and melt down the gold. No one wants to be caught with gold fillings. I had two people come in today to ask me to take it out because they don't want the solders to do it. The soldiers don't care if it hurts."

"These people are monsters," Grandma said. "Is there no end to their evil ways?"

As the family talked, they heard a knock at the door. Grandpa opened it. A wiry man in a Polish postal worker uniform came in. "I'm Arturo," he said. "I'm your postal deliveryman."

Grandpa shook his hand. "We haven't received any mail for about two months, and we haven't received any mail here at all. I don't think there is anyone out there who wants to write to us."

"Well, if anything comes for you, I will bring it to you. You don't have to pay me. I am paid out of community funds. I just wanted to get your name so if I get a letter with your name on it, I will know what to do with it."

"We are the Biebersteins and the Szyncers," Irena replied. "The Szyncers are my parents."

"You're the dentist, right?"

"Yes, I am. I just opened an office downstairs."

Arturo nodded, "I've heard about it. I want you to know that I am sympathetic to the Jews. If you need to get anything in or out of the ghetto I can help you. If you need anything let me know. I will do what I can."

"Thank you so much," said Grandpa. "Actually, there is something you might be able to help us with. We are looking for two teenage girls. They were living with us the day we were told to move into the ghetto. We don't know what happened to them. If you could find out what happened to them we would be very relieved."

"What are their names?"

"Rachel and Sarah Goldstein."

The postman nodded and turned toward the door. "I will see what I can find out. You folks have a nice evening. Remember, if you need anything, ask me, and I will do what I can to get it for you. These Nazis are scum."

After he left, Grandma said, "I don't think I trust him. Something about him doesn't seem right."

Irena said, "I was thinking the same thing. I don't want to judge someone unfairly, but something about him was off."

Grandpa waved his finger in the air and said, "Be careful of *lashon hara*. You might be right, and it is good to be cautious, but at this point we have no reason to suspect he is dishonest. He may be a righteous Noachide."

Cass knew Grandpa was right, but he too felt uneasy about Arturo. Something was odd about him. Maybe it was the way his eyes seemed to shift and dart around the room, almost like he was surveying the apartment for a later crime. Though he also felt uneasy, Cass would not disagree with Grandpa. That would not be respectful.

The following morning Cass and Thaddeus went to the neighborhood market for some produce. When they turned the corner at the intersection, they saw a line of about forty Jews. On the other side of the street, they saw another line of Jews passing in the opposite direction.

"What's going on?" asked Thaddeus of a man standing in front of them at the back of the line.

"They're looking for jewelry and gold tooth fillings."

Thaddeus replied, "My grandpa told us about this last night. He said if they find a gold filling, they actually pull out the tooth."

"Yes, they've pulled out three already this morning. It was horrible to hear the people scream. The Nazis laughed at them. I hate the filthy Nazis. I want them all to die a slow and painful death."

Cass and Thaddeus waited in line for nearly an hour and saw the soldiers pull teeth from a man and a woman. As they stood in line they looked around to ascertain how many soldiers were in the vicinity. They saw two at each of the two inspection points and one soldier in the middle of the street to make sure no one ran. "Don't forget what we learned from Ari," Thaddeus said. "Always be vigilant to know the strength of the enemy."

Cass nodded.

Eventually there were only five people between them and the soldiers at the checkpoint. An attractive young woman walked up to the soldiers. "Hold out your hands," one of them said gruffly. The young woman complied, revealing a gold ring on her left hand.

"Remove the ring and give it to me," the soldier said.

"But it's my wedding ring. I can't give it up."

The soldier punched the woman in the face, knocking her to the ground. A man standing near her helped her to her feet.

"I'm not going to ask you again."

The woman began crying as she attempted to take off her ring. She could not remove it. The soldier grabbed her left hand and began twisting the ring back and forth. "If we can't get it off, I'm going to cut off your finger." When he saw that he could not remove it, he pulled a knife from his belt and began cutting her finger. The woman was screaming and crying. Everyone on the street turned to see what was happening.

Thaddeus said, "This is what we trained for."

"What?" Cass asked.

"This is it," Thaddeus said and looked at Cass. He suddenly bolted toward the soldier who was cutting the woman's finger. In one motion he shoved her aside and grabbed the soldier's wrist and the hand that was holding the knife. Forcefully, with both of his hands using a cavalier wrist grip, Thaddeus torqued the knife upward, shoving it into the soldier's throat, just as he had learned from Ari.

As soon as Thaddeus ran toward the soldier, Cass reached into his pocket, pulled out a sharp six-inch ice pick that he carried for safety, and ran toward the other soldier, who was sitting behind a table and writing down the names of the people being inspected. Before the soldier could stand up, Cass jumped on the table, landed in a kneeling position, and slid up to his face. He quickly stabbed the icepick into the soldier's left eye and then his right eye. The soldier screamed in pain then stood to his feet with his hands covering his bleeding eyes. Cass grabbed a wooden club from the soldier's belt and struck him in the head until he went down. The soldier in the street ran to assist the Nazi soldiers. Thaddeus grabbed a rifle that was leaning against the table, raised it, and shot the soldier in the groin.

The stunned soldier stopped in the middle of the street and grabbed his crotch. Seeing that his hand was covered in blood, he looked at Thaddeus, who chambered another round in the rifle and fired a second shot, striking him in the head. The crowd began to cheer. The two soldiers on the other side of the street tried to run away but were overtaken by the crowd, who began beating them. Thaddeus and Cass stood in the street and were overwhelmed by their own amazing display of close-quarter combat skills. The crowd gathered around them cheering and praising them. Then the crowd dragged the other two soldiers over and threw them on the ground in front of Cass and Thaddeus. "What should we do with these two?" asked a man. Everyone grew quiet as they waited for the answer.

Thaddeus replied, "We have no choice now. If we let them live, they will report this, and the Nazis will come in and kill everyone."

"Kill them," a man in the crowd shouted.

Cass and Thaddeus did not respond. Although they could not do it, they knew that there was no alternative. A man in the crowd took the pistol from the belt of one of the soldiers and pointed it at his head.

"Nein, nein," the soldier shouted and held up his hands as if to stop the bullet. The man pulled the trigger, shooting the soldier in the head. He pointed the gun at the soldier next to him and shot him in the head. The last soldier still alive was on his knees on the ground holding his eyes with the palms of his hands. The blood was running through his fingers. He was shot in the head as well.

After all of the soldiers on the street were lying dead, the crowd became silent. They stood looking at Thaddeus and Cass for instructions. Though Thaddeus was barely in his teens and Cass was even younger, they were suddenly looked to for guidance. "What should we do with their bodies?" asked the man who had shot the soldiers with the pistol.

Remembering what they had learned from Ari, Cass said, "Throw their bodies in the sewer where they belong. Pour petrol on the bodies and burn them. The rains will carry the bodies out to the river. When the Nazis ask what happened to them, you will all say you don't know anything about it."

The crowd roared and again cheered Cass and Thaddeus. An old rabbi walked up to them and said, "God's hand is on your shoulder."

Cass felt a hand on his shoulder. He turned and saw Shmuel. "No, that's Shmuel."

Though he did not intend his words to be humorous, the crowd roared with laughter.

Then Shmuel said, "You need to run to your apartment. There could be anyone in this crowd who might report you to the Nazis if they figure out who you are."

Cass and Thaddeus nodded and then noticed the crying woman whose finger had been cut in an attempt to remove her ring. Blood was dripping on the ground. They walked over to her. Thaddeus said, "Come with us. My grandfather can help you."

A group of men disposed of the bodies as Cass had instructed. The rest of them followed Cass, Thaddeus, and the crying woman back to Grandpa's dental office. The crowd waited outside as the boys took her inside. Grandpa stopped the bleeding. He was able to save her finger. When they emerged from the building with her about forty-five minutes later, the crowd cheered again.

The following day the Nazis canvassed door-to-door, asking what had happened to the soldiers. Although there were nearly eighty witnesses in the street that day, not one person told the Nazis what had happened. From that day forward, when Cass and Thaddeus walked the streets, people would step out of their way, smile, and lower their heads in respect. The Jews had found heroes in the ghetto.

Cass and Thaddeus did not think much about what had happened. They did what Ari had taught them to do. Word spread through the ghetto that God had raised up two young men to fight the Nazis. Some compared them to Joshua, which made Cass and Thaddeus laugh. While this was not an isolated event in the ghetto, it was the first time such force had been shown by boys as young as these brothers. For days, people talked of nothing else, though everyone was careful not to say who it was who'd attacked the soldiers. A new sense of hope filled the ghettos. Some have wondered if this was one of the events that eventually triggered the ghetto uprisings.

One day several men appeared at the door of the Bieberstein apartment carrying rugs rolled up into long tubes. They asked to enter, and when they did, they unrolled the rugs, revealing the five rifles that had been taken from the Nazis soldiers who were killed. They also had boxes of ammunition.

"We decided that you should keep these for when the time is right," one of the men said.

CHAPTER

18

TIME PASSED SLOWLY for Rachel and Sarah in the Treblinka prison camp. Each moment seemed an eternity. They tried to encourage each other with words of hope that somehow the Biebersteins would find and rescue them from this horrible situation, but each evening they went to sleep realizing the futility of this hope. They were on their own. The barracks remained bitterly cold even after spring's arrival was scratched on the wall calendar the prisoners kept. The single wood-burning stove provided barely enough heat to keep water from freezing, much less to comfort a dying soul. It did not take long for the prisoners to realize that the best place to bed was nearest the stove. In an effort to find warmth, many of the women would take their blankets and sleep on the floor around the stove. Sometimes they would cuddle together in groups of three or four to share the warmth created by body heat. Though the floor was uncomfortable, at least they could find some warmth, and clearly the cold was less comfortable than the hard wooden floor.

On an otherwise uneventful spring morning, Rachel and Sarah awakened to the ominous but familiar sound of an officer shouting in German. "Get out of bed, you lazy Jews. Get up before I shoot you all. Today is a workday. Today is not Shabbat, at least not in Treblinka."

The women in the barracks quickly jumped out of bed and stood at attention. The officer walked through the barracks followed by several guards. "You"—he looked at one of the young women—"go stand by the door."

"Why?"

"Because I said so," shouted the officer. "If you need further explanation, I will cut off your ears."

"Why do you hate me?" asked the young woman. "You don't even know me."

The officer just stared at her for a moment, as if he was not aware she had spoken to him. The young woman walked quickly to the entrance of the barracks and stood by the door. The guards continued through the barracks, looking at each woman as if they were inspecting beef.

"You," he shouted at another young woman. "Get over by the door." He continued to walk through the barracks until he came to Rachel. He stopped and rubbed a smudge off Rachel's chin. Then he looked at Sarah for a moment. Looking back at Rachel, he smiled. "Go stand with the others. You are chosen."

Terrified and uncertain how to respond, Rachel walked across the room and stood by the two other women next to the door. She glanced at Sarah, who looked at her with an expression of fear. The officer went to the door. "You three, come with me. The rest of you line up in front of the barracks for roll call."

The guards left the barracks, followed by the three women. The rest of the women went out to the yard and lined up in front of the barracks. Sarah watched as Rachel and the other two women followed the guards toward the front gate. "Where are they going?" she asked Olga.

"I don't know," Olga said softly. In reality they both knew Rachel had been taken for the target practice games.

Rachel obediently followed the guards to the front gate. When they arrived, the guard instructed the women to go into a building. In the building, Rachel saw about a hundred women, sitting on the floor wrapped in blankets. Most were sitting quietly. A few were talking softly among themselves. There was no heat in the building.

"Why are we in here?" Rachel asked as she sat next to one of the women sitting on the floor. The young woman looked at her but did not answer.

Rachel looked at another woman sitting across from them. "Why are we in here?"

The woman replied, "We are for target practice."

"Why do they do that?" Rachel asked.

"Because they are Nazis. That is what Nazis do."

"Do you mean they are going to shoot at us?"

The young woman nodded. "They shoot about ten of us every day. Then they bring in another ten so they always have plenty to shoot."

"What is your name?" Rachel asked.

"Tzvi," the young woman said.

"I thought Tzvi was a boy's name."

Tzvi laughed. "Right now I don't care. Maybe Papa was drunk."

"How long have you been in here?"

"About two months. I have been lucky not to be chosen for target practice. I'm just waiting until the day I'm called."

Rachel sat quietly as she waited to see what would happen next. In a few moments, the officer came back in and instructed everyone to stand up and disrobe. All of the prisoners complied. There was no alternative. The brisk spring morning air was chilly but not cold, though it chilled to the bone. The prisoners were instructed to walk into the yard and stand in front of the gate. Again they complied. They were led out of the gate to an area inside a fence that was about one acre in size. They were told to sit on the ground just outside the fence. The ground was muddy and cold. They sat naked in the mud. Fearful of getting caught talking, Rachel decided not to ask any more questions. She could feel the cold muddy water in which she was sitting.

After about twenty minutes, the women saw a group of naked men walking toward them. The men approached and began walking back and forth in front of the naked women who were sitting in the mud.

"Why are they making them walk in front of us like that?" asked Rachel.

"Because they want the last thing Jews experience on this earth to be humiliation," replied Tzvi.

The men were then instructed to sit on the ground in an area next to the women. The officer walked over to Rachel and shouted, "Go to the fence."

Tzvi began to cry. "No," she pleaded. "Please do not make me do this."

The officer looked at her momentarily then shouted, "Not you, dummkopf, her." He pointed at Rachel. He paused for a moment then said, "I changed my mind. You go with her." Rachel wondered if Tzvi did that intentionally to focus the officer's attention off Rachel and onto herself. Tzvi whispered, "I'm sorry, I tried."

Rachel and Tzvi stood to their feet and walked to the fenced area. To get there, they were forced to walk in front of the naked men sitting on the ground. As they walked, Rachel noticed that not one of the men looked up at them. She thought, *Nothing here is normal. What could cause such a desperate situation? It is as if they are dead.*

Rachel and Tzvi stood next to the gate of the fence. The same officer came over and looked at each of them. Finally, he looked at the soldiers standing near him. "Lugers," he shouted. All of the soldiers took their rifles from their shoulders and leaned them against the wall of the barn. They came back over and lined up in front of the gate and unsnapped the holsters that held their Luger pistols.

The officer walked back to the women. He looked at Tzvi then touched her inappropriately. "You're up," he said.

"No, please, isn't there anything I can do for you?"

The officer looked at her for a time. "No, you are a smelly, ugly Jew pig. What could you do for me?"

"I can please you," she replied. "Just give me a chance."

The officer looked at Rachel then said, "I think you could please me. What should I do with her? Should I give her a chance?"

Rachel nodded, not fully understanding what his words meant. "Yes, please give her a chance."

The officer nodded and smiled. "Okay, I will give her a chance, and if she doesn't please me, I will shoot her, and then I will give you a chance."

Rachel looked down at the muddy ground. *Does it really matter? We are all dead anyway.* She remembered what Olga had told her about Rassenschande. Nazis are forbidden to have relations with Jewish women, and when they do, they have to kill them so they don't produce children who would be tainted with Jewish blood. *Tzvi is dead.*

The guard motioned for Tzvi to follow him across the muddy yard to the officers' quarters. Rachel watched as the guard walked with Tzvi, still naked, into the quarters. She wondered if she would ever see Tzvi again.

Maybe this would give Tzvi a chance to live and possibly even to live well in Treblinka.

A short time later, a different officer came over to the naked women. Looking at a young blond girl sitting near the gate, he pointed at her. "You, stand up and come over here." The young woman complied.

"How old are you?"

"Twenty-three."

"Twenty-three is a good age to die," said the officer.

The young woman looked down at the muddy ground.

"Are you ready to die?" the officer shouted.

The young woman said nothing for a moment then replied, "If God chooses this day for me to die, then I am ready to die."

"Stupid Jew pig with your stupid Jew God." The guard kicked her in the stomach with his heavy boot. She dropped to the ground and vomited.

"Get up, Jew whore," he shouted.

Wiping her mouth with muddy fingers, the young woman stood to her feet in front of the officer. The officer pointed to a soldier standing in formation. "Shoot this pig," he said. Then he shoved the young woman into the muddy fenced area and shouted, "Run, slut."

The naked girl ran as fast as she could into the muddy field. She began to run in a zigzag formation across the center of the field, slipping and sliding in the mud. The soldier unholstered his Luger and attempted to sight the weapon.

"Shoot sometime today," the officer shouted. "If we were in combat, you would be dead by now. Maim her."

The soldier aimed his pistol and fired at the girl. He missed. The other soldiers laughed hysterically and began shouting at the soldier who missed. The soldier then aimed a second time. The bullet struck the young woman in the buttocks, and she landed on her back in the mud. The soldiers roared with laughter as the naked woman lay in the mud screaming and writhing in pain. "Shut up that filthy Jew," the officer shouted.

The soldier aimed his Luger at her head and fired. The bullet struck its mark, and the young woman was dead.

Rachel was in shock. She could not believe what she had just witnessed. The officer walked over to the naked women still sitting and grabbed one of them by the hair. "You're up. Run."

The woman ran into the muddy field and tried to dodge the bullet of the soldier. Perhaps the woman believed that if she performed well enough, she might be spared, though that had never happened before. Soon, the officer shouted, "Kill," and the girl was shot dead by a soldier.

Rachel watched this spectacle several more times that morning. Eventually she asked a woman next to her. "Why don't they shoot the men?"

"They do, just not as many. The soldiers like shooting the women more than the men."

Rachel could not fully understand the reason for the difference in the treatment of men and women. It was all death to her. She was old enough to know, however, that the difference stemmed from some perverted sexual fetish. She tried to understand how these guards could ever shoot a naked woman running for her life across a muddy field. She knew she could not ever do it. *Why am I different from these people? Is this the difference between Jews and gentiles? Is this the difference between men and women?*

After shooting several more women, the officer instructed the rest of them to go back inside the camp and sit on the ground. He then instructed several men to stand by the gate in the fence of the killing area. One by one he instructed them to run into the fenced area, and one by one they were shot. Eventually the rest of the prisoners were instructed to go back into the buildings. Rachel realized that she had survived another day.

The following morning, the same group of women and men were again told to disrobe and stand next to the gate of the fence of the muddy field, where they would be required to run for their lives. As they waited Rachel saw the officer come from the officers' quarters with Tzvi, who was wearing new prisoner clothes. She had bathed and was clean. Rachel wondered if she was now going to assist the Nazis in their persecution of the Jews. As the officer and Tzvi approached, Tzvi looked at Rachel with a blank expression. She smiled slightly then walked past Rachel and through the gate into the muddy field. *What is she doing?* Rachel wondered.

Tzvi walked to the center of the muddy field, then turned around and faced the officer who had stopped at the gate. He unsnapped the flap of his holster, removed his Luger, pointed it at Tzvi, and shot her in the head. He looked at Rachel and said, "She didn't please me. Can you do better?"

Rachel knew that no matter what she did, she would be killed.

The officer motioned for Rachel to come and stand next to him as he put his Luger in its holster. Rachel noticed that he did not snap the holster flap but left it loose. She walked over and stood next to him as he ordered another Jewish woman to prepare to run in the field. She thought about the time Ari took the pistol from the officer in the street in Warsaw and shot him with his own gun. She remembered how he ran like the wind to escape the Nazi soldiers who were chasing him. *I wonder if I could slip his gun out of his holster without him knowing it. He seems distracted by the women being shot.* She got closer to him until she was actually touching him. He looked at her and smiled. "Now that is more like it. You Jewish girls don't know what you are missing."

Rachel looked behind her. Everyone was focused on a girl who was running in the field and trying to avoid the sting of the bullet. She stood next to the officer and realized she did not even know his name. *It is better that way,* she thought. She slowly lifted the flap to his holster with one hand and removed the Luger with other. She realized that she did not know how many bullets were in it or even how many bullets it held. The officer felt something as she lifted it from his holster. He instinctively touched the holster with his hand. Realizing the holster was empty, he quickly turned toward Rachel to see her pointing the gun at him. Before he could reach for it, she fired, shooting him in the chest. As he fell to the ground she fired a shot at one of the soldiers who was standing near him. She missed. She realized that she would not be able to hit her target unless she stood right next to it. She didn't know how to aim the gun. She ran toward the soldiers firing one shot after another. She was able to hit three of them before they opened fire on her. Rachel fell to her death that day, but she took four German soldiers with her.

Sarah was lying on her bunk after working a day in the field, when she heard the news about Rachel. She cried bitterly throughout the night. Now she was alone. There were other women in the barracks with her, but it wasn't like having Rachel there. As she lay in the bed crying, she thought about Rajmund. She wondered what he was doing now. She remembered how he promised her that if the Nazis ever invaded, he would fight them to the death. She wondered if he kept his promise. She longed for the days when she used to sit in the dining room of the Bieberstein mansion with Rachel, Thaddeus, and Rajmund. She remembered how much she loved

Rajmund and had thought that someday they would be married. Now everything was ruined. Rachel was dead; Rajmund and Thaddeus might be dead too. When the food rations were brought in, Sarah didn't get up to retrieve any for herself. She simply wanted to die. She thought that perhaps if she did not eat, she would die. Then this would all be over.

In the Oval Office at the Whitehouse in Washington, DC, Franklin Roosevelt, the president of the United States, discussed the crisis in Europe with General Douglas MacArthur and Brigadier General Dwight Eisenhower. Eisenhower had served as the chief military aide to General MacArthur and thus found himself in the president's inner circle.

Roosevelt sat in his wheelchair looking out of the Oval Office onto the south White House lawn. "I never dreamed I would be facing major wars in multiple theaters simultaneously. I need to know that we have the best men in play everywhere we find ourselves fighting."

"We'll do everything possible to get this under control, sir," said MacArthur.

"I know you will." Roosevelt was silent for a time as he continued to look out the window, creating an awkwardness in the room. Finally he said, "Ike, I would like for you to accompany General Arnold to London to assess the performance and ability of General Chaney in his charge over the European theater. I have to know that we are well represented in Europe. This whole damned mess is way out of control. Britain, our greatest ally, is depending on our support, and I'm not convinced we have our best talent over there. I want you to give me the truth straight up. Don't hold back anything. If you find what I suspect, then the joint chiefs of staff will replace Chaney. His replacement will be the commanding general of the European theater. Even though you have never held command higher than a battalion, your performance in the Louisiana Maneuvers last year caught the attention of many who believe you are ready for a lead command position. I think you are probably the best man to assess Chaney's performance."

"Yes, sir," Eisenhower replied.

"Chaney, or his replacement, will work on the plans for Japan and Europe. We have a threat even within the United States, and now we are getting resistance from all the softies who are decrying our internment of the Japanese in the States. At first it was only Governor Ralph Carr of Colorado who opposed it, but now people are starting to listen to that jackass. Can this get any worse?"

Roosevelt continued, "Doug, I really need you to clean up the mess in the Philippines. That's why I asked you to come back to the States for this meeting. I need to impress upon you its utmost importance. You know the islands better than anyone we have. The Japanese are all over it like flies on cow pies. We're going to have heavy casualties, but it has to be done. God help us."

"Absolutely, sir. We will hit them with everything we got," MacArthur said. "We're making great strides. It is just a matter of time before we boot their butts back to Hiroshima."

Roosevelt turned his wheelchair around. "I know you two have had your differences, but I believe you have put that behind you. Now there is something else I need to tell both of you. You know about the Manhattan Project to create a usable atomic bomb under the direction of Dr. Oppenheimer."

"Yes, we're both aware of it," Eisenhower replied.

"This is going to fall in your department, Doug. We are anticipating a functioning test of the atomic bomb within three years. That will change the face of the war if we get there first. If we create a functioning atomic bomb, I intend to drop it on several major cities in Japan. That will end this war as far as Japan is concerned."

"Why do you say if we get there first?" asked MacArthur.

"I have something I want to show both of you." Roosevelt wheeled his chair over to his desk, reached in the drawer, and pulled out a piece of paper. "This is a letter from Albert Einstein that I received a few years back." He gave the letter to MacArthur who read it out loud.

Old Grove Rd.
Nassau Point
Peconic, Long Island

August 2nd, 1939

F. D. Roosevelt
President of the United States
White House
Washington, D.C.

Sir:

Some recent work by E. Fermi and L. Szilard, which has been communicated to me in manuscript, leads me to expect that the element uranium may be turned into a new and important source of energy in the immediate future. Certain aspects of the situation which has arisen seem to call for watchfulness and, if necessary, quick action on the part of the Administration. I believe therefore that it is my duty to bring to your attention the following facts and recommendations:

In the course of the last four months it has been made probable - through the work of Joliot in France as well as Fermi and Szilard in America - that it may become possible to set up a nuclear chain reaction in a large mass of uranium, by which vast amounts of power and large quantities of new radium-like elements would be generated. Now it appears almost certain that this could be achieved in the immediate future.

This new phenomenon would also lead to the construction of bombs, and it is conceivable - though much less certain - that extremely powerful bombs of a new type may thus be constructed. A single bomb of this type, carried by boat and exploded in a port, might very well destroy the whole port together with some of the surrounding territory. However, such bombs might very well prove to be too heavy for transportation by air.

The United States has only very poor grades of uranium in moderate quantities. There is some good ore in Canada and the former Czechoslovakia, while the most important source of Uranium is Belgian Congo.

In view of this situation you may think it desirable to have some permanent contact maintained between the Administration and the group of physicists working on chain reactions in America. One possible way of achieving this might be for you to entrust with this task a person who has your confidence and who could perhaps serve in an unofficial capacity. His task might comprise the following:

a) to approach Government Departments, keep them informed of the further development, and out forward recommendations for Government action, giving particular attention to the problem of uranium ore for the United States;
b) to speed up the experimental work, which is at present being carried on within the limits of the budgets of University laboratories, by providing funds, if such funds be required, through his contacts with private persons who are willing to make a contribution for this cause, and perhaps also by obtaining the co-operation of industrial laboratories which have the necessary equipment.

I understand that Germany has actually stopped the sale of uranium from the Czechoslovakian mines which she has taken over. That she should have taken such early action might perhaps be understood on the ground that the son of the German Under-Secretary of State, Von Weishlicker, is attached to the Kaiser-Wilheim-Institute in Berlin where some of the American work on uranium is now being repeated.

Yours very truly,
(Albert Einstein)

"I heard about this letter, but this is the first time I have seen it," MacArthur said.

Roosevelt replied, "This atomic bomb is the only thing that is going to save us, I believe, gentlemen. But Hitler is also working to develop an atomic bomb. As you can see from the last paragraph, our work on the atomic bomb is being repeated at the Kaiser Wilhelm Institute in Berlin. We have to get the bomb before Hitler does, or the United States will be destroyed by the Nazis along with Europe."

MacArthur placed the letter on the president's desk. Eisenhower walked over, picked up the letter, and read it.

Roosevelt continued, "We need to pray to God that we develop the bomb before Hitler does. If we don't, our lives in America will never be the same."

Eisenhower placed the letter back on the desk. "I understand, sir."

After this meeting, Eisenhower left for Britain with General Arnold where they met with General Chaney and Winston Churchill. Churchill expressed his concern that General Chaney might not be right for such formidable opposition as the Hitler regime. Shortly after returning to the States, Eisenhower was appointed to replace Chaney, and MacArthur returned to the Philippines. America was now committed, to the fullest, in the war effort. It was a war that would change the world forever. Unfortunately, for the Jews trapped in the ghettos and the prison camps of Poland, it might as well have been the war to end all humanity. For them, humanity had ceased to exist.

CHAPTER

19

A S DAYS PASSED, Cass and Thaddeus continued their exercises and worked out as often as they could. Irena tried to persuade them both to enroll in the yeshiva that was just across the street from their apartment, but they both felt that they needed to concentrate on fighting techniques to prepare for the day when the Jews would revolt against the Nazis. Many locals had come to believe that Thaddeus and Cass were destined to lead an uprising. They began meeting in Shmuel's apartment to plan the day when they would revolt. Arturo the mailman said he would help communicate their information to other Jews in the vicinity when they needed him to. In reality, they did not plan anything but just talked of the day when the Jews would revolt. Shmuel would often allow Arturo into the apartment when the meetings were occurring. He told the others that Arturo could be trusted. Cass and Thaddeus were not so sure. They remembered how careful Ari had been in deciding who could attend the Krav Maga classes. Whenever they knew that Arturo was going to be there, Cass and Thaddeus would not go to Shmuel's apartment.

Cass still worked in the gun factory as a slave laborer. He wondered if this opportunity was the result of manipulation by Lech and Schindler to help the Biebersteins. His theory was reinforced when he learned that Schindler had begun using Jews to work in his factories, and it was rumored that he had become romantically involved with a Jewish woman. The benefit to those Jews he employed was they that were not sent for extermination but instead would be provided a modest amount of income to support their families. Although he wanted to believe that Schindler had reformed his ways and had become sympathetic to the Jews, he rejected the notion because of his memory of Schindler shooting his dog, Tiny. In reality, he knew that his mother had arranged his job at the gun factory to keep him from being exterminated.

The work in the gun factory was only a few days per week. Cass had weekends off. This allowed him to continue his exercise and training in Krav Maga. Cass soon noticed that the Germans would inspect every twelfth gun and none in between. Like their practice of having patrols at a precise time, it made their actions very predictable. He brought this to the attention of his fellow Jewish workers, who quickly saw this as an opportunity to sabotage some of the guns by installing weak firing pins and weak return springs. The guns would work well for a short time then misfire. It never occurred to the Germans that the workers making the guns were responsible. Instead they blamed the company supplying the metal that was used in making the firing mechanisms.

One Saturday morning after breakfast there was a loud knock at the door. It was a knock similar to the sound heard when Nazi soldiers would arrive to force the Jews from their homes. Grandpa opened the door. To everyone's surprise it was Ari.

"Ari," shouted Cass and Thaddeus almost simultaneously. "What are you doing here?"

Ari came into the apartment and closed the door behind himself. He shook hands with Grandpa. "I learned where you were living, and I wanted to stop by to see how you are. I heard about the incident with the Nazis on the street corner." He looked at Thaddeus and Cass. "They said you were very brave."

"So where are you living now?" Thaddeus asked.

"I am living a few blocks from here, but I learned about this area. I think it might be a better location for a base than where I am now. Fewer Nazis running around here."

"When did you come into the ghetto?" Cass asked.

"It was about two months ago."

"Were you rounded up?" Cass asked.

Ari shook his head. "No, I came in voluntarily. I felt that I was needed in here since this is where our people are now. I have a way in and out of the ghetto so when something needs to be taken care of, I just go out and do it."

"How do you get in and out?" Thaddeus asked.

"I'll show you when you are ready to come with me on a mission. Until then it is better if you don't know."

Grandma offered Ari cornbread and potatoes, which he seemed to enjoy immensely. "Do you know of any vacant buildings where we could operate a training facility?" Ari asked.

Grandpa nodded. "There are several down here. Across the street is a large vacant building that might be good for you."

"I'd like to see it."

"I will take you over in a bit."

They sat in the living room, talking for a time. Eventually Ari asked, "What happened to those two girls who used to live with you, before you came into the ghetto?"

Irena replied, "We haven't seen them in about six months. They were living with us in an apartment over on Chlodna Street. One morning they went to the local grocery store and never came back. We were rounded up that same day and brought into the ghetto. That was right after Hitler's plan to exterminate the Jews was announced."

Ari nodded. "What were their names? Rachel and Sarah, right?"

Cass nodded. "We were told they were taken away in a Nazi staff car. We never saw them after that, and no one knows what happened to them. There is a mailman named Arturo who said he would try to find out for us."

Ari looked up quickly. "Arturo, the goy mailman?"

"Yeah, that's him," replied Thaddeus. "You've heard of him?"

Ari narrowed his eyes. "Don't trust him. There have been several arrests of Jews who had been disclosing information to him. On a couple of occasions, there were meetings that were raided by the Nazis, and everyone was arrested."

"Do you think he was involved somehow?" Grandpa asked.

"He is the one who delivered the letters telling people about the meetings. We are certain he informed the Nazis about the meetings."

Thaddeus shook his head. "I knew there was something I didn't trust about that guy."

"Oh no," Irena said. "He has been attending meetings with Jews in Shmuel's flat."

"How long has that been going on?"

"At least several months," Irena replied.

Ari shook his head and sighed heavily. "This isn't good. Where does Shmuel live?"

"His flat is right down the hall," Cass said.

"He needs to tell Arturo that there will be no more meetings," Irena said.

"I don't know," replied Ari. "Arturo might know that Shmuel is wise to him, and he might give the names of all of the people who have been attending to the Nazis."

"But if they don't do it, eventually Arturo will turn them in anyway," replied Grandma.

"That's true," replied Ari. "I think we should go down and talk to Shmuel and let him know what is happening."

Grandpa nodded. "I agree. Why don't you and I go down?" He went to the door. Ari, Cass, and Thaddeus followed him.

When they arrived at Shmuel's flat, Grandpa tapped on the door. Shmuel opened the door. "Shalom, Dr. Szyncer, Thad, Cass. What a surprise." Shmuel looked at Ari. "Who is your friend?"

"This is Ari," Grandpa said. "May we speak with you for a few moments?"

Shmuel opened the door wider. "Sure, come on in."

As they entered the apartment, they noticed a thin, sickly woman sitting in a chair near the window overlooking the street. She turned and looked toward the men.

"Ari, this my wife, Liba."

"It's nice to meet you."

Liba remained seated. "Thank you. It is nice to meet you as well."

"Liba isn't well." Shmuel sighed.

Ari nodded slowly. "I'm sorry to hear that."

"Please sit. Make yourselves comfortable. I have nothing to offer you except lemon-flavored water."

"We're fine," replied Grandpa. Everyone took seats around the room. "Are you still holding the meetings in your apartment?"

Shmuel nodded. "We meet every other Wednesday evening."

"Does Arturo still come to your meetings?"

Shmuel looked at Ari. "Yes, why do you ask?"

Grandpa continued, "Shmuel, Ari is from an area of the ghetto about six blocks from here. Arturo delivers mail in his area too. He tells us that Arturo has given information about Jews to the Nazis that resulted in their arrests."

"Oh, I can't believe that," said Shmuel. "Arturo delivers messages to our members and helps us in many ways. He even brings food for us sometimes. What have you heard?"

"There are several situations where information was given to Arturo concerning covert operations. Arturo was trusted because he claims to sympathize with our plight. What happened is that those operations were all exposed, and the individuals involved were arrested or killed. We believe that Arturo told the Nazis. We can't prove it, but it has happened three times. It is possible that someone else revealed the information, but Arturo had been aware of all three of those occasions. I think Arturo is attending your meetings to acquire information that he can take to the Nazis. Have you planned any operations?"

"No, we just always talk about it. It is mostly a support group."

Ari nodded. "I think he is attending in hopes that you will plan an operation so he can alert the authorities."

Shmuel stood up and walked to Liba. "I just can't believe it. He has been in our house a dozen times."

"It's probably only because you have not planned anything that no one has been arrested," Ari said.

Liba asked, "What are they saying? Are they saying that Arturo is bad?"

Shmuel nodded. "If it's true, we're all in danger. What if we stopped having the meetings?"

"He will just go spy on someone else," Grandpa said. "Somehow we need to create a test. We have to find out for sure if it is true."

"How can we do that?" asked Shmuel.

The room was silent for a moment. Then Ari said, "I might have an idea. Why don't we feed Arturo some false information and make sure no one else knows about it? That way we can see if he tells anyone."

"Like what?" Grandpa asked.

Ari continued, "Let's tell him something that would definitely cause the Nazis to raid a specific location if they found out about it. Only it will be false information. For example, let's tell him that a truckload of guns and ammo has been delivered to a specific location to be used in an assault against the Nazi militia. They would have to raid the warehouse to intercept the shipment."

"It would have to be a warehouse in an isolated area so no one gets injured in the raid," said Grandpa.

"I think I know just the place," Shmuel said. "There is an old abandoned warehouse about a mile from here. No one lives in the area that I know about. It is run-down, and it is precisely the kind of place where someone would hide a shipment."

"I like it," said Ari. "I think it will work. Then we will find out once and for all whether Arturo is the mole. Now, we can't let a single person know about this. Because if anyone else knows, we can't be sure that the information came from Arturo."

Shmuel said, "I'll tell him when I see him on Wednesday afternoon. That is his delivery day. That's why we hold the meetings on Wednesdays— so he can always attend."

Grandpa leaned back in his chair. "I'm concerned about one thing. If it turns out that Arturo really is the mole, and the Nazis find out they were set up, are they going to retaliate against you?"

"They might," said Shmuel. "But it's a chance we'll have to take. Let's just hope we're wrong, and he's not the mole." He looked at Liba. She had fallen asleep. "It would be better if I do it rather than anyone else. You're all much younger and have many years left. I'm seventy-eight, and our doctor says Liba won't last much longer."

"Your life is just as valuable as everyone else's," Grandpa said.

"Even so, Arturo knows me best. I'm really the only one who can give him such a message that he'll believe. I'll give him a note to deliver to a flat somewhere."

Ari stood up. "Why don't we walk over and look at the location. We'll need to have someone watching from a distance to see if they show up to raid the building."

Grandpa stood up and walked to the door. "Good idea. There are abandoned buildings all around the one we're thinking of. We could position ourselves at several locations in other buildings to see if the Nazis show up."

The men and boys walked to the abandoned warehouse. The streets were barren. The buildings around the warehouse were empty. "I wonder why there's no one using these buildings as living space," said Ari.

"They are all warehousing structures, so they wouldn't serve well as apartments."

The group walked to a large empty warehouse. Grandpa said, "This is the building Shmuel was thinking of." He walked past several large garage doors and went inside. "This is called the Tobben warehouse. It was abandoned before the last war." The inside of the building was empty except for pallets and pieces of debris. After walking through the building, they went back outside.

"This will be perfect," said Ari. "All of these buildings are abandoned?"

"Yes," replied Shmuel.

They stood in the center of the street looking in all directions. Ari pointed at a building on a corner. "Someone can watch from that window there." He pointed at a building on the other end of the street. "We can put someone there too. We will need to explore those buildings for escape routes in case they decide to check the neighboring buildings as well."

"I think those would be good vantage points." Grandpa pointed down an alley next to the abandoned warehouse. "If we put someone in the building at the end of the alley here, that will allow us to see all access points to the warehouse."

The team spent the afternoon exploring the neighboring buildings. When they were satisfied, they returned to Shmuel's apartment, where they finalized the plans. Shmuel wrote a note telling about a planned attack.

"Shalom, Eben, 400 Mauser 98k rifles with an ample supply of ammunition have been delivered to the Tobben warehouse on my street. The army will stay there tonight, Wednesday night. The Resistance will launch the first assault Thursday evening as planned. Please notify everyone in the network to get there before midnight tonight. The doors will not be opened for anyone after midnight. We will need every man. Shalom, Shmuel."

The following day, Wednesday morning, Shmuel said to Arturo, "We're finally going to make our move. Weapons have been delivered to the Tobben warehouse. Do you know where it is?"

"Yes, I do."

"Would you deliver this letter to my cousin, Eben? He needs to get it before noon today."

"Where do I deliver it?"

Shmuel handed Arturo the letter. "There is an apartment building next to Nozyk Synagogue. Just go inside and slip it under the door of the first apartment on your right. The door will be locked, and no one will answer, but Eben will retrieve the message." In reality it was a vacant apartment that Shmuel owned.

"I'll deliver it." Arturo went downstairs to his bicycle and immediately rode to the German officers' building three miles from the apartment. He went into the building across the street and walked up to an apartment on the third floor. He went into the apartment and raised the blind, which was his routine signal to the Nazis that he had a message.

A short time later, the letter was retrieved by a little boy and taken back to the officers' building. A short time after that the boy returned with a map of the area of the ghetto. "The general says you are to circle the Tobben warehouse on this map."

Arturo circled the Tobben warehouse, and the boy took it back across the street to the Nazi building. Unbeknownst to the Germans, Grandpa, Ari, Thaddeus, and Cass had already taken their lookout positions in the abandoned buildings. Grandpa was in a building a block from the warehouse where he could watch from a window on the fourth floor. Cass and Thaddeus were in a building on the opposite end of the street where they could watch from a window on the third floor, and Ari was in a building at the opposite end of the alley.

At Treblinka I, Sarah grieved the loss of her sister. Two weeks had passed since Rachel lost her life, taking as many Nazis with her as she could. Word spread quickly through camp of Rachel's heroic last feat. She became a hero among the prisoners. Sarah wondered if the Nazis would retaliate against her for her sister's actions. So far, nothing had been said by the guards. She decided that she would be ready for whatever happened. She had been in the camp for five months now. Her weight had fallen to a hundred pounds on her five-seven frame; she looked emaciated. She was not alone; the other women in her barracks had likewise fallen to a fraction of their normal weights. They were allowed to shower once per week, which was not nearly enough, given the heavy workload. Bacterial rashes were common among the women. When a woman became too sick to work, she would disappear from the barracks and a new prisoner would be brought in.

Sarah worried about what clothes she would have in the winter. She had not received a new supply of clothing since she arrived at the camp. The dress she wore was torn, and the material was wearing thin. Although she was relieved that summer had arrived and she no longer felt the bitter cold, with more daylight the prisoners were required to work longer days. Sarah worked in the fields just outside of the camp. She was told the crops were sold in the cities to raise money to pay the salaries of the guards and officers at the camp. She soon learned that she could not believe all of the many stories she had been told. Some were based on certain factual events, and some were misinterpretations of events that had occurred. Sarah simply knew they were not always reliable.

At Treblinka life was harsh. Most of the prisoners hoped, at least in part, they would die; yet, they struggled on in the hope that they would be freed and could go back to their former lives. In reality, no one believed they would survive Treblinka. It was a terrible place that had snatched them from their former lives like a hole of death. While most of the prisoners in Treblinka were Jews, some were physically or mentally handicapped people. Others were segments of society the führer considered undesirable, such as gypsies. The price for vagrancy in the new empire was often death or imprisonment in a concentration camp.

Although it would not become the topic of history books until over fifty years later, sexual abuse was rampant in the camps. Dozens of women disappeared from the barracks at Treblinka every day and were never seen again. No one knew what happened to them, but the suspicion was that some were taken for a night of pleasure and executed the following

morning. In truth, that is what was happening to them. Others were taken away for target practice or simply physical torture for the amusement of the guards. Sarah tried to make herself as unattractive as possible, and as her weight began to decline she felt a little less threatened with the possibility that she might become a victim of this strange sexual exploitation. She remembered studying chapter 8 of the *Laws of Kings and Their Wars*, by Rabbi Maimonides, who was more commonly known as Rambam. She had learned that a woman who was a captive of war living in a man's house was to make herself unattractive so he would not desire her. For three months he was not to touch her; then, if she wanted to convert to Judaism, he could marry her, otherwise, he was to set her free. Sarah would use this method of being unattractive to avoid being desired by the guards.

Two questions clouded Sarah's mind after Rachel's death. First, would she survive this ordeal? And second, did she want to survive? She did not know the answer to either question. She only knew she was miserable and did not want to be at Treblinka. She wanted to be at home with her parents studying at the yeshiva, but she knew she would never have those days again.

Photograph left to right, Casimir Bieberstein, Major Szymon Bieberstein (grandfather) and Thaddeus Bieberstein. Major Bieberstein was in the Polish Army and later became a Colonel in the Soviet Army. Circa 1936

Photograph left to right Thaddeus Bieberstein, Major Szymon Bieberstein, Casimir Bieberstein. Circa 1937

Photograph left to right Sigmund Bieberstein, Casimir Bieberstein, Thaddeus Bieberstein in front of Bieberstein mansion. Circa 1937

Photograph left to right, Thaddeus Bieberstein, Casimir Biebers (Bieberstein). Circa 2004.

Photograph Casimir Biebers (Bieberstein) and grandson Mark Biebers. May 2012

Painted portrait of Irena Bieberstein, Circa 1958.

Irena Szyncer (later Irena Bieberstein), Circa 1914 at the age of 20

Photograph of Irena and Sigmund Bieberstein, Circa 1958

Photograph of Bernard Szyncer (Uncle Bernie), Circa 1949

Katharine Sergava Sznycer, the wife of Bernard Szyncer. She
was in the original Broadway cast of Oklahoma and went
on to a successful career on Broadway. Circa 1948.

Photo of Bernard Szyncer and sister Irena
Szyncer Bieberstein, Circa 1938

Photo of Thaddeus Bieberstein, 2004

Photo of Major Szymon Bieberstein who later became a Colonel in the
Soviet Army. He was the grandfather of Casimir Bieberstein, Circa 1928.

Joyce (McGregor) Biebers, United Airlines Stewardess, Wife of Casimir
Biebers (Bieberstein) Mother of Thomas Biebers, Newark, New Jersey 1960

Photograph of Mark Biebers at Tombstone of Casimir
Biebers (Bieberstein) his grandfather, 2014

Photograph of Tombstone of Casimir Biebers (Bieberstein) 2014

Casimir Biebers's (Bieberstein) Certificate of US Naturalization

Photo of Cass's dog Tiny (Fuji)

Photo of Casimir Bieberstein's border papers

SURVIVORS OF THE
S H O A H
VISUAL HISTORY FOUNDATION.

10 June 1996

Casimir Biebers
1875 Alessandro Trail
Vista, CA 92084

Dear Mr. Biebers,

In sharing your personal testimony as a survivor of the Holocaust, you have
granted future generations the opportunity to experience a personal
connection with history.

Your interview will be carefully preserved as an important part of the most
comprehensive library of testimonies ever collected. Far into the future,
people will be able to see a face, hear a voice, and observe a life, so that they
may listen and learn, and always remember.

Thank you for your invaluable contribution, your strength, and your
generosity of spirit.

All my best,

Steven Spielberg
Chairman

MAIN OFFICE · POST OFFICE BOX 3168 · LOS ANGELES, CALIFORNIA 90078-3168 · PHONE 818.777-7802 FAX 818.733-0312

Letter from Steven Spielberg to Casimir Biebers (Bieberstein)

CHAPTER
20

C ASS SAT ON a floor next to a window on the third floor of a corner building overlooking the Tobben warehouse the Germans were expected to raid. It was Wednesday evening. Thaddeus was watching the street from a different window. Ari was watching from a corner building at the opposite end of the street, and Grandpa was watching from a building down the alley from the warehouse. From these vantage points they could see if anyone approached the warehouse from any angle. In order to give the appearance that someone was in the building, they had turned on some lights inside. The windows were smoked glass so no one could peer in, but one could see that the lights were on inside. They had put locks on all the doors so the Germans would be forced to kick in a door in order to enter. That would prevent someone from looking in the building before the raid and seeing that the building was empty. Only if the building was raided could they be sure that Arturo was the mole. Someone simply looking inside was not enough.

Around eleven thirty Cass and Thaddeus heard the familiar sound of a military truck. They looked down to the street below and saw a truck stop right beneath the window Cass was looking through. The truck then backed into an alley behind the building Cass and Thaddeus were in, to stay out of sight but from a position where it could observe the warehouse.

Cass whispered, "It looks like they are going to raid. Why else would that truck be here?"

"It looks like it, but we can't be sure unless they actually raid the warehouse," replied Thaddeus.

Cass was nervous. "What if they start raiding these other buildings when they find out the warehouse is empty? Maybe they'll think they just have the wrong building and start looking in these other buildings."

"That's why we worked out the escape route."

Every minute seemed like an hour as they waited in the darkness. Cass looked at the warehouse, which was lit up inside as planned. With all of the other buildings dark around it, the building clearly looked like someone was inside. Suddenly, Cass saw someone walking in front of the building. "Look someone is down there. He is going to the building."

Thaddeus ran over and looked down at the front of the warehouse. "That's Ari. What is he doing?"

Cass said, "He is unlocking one of the doors. He went inside."

"Why do you think he went in the building? What if he is still in there when they raid?"

Cass leaned forward for a better look. "Hey, he is coming out the little door on the other side of the building. What's he doing? From the truck they wouldn't be able to see him come out but would have seen him go in."

"I know what he is doing. He knows these trucks are here, and he wants to make it look like people are arriving. They won't raid before midnight because they are going to want to get as many as they can. He knew he could get in and out before the raid. Now they'll believe that at least one more person has arrived. That was smart thinking by Ari."

"Think about it," said Cass. "We're actually on our first mission as Resistance fighters with Ari."

"That's true. This is a real mission. I think Ari trusts us because of what happened in the street the day that Nazi tried to cut off the woman's finger."

Cass opened the window slightly so he could hear the sounds on the street. "Listen, I hear trucks coming."

Thaddeus walked over to the window where Cass was sitting. "They're coming. I hope Grandpa and Ari hear this too. It looks like we were right about Arturo."

"Look." Cass pointed up the street. "There's a tank, and there must be ten trucks behind it. Why would they bring tanks? Are they going to blow up the building?"

Suddenly Cass and Thaddeus heard the sound of trucks coming up the other street. A tank stopped just short of the intersection, and the trucks stopped behind it. German soldiers poured out of the trucks and began running up the street toward the warehouse.

"Look," shouted Cass. "There's Arturo with those soldiers."

"Shh," said Thaddeus. "Some of the Nazis in the truck may have come into the building. We don't want them to hear us. You're right. That is Arturo. What a liar. Everything Ari said about him is true. How can he pretend to be a friend to everyone while he is stabbing them in the back?"

"How could Lech Wagner betray us the way he did? Some people are just bad," Cass replied. "He not only betrayed us, but he betrayed Zofia. I will never forgive him for that."

"I know, but it was probably Lech who helped us get into better places to live until now. He probably put himself in danger to do that. Maybe he wasn't all bad."

"Maybe, but I blame him for Zofia's death. If he hadn't been such an ass, she wouldn't have had to hide that she was coming to see me. She could have come in normal hours, or he could have brought her."

"Lech is probably devastated by what happened to Zofia. He couldn't have known it would happen. If we someday see Lech again, we have to forgive him."

"Never. I will never forgive him. I loved Zofia. Now she is gone forever."

Cass and Thaddeus grew quiet as they watched trucks approaching from all directions. Eventually all of the trucks came to a stop. Soldiers began jumping out of the them. "Look at all of the soldiers," said Thaddeus. "There must be two thousand of them."

They watched as the Nazi soldiers surrounded the building except for the street directly in front of the warehouse. The tank turned its gun directly on the garage doors on the front of the building.

"Look! They're going to blow the door open," Cass said excitedly.

They heard a loud explosion. The garage doors were blown off the front of the warehouse. Bricks and rubble were everywhere. As the dust settled, hundreds of Nazi soldiers climbed over the debris and ran into the building.

Thaddeus laughed. "That was stupid. Now they have to climb over bricks to get into the building."

Cass and Thaddeus continued to watch as the Nazi soldiers poured into the building. Within five minutes they began to walk back out. The sight of the bewildered soldiers was overwhelming to Cass and Thaddeus who began laughing so hard they could not even speak. They saw the soldiers walking in circles. Officers began shouting at them. Then Arturo walked to the garage doors. An officer came up to him and began shouting at him. He held his arms up as if confused.

The more Cass and Thaddeus watched the harder they laughed. "I had no idea this would be so funny," said Cass.

"I know! This is better than *The Three Stooges*," said Thaddeus, laughing hysterically. "They look so confused."

"It's like the two thousand stooges. What a bunch of ignorant Nazis," said Cass as he wiped the tears from his eyes.

"Shh," said Thaddeus. "I just heard a door slam downstairs. Someone is in the building."

Cass and Thaddeus listened as they heard voices. "They are searching all the buildings. We need to go," said Thaddeus. "Let's use the planned escape route."

Cass and Thaddeus got up and ran to the back end of the building and climbed through the window and out onto the ledge. They looked at the alley below to be sure there was no one there. The truck was parked in the alley but they could not see anyone near it. "You go first," said Thaddeus. "I'll be right behind you."

Cass walked over to a heavy drainpipe, took a firm grip, wrapped his feet around it, and slid down the pole to the ground right behind the truck. He rolled under the truck while he waited for Thaddeus to slide down the pole. Thaddeus also rolled under the truck. Leaning out from under the truck they could see the face of the driver in the rearview mirror. Cass could not control himself as he thought of the confusion of the Nazis, and he began laughing again.

"Stop! They're going to hear you," Thaddeus said. "You have to be quiet. If they catch us, they'll kill us."

Those words sounded particularly funny to Cass, and he began laughing even harder. Thaddeus could no longer control himself, and he began laughing too. The driver, believing he heard something, attempted to open the door to see what was creating the sound, but the truck was too close to the wall of the building, and he could not open it wide enough to climb out. Cass and Thaddeus put their hands over their mouths to block the sound of their laughter. The driver shut the door.

"Let's go," whispered Thaddeus. "We need to get out of here."

"Not yet," said Cass. He reached in his pocket and pulled out a large tomato he was going to eat if they had been forced to stay in the lookout for more than a day. He quickly and silently ran up to the driver door of the truck, jumped on the running board, and shouted, "Achtung!" When the driver turned to see who had shouted, Cass shoved the tomato into his face. He jumped down from the running board and ran down the alley away from the rear of the truck as quickly as he could run. Thaddeus was following close behind, both of them still laughing. They heard the door of the truck banging on the brick wall of the building as the driver tried to get out. Then they heard the engine start. They looked back to see the truck backing toward them. When they reached the street at the edge of the building, they stopped and looked for any sign of Nazi soldiers. Seeing none they ran across the street into an alley that led to the next street over. Hiding in the shadows, they ran toward home.

"I sure hope Grandpa and Ari can get out of there okay," Cass said.

"They'll be fine. They'll probably be home shortly after us."

As they ran toward their home, they saw trucks driving toward their apartment building. They had to move quickly, using alleys whenever possible. Nazi army trucks were all over the streets. The penalty for being out after the eight o'clock curfew was immediate execution, unless the soldier who saw them was in a particularly generous mood. To avoid a Nazi in a bad mood, they needed to get back to their apartment quickly. As they ran, they heard the sound of machine gun fire ahead. Suddenly the street was lighted by a truck turning the corner and approaching them from behind.

"I think that's the truck that was parked next to the building we were in," Thaddeus said.

"Rats, they're going to be mad if they catch us."

They rounded a corner to their left and ran to the alley behind their own apartment building. They could hear the sound of people screaming and shouting from inside the building. They heard more gunfire. Sliding in through a basement window they ran over to the front of the building and looked out the front basement window in time to see the soldiers run out the front door of the building and jump into the trucks. The trucks started and drove away. When they were certain all of the soldiers had gone, they ran up the steps to the third floor. They opened the door at the top of the steps, and could see that the door was opened to Shmuel's apartment. The door to their apartment was locked. They ran to Shmuel's apartment. Shmuel and Liba were lying on the floor in a pool of blood, their bodies riddled with bullet wounds. The walls were covered with blood and were also full of holes. Stunned, they stood there looking at the bodies. They heard the door to the stairs open and looked down the hall. Ari was running toward them. He came into Shmuel's apartment and put his hands on his head. "Oh no. This is awful." He shook his head in disbelief, though this possibility had been anticipated. "Is your grandfather back yet?"

"We haven't seen him," Thaddeus said.

"Let's check on your mother."

As they ran down the hall to the Bieberstein apartment, neighbors began to come out. "What happened?" they asked. "Why were the soldiers here? And why were they shooting?"

"They killed Shmuel and Liba," Thaddeus said.

"Oh no. Was it because of the meetings they were having?"

"Yes," Ari said. "It was because of the meetings and because Shmuel helped expose a mole."

"Who is the mole?" one of the neighbors asked.

"Arturo," Ari said.

"The mailman?"

Cass, Ari, and Thaddeus did not wait in the hall to answer questions. Thaddeus unlocked the door to the Bieberstein apartment, and they slipped inside. They searched every room but could find no one. Then Ari opened a closet door.

Sitting on the floor looking up at them was Irena and Grandma. Irena was holding a loaded rifle prepared to fire. "Oh, thank goodness," Irena said. "It's you."

"What was all the shooting a little while ago?" asked Grandma. "It sounded like it was coming from Shmuel and Liba's apartment."

Ari nodded. "It was. The Nazis shot them because they gave Arturo false information to expose him."

"Oh," Irena said. "Those poor people."

"Shmuel knew the risk, and he wanted to accept it," said Ari. "I know that doesn't make it any easier. I actually thought we would have an opportunity to move them before the Nazis came back for them, but they came straight here after they found the warehouse was empty."

"What will happen to Arturo?" Irena asked.

"He should be executed," said Ari. "He is responsible for the death of hundreds of Jews he ratted out. I think we should just spread word through the community about what happened so no one will trust him in the future. He'll probably soon realize he is not wanted here and will leave."

"I am happy you aren't going to kill him," Irena said. "That would make us as bad as him."

As they talked Grandpa came in. "We were starting to worry about you," said Ari. "While we were gone, the Nazis came and shot Shmuel and Liba."

"I know. I heard what happened when I came up. Somebody needs to take care of Arturo," said Grandpa.

"We were just talking about that," Grandma said. "Ari said we should just let it take care of itself. Everyone will know what he did, and no one will trust him again."

Grandpa nodded. "I really didn't believe that about Arturo, and I didn't want to believe it. I have to admit, though, that nothing surprises me anymore."

"Did you have any trouble getting out of there, Doctor?" asked Ari. "What took you so long?"

"The Nazis came up and searched the building. I hid behind some old furniture until they left. I actually thought they were going to find me."

Grandma hugged Grandpa. "I am so grateful that you are safe."

"I'm grateful we're all safe," he replied. "It's tragic what happened to Shmuel and Liba."

"Yes, it's tragic," Ari said.

Cass listened intently but did not say a word.

It was Wednesday morning, four weeks to the day that Arturo was given the note by Shmuel to take to Eben. Everyone had been told to act normally around Arturo as if nothing had happened. No one had told him that they knew he had been the mole. Even so, he was concerned that he had been found out. People seemed guarded around him. No one seemed as friendly as before, and no one confided in him.

At eight o'clock, Cass sat on the roof of his apartment building with a rifle in his hands. It was a rifle that had been taken from one of the Nazi soldiers the day Cass and Thaddeus protected the young woman whose finger was being cut off. Grandpa had purchased a telescopic sight for the rifle, rendering it a sniper weapon. Cass knew that Arturo would ride his bicycle past the building at exactly eight fifteen as he delivered the Wednesday morning mail. He positioned the gun on the three-foot wall that surrounded the roof and rested on his knees as he waited patiently for the arrival of his target. The wall, in combination with the height of the building, concealed his presence. He could not be seen from any vantage point on any other building in the neighborhood, but he could see for several miles in all directions.

As he waited for Arturo to ride by, Cass thought of Shmuel and Liba. He remembered how kind they were, and he remembered when Shmuel placed his hand on Cass's shoulder the day they fought the Nazis in the street. He remembered how kind Shmuel and his wife were when the Biebersteins first came into the neighborhood and how he helped them settle in. He remembered how Shmuel chose to risk his life to find out if Arturo really was a mole. As he sat on the roof, he thought about all these things.

No one knew Cass was on the roof. He decided not to tell anyone what he was planning, not even Thaddeus. The family had expressed their position that nothing should be done to Arturo. Cass did not agree. Arturo had caused the deaths of hundreds of Jews and could cause the deaths of hundreds more if he was not eliminated. In Cass's mind, his family was wrong. Justice had to be served, and Arturo needed to be neutralized. Cass liked the term "neutralized." He had heard his paternal grandfather, Major Bieberstein, use the term often when referring to the removal of a threat to national security. Cass knew it was a polite way of saying "assassinated." He had no reservations about what he was about to do, and he had no concern that his actions would be wrong in any way. The Nazi government certainly was not going to punish Arturo for what he had done, and the Jews were afraid to punish him, so the responsibility fell to Cass.

Cass saw Arturo in the distance riding his bike up the street toward the apartment building. He was approximately three blocks away. Cass placed the crosshairs of the sight directly on Arturo's forehead. Although he was a moving target, on a bike his movements were stationary except for the forward motion, so sighting was easy. Arturo stopped at the intersection two blocks away. Cass cocked the bolt-action lever and focused the crosshairs on the top of Arturo's head to allow for a slight drop in the motion of the bullet. He waited ten seconds. Then he pulled the trigger. The shot was clean, and Arturo fell backward off his bike and onto the pavement. Initially passersby were startled, but on realizing it was Arturo, they were not concerned for their own safety.

Cass placed the rifle on the rug he had used to carry it to the roof. He rolled the rifle into the rug and carried the concealed rifle back down to the third floor. On the way down he passed a man. He stopped and looked at the rug for a moment, then walked on. Cass entered his apartment and noticed that everyone was still asleep except for Thaddeus, who saw him come in.

"Where have you been?"

"I went for a walk."

"With a rug? Most people walk the dog, not the rug."

"I thought I might want to rest in the park."

"Cass, I know you have the rifle. I heard a shot, and I looked in the rifle cubby. It was gone."

Cass laid the rug on the floor, unrolled it, picked up the rifle, and lifted the floorboard where the rifles were hidden. He put the rifle in the space and replaced the floorboard. He said nothing.

Thaddeus said, "Cass, Arturo comes by every Wednesday morning at this time. Did you do what I think you did?"

Cass did not answer.

Arturo lay in the street by the curb for two days though his bicycle disappeared within an hour. No one took his clothes. By five o'clock in the afternoon his body was covered with rats and scavenger birds. A dog came by and fed on his carcass. Two days later Arturo was barely recognizable except that upon looking closely one could tell he was wearing a Polish postman's uniform when he died. On Friday afternoon a truck came by to pick up the bodies of the dead in the street along with the garbage. Arturo's body was thrown into the back of the truck, along with other bodies and trash, by Jewish slave laborers. For those Jewish slave laborers, this seemed a fitting end for an unfit man.

CHAPTER
21

U NBEKNOWNST TO SARAH, in the world outside of Treblinka, her welfare was a matter of interest to someone she loved very much. SS officers had been coming into the Litynski restaurant, which was very popular among the German officers. This provided an opportunity for Josef Litynski to talk to them about various matters. Two of the officers who had been coming into the restaurant were SS-Obersturmführer Irmfried Eberl and his associate SS-Unterscharführer Willi Mentz. Eberl was a psychiatrist and the SS officer in charge of Treblinka, and Mentz was his deputy. Though a psychiatrist, Eberl believed in mass execution of the mentally ill. Mentz, a sawmill worker before joining the military, had acquired the name Frankenstein because of his horrific acts of murder and abuse. Although Hitler discouraged alcohol use, Eberl and Mentz were known for occasional heavy drinking. Josef served alcohol in his restaurant, and several evenings each week, Eberl and Mentz would take a room at the rear of the restaurant where they could enjoy alcohol without being seen. This gave Joseph and Rajmund an opportunity to speak with them frequently, and eventually, to ask about Sarah and Rachel.

On a Tuesday evening in July of 1942, Eberl and Mentz were in the backroom with Josef and Rajmund enjoying a drink. "Josef, come and sit with us," said Eberl, clearly enjoying the effects of the alcohol. Josef thought this might be the opportunity to inquire about Sarah and Rachel, which Rajmund had been requesting him to do.

"Thank you, Commander, that's very kind of you," said Josef as he walked over and sat at the table with Eberl and Mentz.

"Not at all," said Eberl with a laugh. "You're a friend to me. Besides, this is your restaurant. Here, have a drink." Eberl took an empty glass that was sitting on the table and poured a drink for Josef.

"Commander," said Josef, trying to conceal his nervousness. "I was wondering if you might help me with something." Rajmund, who had been preparing some appetizers for the men, overheard the conversation.

"Anything for you, my friend," Eberl said. "What can I do for you?"

Josef took a drink. "There were a couple of Jewish girls who used to work for me. They worked harder and better than any employee I have ever had. One day, they disappeared. It was a loss for me because those two girls did the work of six girls. If there was a way I could find them and get them back…if it was legal, I mean. I don't know what the law says about that."

"Oh, that is indeed a serious thing you ask. You know after the Wannsee Convention the order came down to exterminate all Jews. That was in January. If you kept them here you would be in violation of a number of laws."

"Oh, I didn't know," replied Josef. "They were such good workers, but I wouldn't want to do anything illegal."

"Hey, Rajmund, did you ever fancy one of these Jewish girls," asked Mentz. "Sometimes when I see them walking around the camp, with no clothes, it gets pretty tempting. I think the Wannsee gang of idiots should have said to exterminate all Jews except the pretty girls. What a waste of good flesh." Eberl and Mentz both laughed loudly. Josef laughed too in order to humor the officers. Rajmund kept his face turned away from the men to avoid revealing his disgust.

Mentz continued, "Think about it, Rajmund. Beautiful women walking around in front of you without a stitch of clothing. You are in complete control of their destiny. You could pull out a gun and shoot them in the head, and no one would say a word. You would be like a boy in a candy store, wouldn't you?"

Rajmund turned around to bring the appetizers to the table. "Yes sir, I suppose I would."

"Now those lunatics in Berlin want to kill all of them, including the beautiful women." Mentz lowered his voice. "You know, we let the guards have their way with the women but only if they execute the women afterward. That destroys the evidence and keeps them from making babies. I think every man should be able to keep about a dozen of these Jewish women for pleasure. Don't you think? Sterilize them so they can't make babies. What would be the harm in that?"

"I don't know, sir."

Mentz continued, "I'll tell you what, Rajmund. You come down to Treblinka, and I will give you a tour. You can see some of the girls I'm talking about."

Rajmund nodded. "Yes, sir."

Eberl took a shot of whiskey and set his glass on the table. "So, Josef, what are the names of the girls you are trying to find?"

"Sarah and Rachel Goldstein."

"When did you see them last?"

"They were staying with a family called the Biebersteins. They all disappeared around January."

Erbel nodded. "Biebersteins. Isn't that the rich Jewish family? He was a publisher who owned a number of other businesses, right?"

"Yes," replied Rajmund. "Do you know what happened to them? I heard they're in the ghetto, but I don't know for sure."

"I will see what I can find out," said Eberl. "I will also see if I can find the girls. If they are in the ghetto, it isn't likely I can find them. If they are at Treblinka, we can probably find them. There are probably several girls at Treblinka with those names, but there would be few who are sisters. If they are at Treblinka we'll find them. The name Rachel Goldstein rings a bell because a girl named Rachel Goldstein was killed at Treblinka a few months ago. She went crazy and grabbed an officer's gun and started shooting everyone. She killed four guards. I have no idea if that is the same Rachel Goldstein. I will do what I can to find out for you."

Later in the evening, as the men were preparing to leave, Mentz turned to Rajmund. "I'm serious. You come down to Treblinka, and I will show you some things that will start your motor. You're about seventeen. You're old enough. Right, Josef?"

Josef forced a laugh. "I don't know if any of us are ever old enough for that."

Mentz snorted. "You boys need to get out more. Have a good evening, gentlemen." Mentz held up his hand as if giving a Nazi salute. "Or as the prisoners say in Treblinka, 'Heil Shalom.'" Mentz and Eberl roared.

Josef shook his head and smiled. "Good night, gentlemen." He closed the door behind Eberl and Mentz.

After they were gone, Rajmund said, "I hope my disgust wasn't too obvious."

"I don't think so," replied Josef. "You should try harder to act amused by their jokes, though. I know it's difficult, but it's very important to find the Biebersteins and the girls so we can help them. Mentz and Eberl may be our only chance to find them."

"I have so much contempt for them. It's hard not to show it."

Josef nodded. "Maybe it is better that you not be around when I talk to them."

"No, I need to be part of this. I will try harder to humor them."

Sarah stumbled on the path as she tried to carry a heavy rock up a steep hill toward a truck partially loaded with rocks. She fell forward and instinctively let go of the rock to break her fall with her hands. The rock landed on her left foot, fracturing the first and second metatarsals. The thin leather shoe offered no protection. Sarah glanced back. A guard was looking at her but said nothing. Though the pain was excruciating, she dared not say anything lest she draw attention to herself. She kept her face turned away from the guard as she grimaced in pain. Slowly she reached down and picked up the heavy rock. She continued up the hill with the rock in her arms.

Sarah did not know how long she would be able to continue carrying the heavy rocks. She had heard that the rocks were being used in construction of Treblinka II, the death camp. As she worked, she imagined that the rocks secretly held bombs that would explode after the building was completed. She pictured cutting open the rocks and inserting bombs with timers that would not activate until the rocks were securely placed in the building's foundation and the structure was complete. Then she pictured the bombs exploding like the bombs that fell on Warsaw on September 1, 1939. While these thoughts distracted her from the horrible task, the only real comfort Sarah had as she carried the rocks up the hill was her faith that the God of Jacob was caring for her.

As the day wore on, Sarah felt that she would never have rest. Finally, when it became too dark to see, the prisoners were instructed to go to their sleeping quarters. They walked single file to the barracks and went inside. Sarah staggered to her bunk. She felt nauseated and dizzy. Her foot ached causing her to limp. She fell facedown onto the bunk and passed out. A short time later she felt someone shaking her gently. It was Olga. Olga sat on the edge of the bed and helped Sarah roll over and sit up on a pillow. She then gave Sarah a small bowl of broth and a piece of bread.

"I don't want it," Sarah said. "I don't want to be here anymore. I want to be with Rachel."

"It isn't time for you to be with Rachel," Olga said. "When Hashem wants you to be with Rachel, he will call you home. And it isn't for you to decide that it is time. He may have a master plan for you."

"But I don't want to go on without Rachel. First I lost my parents and now my sister. Rajmund is probably somewhere having fun with a Nazi girl at this very moment."

Olga held the bowl up to Sarah's lips. "Oh, don't talk like a *shlimazel.*"

Sarah took a sip of the potato broth. "But I am a shlimazel."

"How is your foot?" asked Olga. "I saw you drop the rock on it." Olga loosened the laces of Sarah's left shoe and slowly took it off. The foot was red and swollen.

"Ah," said Sarah softly as she tilted her head back, closed her eyes, and gritted her teeth.

"Oy vey," Olga said. "This doesn't look good. Are you going to be able to walk on it tomorrow? It looks broken. That bone is sticking way up. Let me see your other foot." Olga took off the right shoe and looked at both of the feet for comparison.

"I don't have a choice. If I don't work, I will just get in trouble."

"We could probably get you into the infirmary for a day."

"I don't trust that," replied Sarah. "I have heard what happens to some of the women in the infirmary. I will just have to put the weight on the heel of my foot like I did today."

"You can't do that until it heals. That could be weeks."

"If they find out I have a broken foot, they will just shoot me anyway."

Olga said, "I am going to get some water so you can soak your foot in it. Maybe that will help."

Olga walked over to the stove and picked up a bucket that was sitting on the floor next to it. She walked to the door of the barracks, opened it slightly and looked outside. Seeing no one she stepped out onto the ground and ran across the yard to the pump. She quickly filled the bucket with water and ran back into the barracks.

She brought the bucket over and set it on the floor next to the bunk. She laid Sarah back on the left side of the bunk. She took Sarah's left foot and placed it off the bed and in the bucket. She then lay down on the right side of the bunk next to Sarah. A few minutes later a guard stuck his head in the door and shouted, "Lights out." He turned off the lights and closed the door. Sarah fell asleep.

The following morning Sarah awakened. Her foot was so swollen she couldn't put on her shoe. "What am I going to do?" she asked Olga.

"We have to tell the guards that you can't work today. You can't walk on it like this, and you can't walk barefooted on those jagged rocks."

As they tried to decide what to do, a guard came in. Sarah, who was still looking at her foot, didn't see him come in. "Sarah," he said, "they are going to need you in the kitchen for a few days. They are shorthanded there. They need someone to be the potato peeler. You will have to sit all day, but you can get up and stretch if you need to."

Sarah looked up in disbelief to see the guard who saw her drop the rock on her foot. "Oh thank you so much," said Sarah as a tear formed in her eye.

The guard smiled and nodded. He whispered only loud enough for Olga and Sarah to hear. "Shalom, things will be better for you soon."

Sarah looked at Olga, who laughed. "See? You aren't a shlimazel." Sarah laughed too.

Sarah was escorted by the guard to the camp kitchen where the food was prepared. When they reached the building, the guard even held the door for her, something the guards never did for prisoners. They entered the kitchen, and the guard announced, "This is Sarah Goldstein. She injured her foot and is going to work in here for the time being. She will need to remain seated most of the time until her foot heals. A doctor will stop by later to look at her foot."

"Yes, sir," said an elderly woman who appeared to be in charge of the kitchen.

After the guard left the elderly woman looked at her and smiled. "You must be a very important person."

"Why?" asked Sarah.

"I was hoping you could tell me. You don't know what happened?"

"No, I hurt my foot yesterday, so they brought me here to work."

The elderly woman shook her head. "Do you think someone who hurts her foot really gets light duty? No, they get shot. Somehow you attracted the attention of camp commandant. He is the one who ordered you onto light duty." She walked over to Sarah. "My name is Ellen. And yes, I am a Jew too. I am in charge of the kitchen. We prepare the daily rations for the prisoners and also the food for the guards. I owned a restaurant before I was brought here, and they found out that I have a cooking talent."

"Why is the camp commandant interested in me?" asked Sarah.

"That is a good question," said Ellen. "Clearly it isn't because your sister killed four Nazi soldiers. There is something else going on."

"I don't understand," said Sarah.

"You don't need to. Just count your blessings. I would say there is probably someone powerful on the outside who is looking out for you."

Sarah remembered how the Biebersteins used to receive the anonymous packages with food and money. She remembered how the Biebersteins were allowed to move into a private apartment outside of the ghetto. She wondered if the Biebersteins might be responsible for her apparent good fortune, or maybe the person who helped the Biebersteins. Soon a doctor came in and examined Sarah's foot. Sarah was taken to the infirmary where she was given a warm bath and received surgery for her fracture. Her foot was placed in a cast, and she was instructed not to place weight on her foot. She was moved into the quarters where the prisoners who performed domestic chores lived. They were much nicer than the quarters where Sarah was staying previously. For the first time since arriving at Treblinka, Sarah went to sleep that night without feelings of terror.

In early August of 1942, Josef Litynski and his son, Rajmund, sat at a table in a back room of the Litynski restaurant with officers Irmfried Eberl and Willi Mentz. "You understand that this is highly irregular," said Eberl, clearly intoxicated. "That's why it has to be kept in the strictest confidence. I am doing this for you, Josef, because I like you, and you give us a place where we can enjoy a drink. You know the führer doesn't want us to drink. Just between you and me"—he lowered his voice—"the führer is a jackass." Eberl looked at Mentz and guffawed. Mentz nodded and smiled. Eberl leaned forward and put his arm around Josef. "You are a good man, Josef, and you are loyal to the Reich. I'll do this only because I consider you a friend."

"Thank you, and I appreciate that," Josef said. "Have you been able to confirm that the girls are in the camp?"

"They were at the Treblinka camp. It's a work camp about sixty kilometers from here," said Eberl.

"You said 'were.' Have they been taken somewhere else?" asked Josef.

Eberl drank a shot of Jägermeister. "I'm afraid I have some bad news. The girls were picked up for their own safety in January. They were walking around the streets of Warsaw, which is very dangerous for Jews. They told the SS they had no place to go, so they were taken to the Treblinka work camp where they were both doing well. Unfortunately, due to the stress of everything that has happened, Rachel became ill, mentally. She began saying crazy things, and she scared the other women at the work camp. One day she became completely deranged and grabbed an officer's gun and began shooting soldiers. They had no choice but to shoot her to stop her from shooting others. I'm sorry to say that Rachel was killed. Sarah is still alive at Treblinka."

"Can we pay for her release?"

Eberl laughed. "Why do you want her released? She's a Jew. If you want a pet, why don't you get a dog?"

"As I said when I first asked about the girls, they used to work for us. No one has ever done as much or worked as hard as Sarah and Rachel. That is why we want to get her back."

Eberl looked at Rajmund as if he suspected he wasn't hearing the truth. "As I said, this is highly irregular. I will arrange for her release, but we will need some money to pay for everything. We are going to have to pay some guards to keep their mouths shut."

"How much?" asked Josef.

"Twelve thousand reichsmarks, and this has to be kept in complete confidence. You can never tell anyone we did this. The money has to be in cash because there can be no traceable record that we ever did business."

Josef nodded. "I'll be back in a moment."

"You have our word. We will never tell anyone," Rajmund said.

"This girl must have been a good worker," said Eberl with a laugh.

"Yes, she was."

Eberl and Mentz each had another shot of Jägermeister.

"Well, make sure you don't make a baby with her, or this will get messy," said Mentz with a laugh.

A few minutes later Josef returned with a large leather bag. "There are four thousand reichsmarks in this bag. I'll have the rest tomorrow as soon as the bank opens."

Eberl took the bag and looked inside. "Okay, I know you're good for it. Do you know the village of Treblinka? It is just a few kilometers from the Treblinka camps."

"Yes, I know the village."

"Be there tomorrow night at ten o'clock sharp. When you get to the village, there will be a staff car parked along the left side of the road facing toward you. Park on the opposite side of the road. The driver will open the door and let Sarah out, and you will give him the bag with the rest of the money."

"I understand."

Eberl and Mentz stood up to leave. Mentz picked up the bag. "It was good seeing you again, Josef," he said.

"You too," said Josef.

The following night Josef and Rajmund drove a delivery truck to the village of Treblinka. On the seat next to Josef was a leather bag with the rest of the money. There were two loaded rifles on the floor of the truck. "Do you think we'll have trouble?" Rajmund asked.

Josef replied, "We haven't known Eberl and Mentz very long, and according to the SS men who come into the restaurant, they are as mean as they come. I would say anything is possible. We don't even know if Sarah is alive. If she is, they'll probably deliver her, but if not, then they'll just take the money and go. They know we can't do anything about it."

They drove on silently until they reached Treblinka village. As promised, there was a staff car parked along the left side of the road. Josef pulled off to the right side as instructed. He stopped the truck and opened his door. "Stay in the truck," he told Rajmund. "If they do anything to me, use the guns and get away."

Josef stepped down out of the truck, pulled the leather bag with him, and closed the door. Rajmund picked up one of the rifles and laid it across his lap. The staff car door opened and an SS officer stepped out. He crossed the street and took the bag from Josef without saying anything. He turned around, walked back across the street, and threw it into the front of the staff car. Then he opened the rear door and said, "Get out."

Rajmund leaned forward for a better view. Slowly a human figure in a dress climbed out of the car, but it was too dark for Rajmund to see who it was. The driver climbed back into the staff car and drove away, leaving the passenger standing in the middle of the road. Rajmund jumped out of the truck and ran around the front. He saw a thin figure of a teenage girl whom he barely recognized as Sarah. She was wearing a cast on her left foot.

"Sarah," said Rajmund.

"Rajmund," she said. She reached her arms out to him then fell forward and nearly collapsed in the middle of the road. Rajmund caught her, and he and Josef helped her to the truck and placed her inside. She leaned against Rajmund who held her in his arms. "Rajmund, I thought I would never see you again. How did you find me?"

"The Treblinka camp commanders started coming into our restaurant about two months ago. They found out we had a back room where they could drink in private, so they started coming in all the time. We got to know them, and one day we asked if they would try to find you. They said they would check the records and came back and said you were at the camp, but not Rachel."

"What were their names?" asked Sarah.

"Eberl and Mentz."

"Oh, they're horrible. You have to stay away from them."

"Why?" asked Josef.

Sarah leaned forward. "They murder Jews by the hundreds every day. The bodies are piled up in front of the camp until they haul them away in trucks."

"Are you hungry?" Rajmund asked, trying to distract Sarah from the horrors of the camp.

"Yes."

Rajmund reached into a bag on the floor and pulled out a sandwich and bottle of milk. "Here. We brought this for you."

"Thank you." Sarah took the sandwich and milk and began to eat slowly.

"We need to take her to the hospital," Rajmund said.

"We can't," replied Josef. "What hospital could we take her to? The doctors would call the SS, and they would send her right back to Treblinka. Remember, we can't tell anyone where she came from. Eberl and Mentz would get into a lot of trouble, and so would we. As much as I despise them, they did help us. And they helped Sarah."

Rajmund said, "Sarah, we are going to take you to our truck repair shop. There is an apartment in the rear of the garage. The Nazis are there all the time bringing in their military vehicles for repairs. For that reason, no one would ever suspect that we would be hiding a Jew there. It's the perfect place. It's a nice little apartment. We had some papers made up for you. You need to put them somewhere safe so you can get to them if a Nazi ever sees you. You shouldn't go out at all, but if you do, you need to take those papers with you. From now on you will be Katherine Siefert. That's what your papers say. You were born in Poland in 1928, and your parents were killed in the first bombing. Your father's family was from Munich, and they moved to Poland when he was three. Your mother's maiden name was Zebro. She was born and raised in Poland. Can you remember all of that?"

"I'll learn all of that, but I won't be going anywhere outside of the apartment."

"Yes, that is just in case someone ever finds you back there," Rajmund said. "What happened to Rachel?"

"They killed her," replied Sarah looking blankly into the dark outside of the truck.

Rajmund said, "The Germans told us that she went crazy and grabbed one of the officer's guns and started shooting soldiers."

"Is that what they told you? It's true, but she didn't go crazy. They were going to kill her anyway."

"Why were they going to kill her?" Josef asked.

Sarah raised her head and looked at him. "That is what they do at Treblinka. They kill people. There are two camps. One is called Treblinka I. That's a work camp. That is where Sarah and I were. The other is called Treblinka II. It's about two kilometers away. Treblinka II is an extermination camp. They're still building it, but they're already exterminating Jews there."

Rajmund nodded. "That's what we thought, but the Nazis deny it. If you were in Treblinka I, why did they kill Rachel?"

"They kill people all the time in Treblinka I, but mostly it's a work camp. Treblinka II is nothing but an extermination camp. They killed Rachel because they were going to use her for the game."

"What game?"

"Target practice. They make people run naked in a big field, and the soldiers take turns shooting at them. They were going to make Rachel run, but she grabbed the officer's gun and started shooting the soldiers. She killed three in addition to the officer whose gun she took."

"Those Nazis are scum," Rajmund said.

"Whatever happened to the Biebersteins?" Sarah asked.

Josef shook his head. "We don't know. We've been trying to find them, but so far we haven't been able to. We don't know if they're in the ghetto or at a camp somewhere."

"We'll find them," Rajmund said.

The truck arrived at the Litynski repair shop about an hour later. Josef got out and opened a garage door. He got back into the truck and drove into the garage. The overhead lights were on. There were twenty bays, each of them with a military truck or tank.

Sarah looked at the swastika on the door of the trucks. Rajmund and Josef opened their doors and got out. As Sarah moved toward the passenger door, she asked, "What's this place? Whose trucks are these?"

"This is our garage. We repair trucks," replied Rajmund.

"But these are Nazi trucks. Why are you helping the Nazis?"

Rajmund helped Sarah out of the truck. "I know it's confusing. If we don't repair their trucks, someone else will. By repairing their trucks and serving them in the restaurant, we're able to obtain much important information, and we receive favors. That's how we were able to get you out of Treblinka."

Sarah looked at Rajmund with a blank expression. "I don't understand," she whispered.

"That's how we're going to help the Biebersteins, once we find out where they are," said Rajmund sadly.

Sarah limped into the apartment with Rajmund's assistance. "Once you find them, how will you help them? Who can stand against the Nazis?"

"We will," Rajmund said. "We will stand against the Nazis."

On August 26, 1942, shortly after Sarah's release, Eberl was dismissed as the commandant of Treblinka. The purported reason was that he was not efficient in exterminating the Jews and that he was allowing bodies to decompose in open air, which caused an odor that was offensive to those living in the nearby village of Treblinka. Josef and Rajmund suspected that the real reason for the dismissal was that he was accused of releasing a prisoner in violation of the order to exterminate all Jews. They were surprised to learn that the person whose accusations resulted in Eberl's dismissal was Mentz. Eberl was replaced by SS Officer Franz Stangl, who soon became known as the White Death.

CHAPTER

22

B Y THE FALL of 1942, the large ghetto was suffering a serious shortage of food. Jews were rounded up on a daily basis for concentration and extermination. Working-age Jewish men and women were taken to Treblinka I, which meant that they might be able to work for a while, but the elderly and children too young for work were taken to Treblinka II for immediate extermination. Often the apartment buildings were raided, and entire families were taken. On other occasions, just the children were taken. The community was always told that the adults taken were going to work camps where they would be well fed and cared for, and the children were going to schools where they would study and receive care. The people wanted to believe it, but they knew that many were being taken to extermination camps. They often talked about the ovens in Treblinka II where the Jews were exterminated.

By October the food rations had nearly terminated. People were living on less than a hundred calories per day. There simply was no way to get food. There was no place to grow crops, and no meat was available. Some local merchants were selling something called meat but they did not say what kind of meat it was. The Biebersteins refused to buy it because they believed it was human flesh. People needed every food voucher to obtain the desperately needed food. Dental work was now a necessity that few could afford. The Biebersteins had not received one of the anonymous gift packages for over a year, and they were now starving like everyone else. The ghetto had become the city of death. The Biebersteins survived only on the rations and the small amount of food they could buy from Grandpa's limited dental practice. For reasons unexplained, Cass lost his position working at the gun factory. He was simply told he was no longer needed.

On a chilly morning in October, the SS came through with trucks, rounding up children between the ages of four and twelve years. Although no one said it, everyone knew they were being taken for extermination. Since they were too young to work, they had no value to society. The Nazis had kept meticulous records and knew the names and ages of everyone in the ghetto and where they lived. Cass was just under the age of twelve.

Wearing only a pair of torn boxer under shorts and a T-shirt, Cass was herded into the street with the other children. They were told to stand against a wall and form a row facing their other family members, who were standing on the sidewalk across the street. Cass could see his mother and his brother on the sidewalk looking at him. His mother was fighting to hold back her tears. Notwithstanding his previous displays of valor, knowing that he was going to his death with his mother watching was too much to bear, and Cass began to cry. Then he thought of Ari and what Ari would do in this situation. Ari would try to end his mother's pain. In this effort, Cass thought he might show humor, so he shouted, "Hey, Mom, Thaddeus, why are you two looking so sad? I'm the one going to Treblinka."

Cass's statement was more than she could bear, and Irena fell to her knees crying bitterly. Thaddeus knelt next to her in an effort to comfort her. Cass immediately realized that his attempt at humor was unsuccessful. "I was only joking, Mama," he called. All the children in the line with Cass were crying. Cass wondered why he was being taken. He had been discharged from his job at the gun factory several months earlier. Maybe they had decided to exterminate him, he thought.

As Cass watched his mother, he noticed a German soldier in a military trench coat walk up the street and stop next to Irena, who was still kneeling on the ground with Thaddeus. The soldier looked up the street one direction then the other. He then reached down and took ahold of Irena's arm and helped her to her feet. He then stood talking to Irena and Thaddeus for a few minutes. As Cass watched, Irena pointed in his direction. They appeared to be exchanging something, though Cass could not see what it was. Eventually, the soldier turned toward him. It was Sergeant Arnold Schultz. He remembered how Schultz had helped them when they were moving into their apartment, and again when they were moving into the ghetto.

Schultz walked over to Cass and stood in front of him while facing Irena on the sidewalk. He again looked up the street in one direction then looked in the other direction. He instructed and motioned for the children to step forward. When they did he turned and tapped Cass on the back of the head. "Run," he said softly. Cass did not think he heard correctly and did not move. Schultz quickly looked once again in both directions. "Run back to your apartment. Quickly."

Finally Cass realized he was being rescued. He ran quickly across the street and into the front door of the apartment building that Irena was holding open for him. He ran up the steps to the Bieberstein apartment. Thaddeus and Irena followed him up the three flights of stairs and they ran into the front door of the apartment. Irena closed and locked the front door, and Cass lifted the trapdoor to the compartment where the guns were kept. He jumped down into the compartment and pulled the trapdoor shut above him.

Irena opened the trapdoor slightly. "Stay down there and be really quiet. We will tell you when it is safe to come out." She pulled a rug over the trapdoor then pulled the table over the rug. A few minutes later there was a knock at the front door. Everyone remained silent, and no one opened the door. They could hear the voices of German soldiers going from apartment to apartment looking for more children.

After several minutes Irena finally decided to open the door.

The German officer said, "We are looking for a boy under twelve years of age. We counted, several times, the children who were ready to be transported to the...to the school. There were twenty-seven of them, sixteen girls and eleven boys. Now there are only twenty-six. There is a boy missing. Is there a boy hiding in here?"

"No one is hiding in here," Irena replied.

Hiding in the hidden compartment under the floor, Cass silently took bullets from the metal box that held ammunition and loaded the guns.

He decided that if he was going to die, he would take as many Nazis with him as he could. He remained for nearly an hour in total silence waiting for the trapdoor above him to open and reveal the face of a Nazi. He could hear their boots pounding on the floor as they talked and laughed while searching the apartment. He could hear them talking to his mother. A young officer decided to sit in the Bieberstein apartment while the soldiers searched the building. Taken by Irena's beauty, he began flirting with her. "I wouldn't have any problem with Jewish women if they were all as pretty as you," he said.

Irena forced a laugh. "Oh, you would get tired of me and move on to another girl."

"You? I would never grow tired of you."

The conversation continued. The officer asked Irena questions about her family and who lived there with her.

"It is just my parents, my son, Thaddeus, and me."

"Our records show that you have another son living here. Casimir. He used to work at the gun factory, but they discharged him a few months ago."

Irena nodded. "Yes, Cass got diphtheria and died several weeks ago."

The officer looked at Irena as if trying to discern if she was telling the truth. Finally he looked at the rug under the table and asked, "What's under that rug? Is there a trapdoor under there?"

Irene laughed. "Yes, we hide little Jewish children under the table."

The officer laughed. "Nothing surprises us anymore, so I had to ask."

Standing to his feet, the officer said, "If you see a little boy hiding anywhere, please let us know."

"I will."

The officer walked to the door and said, "Good day, Fraulein."

"Oh, but you forgot, I am married," replied Irena with a laugh.

The officer smiled. "Well then, good day, Frau Bieberstein."

"Good day."

When Irena finally opened the trapdoor, Cass climbed out of the hidden compartment and began looking around the room. He looked at the closed door as if waiting for someone to burst in.

Irena said, "Cass, you can't be seen in the neighborhood now. The Nazis think they have taken away all of the children except one, who escaped. You'll have to stay inside all the time now."

Irena, Cass, Thaddeus, Grandma, and Grandpa sat quietly in the living room for most of the afternoon. They all knew they had come very close to losing Cass. From that day forward, Cass stayed inside most of the time. He would often go out at night with Thaddeus, when he could hide in the shadows, yet knowing that he could be shot on sight for being out after dark. Later he began going out in the day again. He refused to allow himself to be contained in the apartment all of the time.

CHAPTER
23

I N THE FALL of 1942, Cass and Thaddeus officially joined a Jewish Resistance organization known as Zydowska Organizacja Bojowa, founded by a twenty-year-old man named Mordecai Anielewicz. Cass and Thaddeus made a new friend, Yitzhak Weis, also a Jewish boy in the organization. Yitzhak was fifteen years old and met Thaddeus near the apartment where they lived. Like most of the children in the ghetto, he was underweight due to the lack of food. His clothes were ragged and torn, and he wore a gray beret that tilted to the left on his head. His hair was long and unkempt. He was angry about the recent escalation of Nazi activity in the ghetto, and he was ready for a fight.

Early one morning in November, Cass, Thaddeus, and Yitzhak were sitting at the side of Franciszkanska Street. They were hungry and weak. They had been walking the neighborhood, looking unsuccessfully for food. There were many Jews voluntarily walking toward the railroad they had been told would transport them to the work farm. In the center of the street was a long rope, rolled up. One end was hooked to a metal pole cemented into the middle of the street. The other end had a small hook attached to it. On the opposite side of the pole was another rope rolled up, also attached to the pole on one end with a hook on the other end. Each rope was approximately forty feet long. As they sat at the side of the street, Thaddeus asked, "What are those ropes for?"

"They use that to rope off the street at night," replied Yitzhak. "See the hook on the end of the rope? That is attached to the building on that side of the street. The rope on the other side of the pole is hooked to the building on this side of the street. No one is to go past the ropes when they are up."

In front of the pole was a motorcycle with a sidecar, facing away from the pole. People were crossing back and forth in the street by the pole, walking behind the motorcycle. On the motorcycle was a soldier in a long trench coat; sitting in the sidecar was an officer also in a long trench coat. They were facing the opposite direction from the pole watching the people walk up the street toward the railroad station. As they looked at the men on the motorcycle and the curled up ropes, Cass suddenly laughed.

"What are you laughing at?" asked Thaddeus.

Cass did not reply. Instead he suddenly jumped to his feet. Large groups of people were crossing the street in both directions. Cass walked behind one of the groups and was crossing with them. When he reached the center of the street he suddenly stopped and picked up the hook end of the rope that was attached to the pole, and quietly hooked the rope to the belt of the motorcycle driver's trench coat. The driver was unaware. The rest of the rope remained rolled up on the ground.

A man crossing the street saw Cass hook the rope to the belt. He looked at the rope and saw that it was hooked to the pole and that the other end was hooked to the back of the driver by his belt. He smiled slightly, shook his head, and ran away as if he was concerned he would be accused. Cass ran back across the street and sat down next to Thaddeus.

"You didn't do that," Thaddeus said with a laugh.

"Yes, I did."

"Why did you do that? What's going to happen?" asked Yitzhak.

Cass did not reply.

The boys continued to sit at the side of the street watching the men on the motorcycle. As people crossed, once in a while a person would notice the rope hooked to the belt but assumed it had some legitimate purpose and said nothing. Others would laugh. After about forty-five minutes, the officer in the sidecar said something then pointed with his right hand in front of the motorcycle. The driver started the motorcycle and placed it in gear. Upon hearing the motorcycle start, people in the street in front of the motorcycle began to clear a path to allow it to pass.

"Uh-oh," said Thaddeus. "Get ready to run."

The motorcycle driver released the clutch as the road ahead cleared, and the motorcycle jerked forward, quickly reaching a speed of nearly twenty miles per hour. Suddenly, the motorcycle reached the end of the rope, and the driver was jerked backward off the motorcycle by his belt. By the time he landed on the pavement with a thud, the motorcycle had traveled another twenty feet. The front wheel of the motorcycle turned to the left, and the contraption begin spinning in circles in the middle of the street. The officer attempted to stand up in the sidecar to reach the throttle and brake on the handlebar, but lost his balance and fell backward onto the pavement, only to be run over several times by the spinning motorcycle, which eventually straightened its direction and crashed into the building on the opposite side of the street.

Cass, Thaddeus, and Yitzhak burst into laughter as they jumped to their feet and ran around the corner of the building into an alley. They stopped and watched from around the building. The driver who had been jerked off the back of the motorcycle sat up with a groan as he reached behind himself and discovered the rope hooked to his belt. He looked up and down the street in an effort to see who had played such a prank on him.

The officer lay in the street, having sustained more serious injuries than the driver. In obvious pain the driver got to his feet and walked over to the officer, who was slowly beginning to move. Meanwhile, Jews had gathered on both sides of the street to watch this strange sight. Some were laughing quietly, but most quickly left the scene to make sure that they were not mistakenly believed to have been the pranksters who hooked the rope to the driver's belt.

The boys watched from the alley as an ambulance came to pick up the officer who had been run over by the motorcycle. Though slightly damaged, the motorcycle was still drivable, so the driver left on the motorcycle once the officer had been taken away by ambulance. A short time later approximately twenty troops came in the area, on foot, and began shooting at people on the street. Much to their surprise, they were met with return fire from members of the Resistance, who had managed to obtain weapons. In a short time, the German soldiers retreated.

The boys went back to the Bieberstein apartment where they told the family what had happened. They said that they would have participated in the return fire on the Germans but did not have their weapons with them. Grandpa said, "The Resistance is going to have to get serious now. Schultz said that this is what Hitler calls the Final Solution. The Nazis are planning to come into the ghetto and round up everyone for extermination. Yesterday, I asked him to visit Josef Litynski to see if there is anything he can do to help us. If we can't get out of the ghetto now, it will be too late. He said he would try."

"That's great news. I sure hope they can do something to help us get out of here," Grandma said.

The following day, Ari and Yitzhak brought over two potatoes for the family. Irena divided the potatoes carefully to make the pieces as equal as possible, then she gave herself a tiny piece that was left.

"Mama, you need to eat more than that," said Cass.

"I'm fine," she replied. Cass did not believe her but also did not believe he could convince her otherwise.

Just as they finished eating, there was a knock at the door. Everyone looked at one another for a moment. Irena placed her left hand on the doorknob, and with her right hand, she unlocked the door and slowly opened it.

"Hello, Mrs. Bieberstein," Sergeant Schultz said. "May I come in?"

Grandpa rose and walked to the door. "Arnold, come in, please."

Sergeant Schultz entered the room quickly and put his hat on the table. "I have some good news," he said. "I spoke with Mr. Litynski. He is going to help."

"Oh, thank you, thank you," Grandpa said. "Thanks to Hashem. How can he help?"

Arnold continued, "Mr. Litynski was thrilled to hear that you're okay. He wanted me to let you know that Sarah is okay. She's living with them."

"What about Rachel?" Thaddeus asked.

Schultz shook his head. "She didn't make it. She was going to be executed in the Treblinka work camp, but she grabbed an officer's gun from his holster and killed three or four German soldiers before they shot her."

Thaddeus put his hand to his forehead and whispered, "Oh no." Everyone was silent for a time.

Finally Schultz said, "Mr. Litynski wondered why you didn't contact him earlier. He said they have been looking for you all this time."

"It never occurred to us he could help us in here," Grandma said. "We thought of contacting him for the first time when we learned about Hitler's Final Solution for the Jews in the ghetto."

Schultz nodded. "Let me tell you the plan. Mr. Litynski's going to say he needs laborers for his business. He will say he needs them to help clean in the restaurant and in his garage. Because these are low-skilled labor jobs, anyone will be able to do the task. He has been given permission to take five Jews per day from the ghetto then bring them back at the end of the day. He'll be here tomorrow, only instead of taking five, he will take seven. He has constructed tool compartments on each side of the truck where two of you will hide. He'll take the truck to the garage where the hiding passengers will get out and go into the apartment behind the garage. In the evening, he'll bring the five workers back. The following day he'll take five more plus an additional two hidden passengers, and the same the day after that. Within three days you'll all be out of here."

The Biebersteins looked at one another in disbelief. How could it be that they could actually get out of the ghetto so easily and so quickly? "Thank you so much, Arnold," said Irena. "You have saved our lives."

"I did what any good person would do," he replied. "Be ready tomorrow morning at seven o'clock. Two of you can leave. The truck will come around the back of this building into the alley. On each side of the truck is a large toolbox with a fake floor. One of you will crawl into the toolbox on one side and one of you will crawl into the toolbox on the other side. Then the fake floor will be lowered on top of you and the tools will be placed on the fake floor. The Litynskis are trusted so no one will stop to inspect the toolboxes. The truck will then come around to the front of the building and will pick up five Jews who will ride in the back of the truck. The toolboxes will be locked after you are in, and if anyone asks to inspect them, Mr. Litynski will say he left his key at the garage."

Everyone stood looking at Sergeant Schultz in excited disbelief. "Can this be true?" Grandpa asked.

"Yes, it's true. Tonight you must decide who will go first."

After Schultz left, Grandma looked at Grandpa and their grandchildren. "Cass, you and Thaddeus have to go first. You are the youngest. You have the longest lives ahead of you. The Nazis are coming any day. We need to get you boys out first."

"No," Cass said. "I'm not leaving until the last Jew is gone. There's an uprising coming, and I am going to be part of it."

Thaddeus said, "I'm not staying here. I want to get out as fast as I can."

Irena said, "Cass, they are killing Jews every day. We can all get out safely. It won't do any good for you to stay in the ghetto and die. You can fight from outside of the ghetto."

Cass protested, "But the fight is here in the ghetto. This is where the Jews are. I trained for this for years. This is all that matters to me now. I have to stay here and fight. I am not leaving as long as there is a Jew alive in the ghetto."

Irena shook her head. "No, Cass. You can't stay. If you don't get out now, you might not ever get out. Don't you remember how scared you were just two days ago when you were going to Treblinka?"

"I wasn't scared at all. I was ready to die if it came to that. I had all the guns loaded, and I was ready to come out shooting. It will be okay, Mama. I'll get out, but I'm going to fight as long as I can."

Finally Ari said, "He can stay with me. We'll take care of him. We really could use someone with his skills."

Grandpa listened to the argument. Finally he said, "Irena, these are times like we have never seen before. This is the worst time in Jewish history. Even under Rome we didn't suffer the way we are suffering today. Ordinarily, I would agree with everything you are saying. But in these times, I think Cass needs to make his own decision about what he is going to do. Even if we are all able to get out, how long will it be before we are identified as Jews and taken to some other prison to be exterminated? Cass is doing what he believes God has called him to do. You have to let him go, Irena."

Irena began to cry. "I can't. He's my baby."

Grandma put her arms around Irena. "Papa is right," she said. "No one is safe anywhere. Unless something is done, we're all going to die anyway. You might as well let him take his last chance trying to right the wrong."

At last Irena nodded. "Okay, you and Papa get out first in the truck tomorrow. I'll come the next day with Thaddeus." She looked at Cass. "I don't want you to do this."

"I'll be okay, Mama. It is what I want to do. This is why I live."

"Okay, I know I can't stop you, but you are still a child to me. You are only eleven years old."

"We'll take good care of him," Ari promised. "I'll watch out for him like he's my own little brother."

Irena nodded silently.

The following morning at seven o'clock there was a knock at the door. Cass opened the door to see Sergeant Schultz and Rajmund. "Rajmund," he said excitedly.

"Cass, you're still alive."

Irena came to the door. "Rajmund, it's so good to see you."

Rajmund and Sergeant Schultz came into the apartment. Rajmund hugged Thaddeus. "Thad, I didn't think I would ever see you again. Sergeant Schultz found us and told us where you were. We came up with this plan to get you out, but we can only take out two of you each day."

"We talked about that," said Irena. "Grandma and Grandpa are going to go with you first."

"Okay," replied Rajmund as he motioned for them to follow. "Papa is downstairs with the truck. He's behind the building. Follow me."

Grandpa and Grandma followed Rajmund and Schultz out the door and down the steps to the rear of the building. There they saw the truck. Rajmund opened up a cover of a toolbox that was mounted on the right side of the truck. He motioned for Grandma to get in. She complied. Once she was in the truck, he told her to lie flat on her back. He lowered the fake floor in place above her. He then retrieved tools from the bed of the truck and placed them on top of the fake floor.

After Grandma was securely in place Rajmund walked around to the other side of the truck and assisted Grandpa in getting into the toolbox. He placed the fake floor above him as he had with Grandma and filled the toolbox with tools. Once they were securely in place he climbed into the truck where Mr. Litynski was seated behind the steering wheel. Schultz climbed in next to Rajmund. Mr. Litynski started the truck and drove around to the front of the building where five laborers climbed into the back of the truck. They drove toward the front gate of the ghetto. As Schultz had promised, they were not stopped or questioned by anyone as they left the ghetto.

At the Litynski garage, Josef pulled the truck inside. Rajmund got out and closed the door behind him. Josef opened the back of the truck and asked the Jews to get out and follow him. He took them into a cafeteria area of the garage and closed the door behind them. Once Rajmund was sure they were all in the cafeteria, he opened the toolboxes and helped Grandma and Grandpa out. As they stood and looked around the garage, Grandma began to cry. "You have saved us," she said to Rajmund.

Rajmund said, "Follow me."

Grandma and Grandpa followed him to the apartment in the back of the garage. When he opened the door they saw Sarah sitting at a table. She stood up and looked at them, began to cry softly, and then said, "Oh." They went to her, and she hugged both of them simultaneously. Rajmund stood silently next to them for a while.

The following morning, Cass quietly helped Rajmund place the fake floor of the toolbox above his mother who was lying in the bottom of the box. She reached up and took ahold of his wrist. "Live for me," she whispered.

"I will, Mama," he said softly as he lowered the floor above her. "I will survive."

She let go of his wrist. "I love you, Cass."

Cass and Rajmund quietly placed the tools on the fake floor above Irena. They then walked around and looked at Thaddeus, who was lying in the bottom of the toolbox on the other side of the truck. "I have to admit I am going to miss your pranks," he said.

Cass laughed, "Don't worry, I don't have a rope hooked to your butt."

"I'm glad about that," Thaddeus replied as they lowered the fake floor down on him.

After placing the tools on top of the fake floor, Rajmund looked at Cass and asked, "Are you sure you don't want me to come back for you tomorrow? You don't have to stay here."

"Yes, I do," Cass replied. "This is why I live."

Rajmund nodded, then laughed. "Well, maybe in a few weeks we can go Nazi hunting together. If you change your mind, just tell Sergeant Schultz, and I'll come and get you out."

CHAPTER

24

ON JANUARY 18, 1943, the Nazis began rounding up the fifty thousand Jews remaining in the ghetto, reportedly to take them to a labor camp in the Lublin district of the General Government. Many of the Jews, however, believed that they were going to Treblinka for extermination. Others knew this to be true. The following day, Cass, Ari, and Yitzhak crouched on the roof of a four-story building on Zomenhof Street, accompanied by several hundred Jewish men and boys situated on rooftops and in buildings around the neighborhood. Below them was a large group of Jews voluntarily walking toward the railroad station under the belief that they would be given an opportunity to work in a factory.

Watching the German soldiers approach, Cass wondered how many could be killed before they returned fire on the Resistance. The soldiers walked toward them on the street below in single file as the Jews walked in the opposite direction on either side of them. To Cass seemed like lambs walking to the slaughter. "This is it," he said quietly.

"Shh," Ari nodded and put his finger to his own lips, reminding Cass to whisper. "Are you okay?"

Cass nodded. "I'm ready for this."

Suddenly a shot rang out. Cass looked at a young boy on a nearby rooftop who seemed puzzled that his gun had discharged. The German soldiers began looking around to see where the shot had originated. Cass yelled, "Up here, dummkopfs!"

An officer shouted, "Who's shooting?"

Cass aimed his rifle at the officer. "I am."

The officer heard the shout and looked up at Cass for only a brief moment before Cass pulled the trigger, shooting him squarely in the face. The stunned German soldiers were caught completely off guard.

Many of the Jews who had been walking did not know what to do so they crouched down in the street to avoid flying bullets. Some began to run for cover. It was pandemonium in the streets. The Germans attempted to fire back but were overwhelmed by the surprise. Anielewicz and a group of Resistance fighters rushed out of buildings and into the street and opened fire on the German soldiers. This was the first time the Germans had seen the Jews in the ghetto fight back with such force; at first they did not even realize they were Jews.

Right below them on the sidewalk, Cass saw a dozen German soldiers trying to hide behind a steel plate they had lifted from the street. They crouched behind the plate to avoid the barrage of bullets flying through the air. Cass grabbed a pint whiskey bottle filled with petrol, a kerosene-saturated piece of cloth protruding from the top. He lit the cloth with a Zippo lighter Ari had given him and threw the bottle at the men hiding behind the plate. The cloth blew out while hurtling toward the men. The whiskey bottle hit the top of the metal plate and broke spewing petrol on the soldiers who looked around as if puzzled by what had saturated them. Ari picked up a gallon whisky jug filled with petrol, ignited the cloth protruding from the top, and heaved it with both hands directly down at the soldiers behind the steel plate. The jug exploded covering them with burning petrol. The soldiers began screaming and running, and some rolled on the ground to put out the flames to no avail as they burned to death. Yitzhak aimed his rifled at one of them.

"Don't shoot him," Ari said.

"But he's suffering," Yitzhak protested.

"We can't afford to waste the ammo."

257

Cass looked at the soldiers screaming in pain, but he knew Ari was right. As harsh as it was, these men were already dead. The bullets needed to be saved for those capable of fighting in the future. Across the street was a German soldier hiding behind a wagon, firing on unarmed Jews who were running for cover. Ari quickly aimed his rifle and shot the soldier in the torso. Before he hit the ground, Cass and Yitzhak both shot him as well. As he lay motionless, people ran over and began kicking him; others tried to assist those he had shot.

That day, the Resistance fighters suffered heavy losses, as did the German soldiers. After a lengthy battle in the streets, with the Jews maintaining an upper hand, the Nazis ran up the street to retreat from the assailants. The Resistance did not relent but instead shot as quickly and accurately as possible to kill as many retreating Nazis as they could. After the soldiers were gone the Jews ran into the street dancing and shouting. They discovered numerous soldiers lying in the street. Those still living were abruptly eliminated with a single shot to the head. For the Resistance, this was their first victory against the Nazis. They collected the weapons and ammunition and celebrated with vigor, notwithstanding their own heavy losses. Perhaps overcome by confidence, they saw this as a turning point in the war with the Germans. They took the weapons from the dead soldiers and piled their bodies in the street to block the Germans who would arrive in the morning.

The Resistance fighters went to sleep early that night anticipating an early morning German assault. They awakened before dawn and took their posts on the streets. Cass, Ari, and Yitzhak went back over to Zomenhof Street to join Zuckerman's fighters there. Zuckerman and his team had been fighting on the Aryan side of the wall but slipped into the ghetto through the sewers. They took positions in the buildings and on the rooftops. As anticipated, shortly after sunrise, a large army of soldiers in trucks and on foot entered the ghetto and made their way toward the area of the altercation the day before. Everything remained quiet as the German soldiers set up strategic locations where they sought to overcome the Resistance fighters. Unbeknownst to the soldiers, Resistance fighters were hiding in the buildings and on the roofs directly above the soldiers. Thus, the soldiers were surrounded by a smaller number of Resistance fighters who had set them up for an ambush.

When the signal was given, the Resistance fighters opened fire on the soldiers in the streets below. It was a brutal ambush, and the Germans quickly retreated in an effort to escape the fire. Cass, Ari, and Yitzhak ran into the street with other fighters and chased the German soldiers for several blocks as they fled the ghetto. Once again, the Germans suffered many losses and the Resistance fighters lost far fewer than the day before. That night they slept in a building at the intersection of Zomenhof and Mila Streets, where they had built a bunker. This would be their stronghold for the duration of this uprising.

Zuckerman and Anielewicz sat near a stove in a building where they had decided to spend the night. Around them were two dozen Resistance fighters, including Cass, Ari, and Yitzhak. Zuckerman looked around the room at each of the fighters. He opened a duffel bag and took out a couple of loaves of bread. He broke off a piece of bread then passed it to those on each side of him. "Everyone break off a piece of bread. I took this off one of the Krauts we shot. I don't know if Nazi food is kosher, but it is all we have."

The group chuckled. Cass was surprised to hear a woman's voice.

Zuckerman said, "I don't know why he was running around with bread, but I am happy he was."

An elderly man said, "I didn't know we had women with us. How many women do we have?"

A woman said, "Obviously, I am."

"Me too," said a second.

"And me," said a third.

The room fell silent. Eventually the elderly man asked, "How old are you girls, and what are your names?"

"Twenty-three. My name is Helena."

"Seventeen. I am Golda."

"I am fourteen. My name is Hadassah."

Anielewicz said, "I'm honored. Thank you, ladies, for fighting with us. Where are your families?"

Hadassah replied, "Mine are gone. They left on the train."

"Why didn't you go?" asked Ari.

"They were taken when I was not in our flat. Our neighbors told me."

Ari nodded. "How about you, Golda?"

"Mine are still living here in the ghetto."

"Mine left on the train too," Helena said.

Ari passed the bread to Cass who broke off a small piece.

"Take more than that," said Anielewicz. "We don't know how long we are going to be holed up here."

Cass broke off a second small piece of bread then passed it on to Yitzhak.

"How are you fellows doing?" Ari asked Cass and Yitzhak.

Cass nodded.

"I'm okay," replied Yitzhak. He passed a bottle of gun oil to Cass along with a piece of string and cloth. Cass tore off a piece of the cloth and tied the string around it. He then put gun oil on the cloth and pushed into the barrel of his rifle with a metal ramrod from an old flintlock rifle. He pulled the cloth through the barrel then pushed it in several times. He then took the cloth, put more oil on it, wiped the outside of the barrel, and then wiped the stock. He then passed the string, oil, and ramrod to the person next to him who used it to clean his rifle.

"You're pretty young," Helena said, looking at Cass. "How old are you?"

"I'll be twelve in March," Cass said as he took a bite of his bread.

"You're even younger than me," said Hadassah. "Where's your family?"

"My father left Poland in 1939 to go to America. He was planning to bring us over once he got settled, but because of the war, he couldn't get us out."

"What about your mom?" asked Helena.

"My grandparents, my mother, and my brother all got out of the ghetto a few months ago."

"How did they get out? Why didn't you go?" Hadassah asked.

Ari replied, "Cass didn't go because he wanted to stay and fight Nazis. Cass shouldn't go into detail about how they got out. If any of us got captured, the Germans could torture us to find out information."

"Wow, you chose to stay in the ghetto and fight? That's amazing," said Helena. "I wish more people were like you. We would have a huge army."

The following morning everyone awakened to shouting voices. "The Nazis are coming back!"

Everyone grabbed their weapons and ran outside. Looking up the street, they could see German military trucks. They ran to their strategic positions as the trucks approached. Soon they were fighting again. Day after day the battle raged on. The Germans were surprised at the resistance, which was something they had never expected. Helena felt a need to protect Cass and soon had adopted a motherly role over both Cass and Hadassah. Every evening after the fighting stopped, she would spend an hour or so searching for food to make sure Cass and Hadassah had enough to eat. Sometimes they would go with her. By the first week of May, thousands of Jews had joined in the fight against Nazis. Some of them did not even have weapons but fought with rocks and sticks. The battle was fierce, and the Jews were heavily outgunned, but they fought with every bit of strength they had. Thousands died in the battles that often carried on until late at night and started early in the morning.

By May 8 the Resistance had lost nearly ten thousand fighters whereas the Germans had lost only a few hundred. The fighting was especially intense that day, and the Germans had almost reached the stronghold at the intersection of Zomenhof and Mila Streets. Cass was sniping from a roof. Suddenly he heard loud screaming and saw hundreds of people running away from Zomenhof Street. He ran down to the street to find out what was happening. He grabbed a Resistance fighter running past him. "What's going on?"

The fighter stopped for a moment and shouted, "The Germans took the stronghold at Zomenhof and Mila. Mordecai Anielewicz was killed. We're retreating."

Cass felt a hand on his shoulder. He turned around and saw Helena with Ari and Yitzhak. Helena was crying. "Let's go," Ari said.

"Where are Hadassah and Golda?"

"They were killed when the Germans broke the stronghold at Zomenhof and Mila," Ari said. "Let's go."

By May 16 the Resistance had lost over thirteen thousand fighters. The Germans had lost only three hundred. Late that evening, the Resistance surrendered. Many ran for safety away from the fighting area. Forty-two thousand Jews were captured and taken to forced labor camps at Poniatowa, Trawniki, and Lublin/Majdanek. Seven thousand were sent to Treblinka II for immediate extermination. Many of those who were captured were summarily executed. That was the end of the uprising of 1943. To add insult to injury, the Germans destroyed the Tlomackie

Synagogue, which had been a place of worship for Polish Jews for over a century. The Germans then began systematically destroying the entire ghetto with tanks and demolition materials. Thousands of Jews were rounded up and killed, and thousands more were taken to Treblinka for extermination. Some survivors hid out in the remaining buildings in the ghetto, moving from location to location as the German tanks came in. Most of those who survived and were not captured fled the ghetto to the Aryan side, where they tried to find anyone who would assist them. Many were turned in to the German authorities and were incarcerated or executed. Eventually, only about twenty thousand Jews remained alive in Poland. Before the war, approximately 350,000 Jews lived in Warsaw, comprising approximately 30 percent of the city's population of 1.3 million.

CHAPTER
25

THE SUMMER OF 1943 seemed like a vague nightmare for Cass. After the uprising, the remaining Jews began hiding in the buildings that had not yet been destroyed. As the tanks rolled through destroying the buildings, the Jews would move to other buildings in an effort to stay one step ahead of the Germans. Through the years of the occupation, some of the Jewish families had planted gardens on the roofs of the apartments where they lived. Occasionally, these gardens were spotted by German gyro planes and were burned or bombed, but many of them continued to grow and produce a limited crop. It was only these gardens, and food that was smuggled in, that kept some of the Jews alive in the ghetto that horrible summer.

Cass, Ari, Yitzhak, and Helena were hiding together in a flat in a partially demolished building where Helena had lived before the uprising. On the roof she had a garden that provided the limited crop that she had canned and stored from the year before. Helena seemed attracted to Ari, who showed no interest in her overtures. He was polite but acted as though he did not perceive her interest in any way. One morning Ari, Cass, and Yitzhak went in an old abandoned piano factory looking for supplies they could use in the war against the Nazis. As they rummaged through boxes of finely cut ivory keys, Yitzhak asked, "Ari, do you like Helena? I think she likes you."

Ari shook his head but made no audible response. Cass, who was standing next to Yitzhak, whispered, "Ari's married."

Later that morning as they continued to look through the abandoned piano materials, Cass asked, "Ari, whatever happened to Leah? I haven't seen her since we lived in the apartment on Wilanow Street."

Ari continued to work in silence for about thirty seconds but finally said, "The Nazis took her to the work camp."

Cass did not say anything. Ari continued. "I was on a mission one day. I had been gone for two days. When I got home the entire street was vacated. I asked the neighbors on other streets what happened. They told me that a truckload of troops came in looking for me. When they couldn't find me they rounded up everyone on the street and took them away. They told those left that they were taking them to a work camp. I never saw Leah again."

"I'm sorry to hear that, Ari," said Cass. "Leah was really nice." Cass realized that he had used the past tense, so he corrected himself. "She is really nice."

As they continued to rummage through the materials in the piano factory Cass found some large spools of metal wire. "What's this?" he asked.

Ari and Yitzhak came over to see what Cass was looking at.

"I know what that is," Ari said. "That's piano wire. Those are the strings that go inside the piano. That spool you have is large. There might be five hundred feet of wire on that spool."

"How strong is it?" asked Cass.

Ari replied, "The thicker wire is used for lower notes. It can support a lot of weight."

Cass rolled a spool of heavy gauge wire across the floor causing the wire to unroll. "It's all connected as one long piece. I have an idea."

Ari nodded. "Yes, that's how they make it. What's your idea, Cass?"

Cass laughed and shook his head. "What if we string this wire across the street where the motorcycles come on the morning patrol."

Ari and Yitzhak both laughed. Ari replied, "You and your motorcycles, Cass. I don't know what we are going to do with you. I like the idea, though."

"I do too," said Yitzhak. "It probably won't kill anyone, but it will be fun to see them fall off their motorcycles. Did I ever tell you about the time Cass hooked the rope to the belt of the soldier on a motorcycle?"

"No, but I heard about it," Ari said. "We're going to have to find a way to get that heavy spool of wire back to the flat. It probably weighs two hundred pounds. I suppose the three of us can carry it. We will have to watch for Nazis though. They won't like it that we are carrying supplies."

Later that afternoon, they returned to the flat carrying a large spool of heavy-gauge piano wire. Helena asked, "What are you doing?"

Cass laughed. "We have a plan."

Ari said, "Early tomorrow morning we're going to string this wire across the streets where the Nazis ride in on their motorcycles."

Helena looked at him with a puzzled expression.

Ari lifted the end of the wire from the spool. "You know, to knock them off their bikes."

Helena began laughing. "Is it strong enough that it won't break?"

Ari replied, "We're going to string several wires across. They won't see them in time to stop. Several wires across the street will be strong enough that they won't break."

"Whose idea was this? Let me guess. Cass?"

Yitzhak and Ari both laughed. "Yes, it was Cass's idea," Ari said.

"Where do you come up with these ideas, Cass?" she asked.

"They just pop into my head."

Helena replied, "Well, you guys be careful. You don't want the Nazis seeing you put up those wires."

Later that afternoon, Cass, Yitzhak, and Ari walked over to Zomenhof Street. They had to walk past several guard posts. They found a location where they decided to string the wire. Every morning a patrol, consisting of several motorcycles driven by Nazi soldiers, often with officers in sidecars, would ride down the street just as the sun was starting to come up, but before it was fully daylight. They would string the wire there to catch those riders.

When there was no traffic, Ari gave one end of a wire to Yitzhak and said, "Hold this. Stand next to that pole." Yitzhak took the wire in his hand and held it as Ari ran across the street with the other end of the wire. Ari ran about ten feet past the pole on the other side of the street. He quickly cut the wire so that it extended about ten feet past the curb on either side when stretched across the street. He ran back to Yitzhak and Cass and they walked back to the flat.

Ari cut two more wires the same length as the piano wire that had been used for measuring. "How are we going to hook the wires to the pole?" asked Cass.

Ari reached into his pocket and pulled out some metal clamps. "With these," he said handing a clamp to Cass and another to Yitzhak.

"What are these?" Yitzhak asked.

"These are wire clamps. We wrap the wire around the pole and twist it with a pair of pliers. Once we have about a foot of the wire twisted together, we slip the clamps over the wire right up next to the pole and tighten the clamps. It would be strong enough to hold several men up in the air."

"Where did you get those?"

"I found them at the warehouse. I also found these." Ari held up a pair of pliers.

"Dinner is ready," said Helena as she walked in with a plate of tomatoes, potatoes, and squash. "These are from the roof garden. They are the first crop this summer."

Everyone ate slowly. They had not had much to eat for several days, and they knew that rapid food consumption after a period of hunger could be dangerous. They all ate more than they should have eaten that night, but they enjoyed the meal.

At five o'clock the following morning, Ari, Yitzhak, and Cass ran to Zomenhof Street. They quietly slipped past the guard shacks, which they realized were vacant. They knew there would be no traffic before the motorcycles came through. They quickly connected the wire as they had discussed. For extra strength they used three low-G strings and wound them around one another. Then they tied them off at the poles as they had planned.

After they completed stringing the wire across the street, they stood back and looked at the rig. The wire was completely invisible from the direction the riders would approach.

"We'd better hide," said Ari. "They'll be here…uh-oh." Ari pointed up the street.

There were some guards walking up the sidewalk toward the wire. Ari and the others hid in the shadows as the guards approached. Nervous, they remained completely silent as the guards neared the wire. They all felt relieved as the guards passed by unaware.

They stayed in the shadows. Then Ari said, "Listen, the motorcycles are coming now. Let's go to Mila Street. We can watch from behind that guard shack."

They ran up the street to the intersection of Mila and Zomenhof, where they hid behind an abandoned guard shack that had been built in the street. As they looked south on Zomenhof, they could see the headlights of the motorcycles traveling at about forty miles per hour.

"What do you think will happen?" asked Cass. "Do you think the lines will break?"

Ari shook his head. "No, they are very strong. I think it will knock them off their motorcycles. And at forty miles per hour, they might even break a few bones."

They leaned around the walls of the shack watching the motorcycles approach the wire. Cass could see that the first motorcycle had a sidecar. There were two others without a sidecar then a fourth with a sidecar. The driver of the first motorcycle looked like the soldier Cass had pranked a year earlier by hooking the rope onto his belt, and the passenger in the sidecar looked like the same officer who was in the sidecar that day. As he continued to watch, Cass almost felt a bond with the driver of the motorcycle. He felt a moment of compassion. *I wonder what he would say if he ever learned I was the one who pranked him. Now I am going to prank him again.*

Suddenly the first motorcycle reached the wire. It all happened so fast. They were not expecting what actually occurred. The wire struck the driver's neck, instantly severing his head. The motorcycle swerved left as the driver's head fell into the lap of the officer in the sidecar. The headless body fell backward off the motorcycle onto the pavement.

The second motorcycle reached the wire. Seeing what happened to the first motorcycle, the driver attempted to duck. As the wire hit his helmet, he too was knocked from the motorcycle. The driver of the third motorcycle held up his hands to protect his face, only to have his hands severed at the wrists. As the wire hit his helmet, the stress finally overcame the wire, which snapped in two.

The fourth driver skidded to a stop to avoid what might be ahead. He looked up the street and saw Ari, Cass, and Yitzhak running toward the intersection of Mila and Zomenhof. He pointed at them. The officer in the sidecar raised an MG42 machine gun and fired at them. He then shouted and pointed. The driver immediately placed the motorcycle in gear and set out in pursuit of the three men. Ari, Cass, and Yitzhak ran up Mila Street, turned right, and sped down Dubois. They could hear the motorcycle approaching. They looked up the street and saw no place to hide. They attempted to open a few doors, but the buildings were locked.

Ari saw an iron sewer grate at the edge of the street. "Help me lift that."

"We can't lift that, it weighs at least two hundred pounds," Yitzhak protested.

"Let's try."

Cass reached down and began lifting, assuming that Ari intended for them to jump into the sewer to hide. They were able to break it loose as they could hear the motorcycle nearing the corner and slowing slightly to turn. Suddenly, Ari began spinning in circles while holding the sewer grate in his hands, as if he were holding a giant discus in the Olympic Games. As the motorcycle turned the corner he leaned into the direction of the sound of the motorcycle and released his grip. The iron grate flew through the air and struck the motorcycle driver squarely in the chest. As he fell from the motorcycle his hand released the throttle, and the motorcycle slowed dramatically. The officer in the sidecar fell forward. As the motorcycle passed Ari, he calmly reached down and lifted the machine gun from the officer's hands. The officer immediately jumped from the sidecar and ran up the street. Perhaps in a moment of mercy, or simply amusement, Ari did not shoot the fleeing officer. Instead he laughed and fired the machine gun in the air to startle him. By this time several Jews who had been hiding in the nearby buildings came into the streets to see what was happening. Those who saw Ari strike the motorcycle driver with the sewer grate were telling the others what happened. Someone shouted, "Samson." Ari shook his head and laughed. "These guys see the Tanakh in everything."

Looking in the sidecar, Cass found boxes of ammunition for the machine gun. Ari jumped on the motorcycle and said, "One of you get in the sidecar, the other get on the bike behind me."

Yitzhak looked at Cass and laughed. "We aren't going to do this."

"Yes, we are," Ari crowed. "We just got a motorcycle."

Cass climbed on behind Ari and Yitzhak jumped into the sidecar. As they sped down the street, Cass looked back and noticed that a crowd of people had gathered around the motorcycle driver who had been knocked off the bike with the sewer grate. They were kicking and stomping him. *He won't live long*, Cass thought.

The three rode around on the motorcycle for about ten minutes then parked it in an abandoned warehouse near the flat where they were staying. They put it in a locked room with a steel door. "We might need this later," Ari said. "And we'll definitely need the machine gun."

Later that night Cass sat on the floor of their flat. He felt sadness for the motorcycle driver who was beheaded by the piano wire. He realized that he had thought of that soldier often after the day he'd hooked the rope to his belt. Cass had convinced himself that the motorcycle driver might actually be a kind fellow, much like Sergeant Schultz. He found it strange that he actually had compassion for a Nazi. *Maybe I'm not thinking right because I don't have enough food.* The strangeness of the times was overwhelming.

Cass went to sleep late that night. Sleep remained fleeting until the early morning hours. Finally, at two o'clock, he felt himself drifting into slumber, only to be awakened by a knock at the door. No one else seemed to hear the knocking sound. Crawling out of bed, Cass went to the door of the flat. Slowly opening the door, he saw a figure of a young girl he thought he knew, standing in the shadows. As his eyes adjusted to the darkness in the hallway eventually he could distinguish an apparition that resembled Zofia. Wearing a dress like the one Zofia wore the last day he saw her alive, she seemed to engulf Cass with her beauty and kindness. She slowly reached her hand out to him. Initially frightened, Cass overcame his trepidation and reached his hand to her. Their hands touched, and Cass was instantly transported to a place of comfort. In his heart, he knew it really was Zofia. He pulled her into the light of the room. She seemed so beautiful. She didn't speak, but he heard her thoughts. *Go see Mama and*

Thad. Cass blinked to clear his eyes to see more clearly, but when he opened them, Zofia was gone.

Cass returned to his room realizing he had been dreaming. He lay on his bed and fell asleep again. He had another dream. In this dream, he saw the soldier on the motorcycle approaching the wire strung across the street. As he watched, in his dream, he saw the driver's head being severed by the piano wire then falling into the sidecar. The motorcycle came to a stop. Cass walked over to the motorcycle and looked in the sidecar. The rider in the sidecar said nothing. He looked up at Cass and held up the severed head. Cass looked away, not wanting to see the head. The rider in the sidecar held it closer to his face so he could not look away. Knowing what he would see, Cass looked at the severed head, and saw the face of Zofia. Immediately awakening, Cass jumped from the bed and ran into the living room, screaming, "I killed Zofia. I killed Zofia!"

Helena jumped out of bed and hugged Cass. "Cass, you're having a bad dream."

Ari ran into the living room. "Whoa, Cass, you're dreaming. Sit down and catch your breath."

"No," Cass wailed. "Zofia died because of me. She was coming to see me when she was killed by the Nazis. That's what I have been trying to understand all this time."

"But it wasn't your fault, Cass," said Ari. "You didn't ask her to come to see you. She came because she wanted to."

"But if it wasn't for me, she wouldn't have come, and she wouldn't be dead today." Cass burst into uncontrollable sobs. "Zofia died because I killed the soldier with the wire and because I killed the mailman and because I killed the Nazis in the uprising."

Ari said, "No, Cass, those things happened after Zofia died. They didn't have anything to do with Zofia."

"They did," Cass replied. "When one person dies, part of everyone dies."

Helena held Cass in her arms and rocked him. "Let it out, Cass. You're finally breaking through. All this time you have repressed your loss of Zofia, and now you're finally letting it out. This is good for you. It hurts, but it's good for you."

After about twenty minutes Cass began to calm down. Yitzhak walked out of his room into the living room. "What's going on?"

"Cass had a bad dream about Zofia," replied Helena.

"Are you okay, Cass?"

Cass did not reply.

Ari asked, "So, Cass, what was the dream? Did she tell you something?"

Cass nodded.

"What did she tell you?" Helena asked.

"She told me to go see Mama and Thaddeus."

Ari nodded his head. "Then we'll go see Mama and Thaddeus."

CHAPTER
26

O N A SATURDAY evening in late May 1943, Helena, Cass, Ari, and Yitzhak sat at the kitchen table, in a flat in the partially demolished building where they were living, looking at diagram of the sewer system surrounding the Warsaw Ghetto. Ari pointed at a circle on the diagram. "This is the sewer grate in the street by the western wall of the ghetto. These lines represent the sewers in the city." Ari pointed at a broken line running across the page. "This is the western wall of the ghetto," he said.

"Where did you get this diagram?" asked Helena.

Ari leaned against the table. "Yitzhak Zuckerman and his team have been working on it for several years. He was able to get his hands on records from the public works department for a lot of it. The rest of it he constructed by exploration. We now have the ability to get in and out of the ghetto as easily as walking through an unlocked door, and the Germans are none the wiser. We are going to use these sewers to move weapons in the next uprising."

"When will the next uprising happen?" asked Cass.

"Soon." Ari replied. "And we need to be much better prepared than we were in the last uprising. Also, this time, it won't be just Jews uprising. We are going to be joined by thousands of Poles throughout Warsaw, and we are going to coordinate with the Soviet and the British armies."

"Are the Soviets any better than the Nazis?" Helena asked. "I've been hearing that they exterminate undesirables just like Hitler does."

Ari nodded. "They probably aren't any better than the Nazis. They may be worse. Hopefully, once the Germans are driven out of Poland, the Soviets will leave, and we'll go back to governing ourselves as we did before the German invasion. If we don't fight, they'll probably just see us as weak, and they'll be more motivated to occupy Poland."

Ari continued, "See this circle here on the map? This is the sewer right outside of the Litynski truck repair shop where your family is staying, Cass. We can go there."

"How will they know we're coming?"

"Zuckerman has been there," replied Ari. "I told him you wanted to see your family, and he mapped out the way. We'll have to travel in sewer tunnels all the way once we are outside of the ghetto. Rajmund offered to pick us up closer to the ghetto, but that puts him in too much danger. There's a sewer line that goes into the alley behind the shop, and there's a grate right behind the shop. That's where we will come up."

"What's in the sewers?" Yitzhak asked.

"Just dead, naked Nazis," Cass said. Everyone laughed.

Ari continued, "Actually, there are some tunnels we should avoid because there are some bodies. The odor is horrific. Zuckerman marked those on the map. Also, we have to be careful because the Nazis have put guardrooms in some of the tunnels. They are building an underground network of their own tunnels and some of them connect to sewer tunnels. Zuckerman thinks they are getting wise to the fact that he is using the sewers to smuggle weapons and food into the ghetto."

"When are we going?" Yitzhak asked. "And who is going?"

"Zuckerman told Mr. Litynski that there are four of us living in the flat and he said we could all come and stay in the apartments behind the shop. He said there's plenty of room. He wanted us to know that he would have come in with a truck to get us out like he did Cass's family, but the Nazis won't allow them to bring trucks into the ghetto after the uprising."

Ari continued, "As to when we're going, I think we should go as soon as possible, and before the weather turns cold. One good thing is that the repair shop is not far from the wall of the ghetto. We can get there easily in a few hours running through the sewers. We'll walk to the sewer entrance inside the ghetto just after dark so when we open the grate and go down, no one will see us. We should be there by ten. Zuckerman said to let him know a day or two in advance and he will let Mr. Litynski know when we are coming. Mr. Litynski is going to have two trucks parked in the alley behind his shop. One of them will be parked right over the sewer grate we will come out of. We will climb up and walk behind the trucks, right up to the door. Rajmund will be in one of the trucks watching for us."

Cass asked, "How will we know where we're going in the dark?"

"Zuckerman is going to write numbers on the wall every few blocks. But the numbers will be out of sequence so the Nazis won't know where they are leading if they find them. We'll study the map before we leave, and we will take the map with us in case we get lost. We're going to take a couple of flashlights so we can see where we're going. Zuckerman is going to write the numbers on the wall in this sequence: two, five, three, seven, nine, twelve, eleven, four, one, six, eight, and ten. That way, if the Nazis find them, they won't know how to follow them. We'll follow them in that order, so memorize the order so we'll all know where we're going."

"I wish we could go tonight," Cass said.

Ari replied, "Zuckerman wouldn't have time to let Mr. Litynski know we are coming. Why don't I tell Zuckerman we are coming on Tuesday night? He can let Mr. Litynski know."

Cass nodded. "I think that would be good."

On the following Tuesday evening Helena, Ari, Yitzhak, and Cass took their limited belongings and set out for the sewer grate near the western wall of the ghetto. In addition to their limited supply of clothing, they were carrying guns and ammunition, which they concealed under the clothes they were carrying. After walking for several blocks they came to the grate, opened it, and descended into the sewer. Using the flashlights they'd brought with them, they were able to move quickly through the sewer system. Walking as quietly as they could, keeping discussions to a minimum, they listened for the guards in the sewer that Zuckerman had warned about.

In an effort to be quiet, they avoided the water by walking at the edge of the tunnels. Most of the water was in the center where the tunnel was deepest. Suddenly, Ari turned off the flashlight and motioned for silence. Up ahead they could see a light, and then they heard voices speaking German. The light appeared to be coming toward them. They turned down a different tunnel, where they hid and watched as the light grew brighter. They saw another light approaching from a different direction. Realizing that they were eventually going to have to face one group or the other, they slipped down into a drain that angled down at about ten degrees. They lay motionless on the floor of the drain hoping not to be detected. Eventually, the two groups of soldiers walking in the tunnel met not more than ten feet from where Helena, Cass, Ari, and Yitzhak were hiding. There were two in each group. Speaking in German, the soldiers talked about hating their assignment in the sewers.

"No one is coming down here," said one of the soldiers.

"I know. This is ridiculous," said another as he lit a cigarette. The smoke blew to where the four were hiding. Cass choked slightly. Hearing the faint sound of a muffled cough, one of the German soldiers shone a flashlight in the direction of Cass who was covered with mud. Shining the light directly at him, Cass appeared to be a pile of sewage, as did the others with him. The soldier continued to shine his flashlight at Cass as he tried to adjust his eyes to the darkness. Cass could see the light shining around him as he lay with his face buried in his arms. "What's that?" asked one of the soldiers near him.

"It's a pile of crap," said another soldier with a laugh. "Are you expecting it to fly up and hit you in the face?"

"Then what made that coughing sound?" asked the first soldier.

"It was probably a rat."

"Rats don't cough."

"Of course they do if they have a cold. Are you paranoid?"

"No," said the first soldier. He took his gun from his shoulder and poked Cass with the bayonet. Cass remained motionless.

"Okay, I guess it is nothing," the soldier said. He turned his light, pointing it toward the tunnel in which they were walking and started to move away. Then Cass coughed again. The first soldier immediately turned around.

Ari shouted, "Great, Cass," as he flung a knife into the throat of the first soldier. The soldier dropped the gun, which Ari caught in midair.

He quickly spun the gun around and thrust the bayonet into the second soldier. The other two soldiers were running away. Ari scrambled up the slippery floor of the drain. When he reached the surface he immediately chased after the two soldiers. Because they were running in the water and Ari ran on the concrete area above the water, he caught up with them in a matter of seconds. Running up behind them he jumped, throwing one arm around each of them, and pulled them down into the sewer water.

One of the tackled soldiers shouted in Polish, "Stop, we are Russian."

Ari sat in the sewer water with them. "You're what?"

"We are Russians."

"Russians? What are you doing here? Why were those Nazis talking to you? And why are you in Nazi uniforms?"

"We're exploring the underground network," one of the soldiers said. "We both speak fluent German, and we were briefed on what is happening down here. We killed two soldiers in one of the guardrooms and took their uniforms. We have been exploring down here for about four hours. Mostly, we want to know if the sewer tunnels go under the ghetto wall or if they have been blocked with gates."

"I am Gustaw; this is Yurik." He pointed at his companion.

"I am Ari. The tunnels go all the way through to the ghetto. If you are Russian, why were those German soldiers talking to you? Did they not know you are Russian?"

"No. Because they didn't know us before."

"So why do you want to know if the sewers go all the way through?" asked Ari as Helena, Cass, and Yitzhak walked up behind him.

"We're mapping the system to prepare for an invasion of Warsaw."

"Invasion by who?" asked Helena.

"By Russia, of course," replied the soldier.

"When is Russia planning to invade?" asked Ari.

"Not until after winter. We're not going to try to take a city the size of Warsaw during the winter months when the Germans would have the advantage of shelter. We anticipate the Russian army will reach the eastern side of Warsaw by late spring or summer."

"So how is it you speak Polish?" Helena asked.

"We both grew up in Poland. In fact, we grew up here in Warsaw. Our families moved to Eastern Poland in the thirties. During the first

Russian occupation we were taken to Russia, where we were given Russian citizenship. We joined the Russian army. That's why they sent us back here to explore the sewer tunnels."

"What is it you need to know about the tunnels?" Ari asked.

"We really need to know where they run," Yurik replied.

Ari nodded. "Would you excuse us for a moment? I want to talk to my friends. We might be able to help you."

"Sure," said Gustaw.

Ari walked about twenty feet away in the tunnel and motioned for his companions to follow.

"What are you thinking?" asked Helena.

"Do you think they're telling the truth?"

"I think so," Cass replied. "Why would they lie?"

"So we don't kill them," Ari replied.

"I believe them," Yitzhak said. "Their story is too well put together to have been made up in the last few minutes."

Ari nodded. "That's what I'm thinking too. I believe them."

"Me too," Helena said. "So what are you thinking, Ari?"

"I am thinking we should give them a copy of the map. I made four copies. We can spare one. This would give them what they need."

"What if they are not Russians? What if they are just saying that so we won't kill them?" asked Helena.

"No matter," said Ari. "The Germans already have the map of the tunnels from the Warsaw Public Works Department. If they are Germans, we won't be giving them anything they don't already have. If they are Russians, then what we give them would be extremely helpful. I will tell Zuckerman. I'm sure he would agree with me."

"I say we give it to them," Cass said.

"Me too," Yitzhak said.

"Are we all in agreement?"

"Yes," said Helena.

"All right," Ari said as he walked back toward Yurik and Gustaw. He pulled out a copy of the map. "I want to give this to you. It is a map of all of the tunnels on the west side of the ghetto."

"Are you serious?" asked Gustaw.

"Yes, I am. We believe you are who you say you are, and we want to help you."

"This is amazing," replied Yurik. "We need to know your names so we can tell our superiors. They may want to contact you when we invade. They will probably want to coordinate with you, and they'll want to honor you when the war is over."

Ari paused for a moment then took a pen out of his pocket and wrote their names on the back of the map. "We want to help you when the invasion occurs. This map will tell you everything you need to know about the tunnels. Yitzhak Zuckerman explored the tunnels and created these maps."

"Thank you," Yurik said. "Your contribution to the war effort will not go unrewarded. Each of you will be rewarded."

After they parted company with the Russians, Ari, Helena, Cass, and Yitzhak walked through the tunnels until they came to the grate that was in the alley behind Mr. Litynski's truck repair shop. Ari climbed the iron ladder that led to the surface. Placing his feet squarely on the steps of the ladder, he reached up and took a firm hold of the sewer grate and pushed as hard as he could until it broke loose. He was able to move it to the side. Climbing up, he looked around in all directions to see if there was anyone watching him. He saw a truck door open. Rajmund stepped out of the truck and down onto the ground. He walked over to Ari and reached his hand down to help Ari climb out of the sewer. Ari took his hand and climbed out. "Don't hug me," whispered Ari. "We've been lying in poo." The men laughed.

Thaddeus, who had been sitting on the passenger side of the truck, walked up and whispered, "It's good to see you, Ari."

Ari replied, "You too." He walked to the rear of the truck and looked around in all directions. Seeing that it was safe, he turned around, walked back to the sewer opening, leaned over it, and said, "It's all clear. Come on up."

Helena came up first, then Cass, and finally Yitzhak. Rajmund motioned for them to follow him. He led them into the back door of the repair shop then down the hall to a door that led to a kitchen. He opened the door and said, "Look who's here." Irena and Grandma shrieked and ran to Cass.

"Quiet!" Thaddeus said. "You'll wake up every Nazi in Warsaw." Everyone laughed.

"Even the dead ones in the sewer," Cass said.

Ari said, "Don't touch us. We're filthy. We came through the sewers."

Josef came from his office. "It's great to see you. I'm happy you all made it out okay. I don't know a couple of you," he said, looking at Yitzhak and Helena. He nodded to Ari. "You, I recognize."

"It's good to see you," Ari said. "This is Helena and Yitzhak."

"It's good to meet both of you," said Josef. "You need a place to clean up. There are a couple of showers in the garage where some of the men like to shower after work. If you want to use those showers, we'll get you some towels and some clean clothes."

Rajmund came in with towels and clean mechanics' uniforms. "Here, you can wear these. They're clean."

"Thank you." Ari took the clothes and towels and passed them out to the others.

After they had all taken showers and put on clean clothes, they went into the apartment and sat in the living room with Grandma, Grandpa, Irena, Thaddeus, Rajmund, Josef, and Sarah.

"So what are your plans?" Josef asked.

"We're going to fight again," Cass said. "There's going to be another uprising, only this time it won't just be Jews. The Poles and the Russians are going to fight with us."

"I've been hearing that by customers at the restaurant. The German officers are saying they know it's coming, and I'm hearing it from Polish nationals as well," Josef said.

"This time we're going to win," Ari said.

Josef nodded. "I want you to know that you can stay here as long as you want. Unfortunately, you have to stay hidden back here in the apartments. You can't ever go out into the garage except at night and then only if Rajmund or I give you the all clear. You will have plenty of food while you are here. When the time comes, we'll help you any way we can. We want the Germans out of Poland too."

That evening, Helena, Cass, Ari, and Yitzhak enjoyed a wonderful meal Josef brought from the restaurant. Cass went to bed in a comfortable room with a clean bed and clean sheets. It reminded him of the days when he lived in comfort in the mansion on Pulawska Street. For the first time in years, Cass felt safe, if only for a moment.

CHAPTER

27

C ASS, HELENA, ARI, and Yitzhak decided to stay in the apartment behind the Litynski truck repair shop after leaving the ghetto. During business hours there were large numbers of German soldiers in the shop, which made it the perfect place to hide Jews; it was the last place the Germans would ever look. Cass used the opportunity to work out with Thaddeus, Ari, Yitzhak, and Helena. Sarah attempted to exercise with them on several occasions but found herself flooded with memories of her time at Treblinka, which made it impossible to concentrate.

During the summer, inhabitants of Warsaw talked openly about the imminent uprising against Germany. With promises by Britain that they would drop weapons from low-flying planes, the Poles found a renewed sense of encouragement. Further incentive was provided when Russia promised to invade from the east, just as Cass had heard from the Russians in the sewer. Throughout the city there was a network of people who had decided to join in the uprising. While the first uprising, in 1943, involved a small group of Jews, the uprising in 1944 would involve thousands of non-Jewish Poles. Cass wondered how they would treat his family when they returned to reclaim their homes? Would the Poles show kindness and understanding, or would they use the opportunity to crush the last breath from the surviving Jews? This weighed heavily on his mind as he thought of returning to his home on Pulawska Street.

Every morning Cass, Thaddeus, Ari, Helena, and Yitzhak would awaken at the crack of dawn to begin their daily workout. By noon they were exhausted and would spend the rest of the day relaxing in the flat, except for Cass and Ari. Cass remembered how hard he worked out before they were forced into the ghetto. As his strength began to return, he found himself pushing ten-hour days of exercise as he had in the past. Like Cass, Ari remembered the days of nonstop training that he loved so much. For Thaddeus, too much time had passed, with too much sorrow and too many losses. He found it impossible to regain the strength he had before.

Because the Germans were constantly going house to house looking for Jews, it was decided that the young people were going to have to stay on the move. It was too dangerous for all of them to stay in the apartment behind the repair shop. A large group of people would be too conspicuous. The plan was for them to go from house to house in areas where the Germans were not searching.

Ari said, "I think that's the best plan. If we're all found here, the Germans will figure out that we're in hiding and that we are Jews. Also, by all of us being here, that puts the Litynskis in danger. I have a place where Helena and I can stay for a while. We'll stay in touch so we can get back together when the uprising starts."

Josef said, "I think that's the best plan. My brother is a priest at the church five blocks down on the corner."

Cass asked, "The big one made out of stone with the huge bell tower on the corner?"

"That's it," Rajmund said.

Irena said, "He's been teaching us about Catholicism so that if we are found, we can say we are Catholics and will be able to show them that we know about the Catholic beliefs and practices."

"What if they make us pull down our pants to see if we are circumcised?" asked Cass.

Helena replied, "The girls don't have to worry about that."

Everyone laughed.

Josef said, "If we do a good job of teaching you the catechism, they probably won't check."

Irena said, "We have made arrangements for you boys to stay at the church for a while. Father Litynski will teach you the about the Catholic faith. You will have to pay close attention and study very hard."

Josef said, "I am going to take you down to the church in the truck tomorrow morning. You can stay here tonight. Ari, I can take you and Helena where you want to go too."

Ari nodded. "Thanks."

The following morning, Josef stopped his truck in front of the Catholic church. Thaddeus, Cass, Rajmund, and Josef walked in through the front door, then through the vestibule and into the sanctuary.

A young woman walked up to them. "You must be Cass and Thaddeus. I am Anastasia. I'm Rajmund's aunt." She laughed. "I know. You think I should be older. I'm twenty-four."

"Yes, I'm Thad, and this is Cass."

Anastasia extended her hand to greet them. They shook hands, and she said, "Come this way."

They walked toward the altar. "David, Cass and Thaddeus are here."

A priest walked out of a chamber behind the altar. "Hello, boys. I'm Father Litynski, but you can call me David. I see you looking at my lovely sister, Anastasia. You are wondering how she can be so young and beautiful when Mr. Litynski and I are so much older." He laughed. "Actually, Anastasia has a different mother. Our mother passed away, and our father married a second time. Anastasia is the daughter of his new wife, who is much younger than our mother."

Anastasia walked over to the boys. She stood between them and gave one arm to each of them as she hugged them. "Just think of me as your big sister. Have you had anything to eat tonight?"

"No, ma'am," Cass said.

"Oh, don't call me ma'am. I am Anna," she said with a smile. She led the boys into a kitchen area.

Josef nodded. "I think they'll be fine with her." Then he called, "Boys, we are just down the street if you need us."

"Thank you, Josef," Thaddeus said.

"Yes, thank you."

Josef looked at David. "Let me know if you need anything."

"Will do," David said.

For the next several weeks Anastasia taught Cass and Thaddeus the basic tenets of Catholicism. She taught them the sign of the cross and the phrase "father, son, and holy ghost." She taught them about the sacraments and the common prayers. It all seemed strange to Cass, but he learned it in order to survive. David had told them not to go outside of the church building because it was too dangerous, but boys will be boys. Shortly after going to live at the church, the boys were sneaking out at night to see what matters of interest they could find. One Tuesday evening they decided to go out and try to find a place they could stay when the next uprising occurred. They walked up and down the streets for hours hiding every time they saw a car or soldiers walking.

As they were returning to the church after a night of searching, someone shouted, "Halt."

They stopped walking and turned. "Where are you going?" asked a German soldier who was accompanied by four other soldiers.

"Our dog got out. We were looking for him."

"Are you Jews?"

"Catholic." Thaddeus recited a prayer he had learned from Anastasia.

"I'm not convinced," said the soldier. "Anyone can learn a prayer. Pull down your pants."

Cass knew that the moment they were seen to have been circumcised, they would be shot.

Thaddeus and Cass began running toward the church. The German soldiers shouted for them to stop, but the boys ignored them. The boys cut into an alley behind the church. Father David heard the shouting and opened the rear door of the church. "Come in here," he said. "Quick, crawl under the altar."

Anastasia asked, "What were you doing outside? You know it's dangerous."

The boys crawled into a small compartment under the altar. A few seconds later the rear door burst open, and four Nazi soldiers rushed in. "Where did they go?" asked one of the soldiers.

"Where did who go?" asked David.

"Where did the two boys go? We saw them come in here."

"What two boys?"

"Don't play games," shouted the soldier.

283

Under the altar, Cass looked at Thaddeus and whispered, "What are they going to do?"

Thaddeus put his finger to his lips and mouthed, "We have to be very quiet."

The soldier walked over to Anastasia, grabbed her by the hair, and threw her to the floor. She landed on one leg in a sitting position. "I will give you one more chance," he shouted at David as he pointed his Mauser P-38 pistol at Anastasia. "Tell me where they are, or I will shoot her."

Anastasia looked at David and gently shook her head and mouthed the word "no."

"I will count to three," said the soldier. "One, two, three." He fired two shots into Anastasia's head.

The soldier shrugged. "Well, I guess we were wrong. You wouldn't have let her die if you knew where the boys were." He motioned for the other soldiers to follow him, and they walked out the back door and into the alley, still looking for the boys.

David went to his sister and lifted her head. Seeing that she was already dead, he made the sign of the cross over her and whispered a prayer. He held her for several moments, then walked over to the altar, pulled back the curtain, and said, "Come on out, boys."

Cass and Thaddeus crawled from under the altar. "They may be back. You need to run." He walked over to a side door and looked out. "The soldiers are on the other side of the building. Run fast to your apartment. Stay in the rest of the night."

Cass and Thaddeus ran down back alleys all the way to the truck repair shop. They ran into the apartment and told everyone what had happened. Josef and Rajmund were devastated. "I need to go see if David is okay," said Josef. He and Rajmund got into a truck and drove to the church, where they found Anastasia on the floor with David kneeling next to her. Josef cried.

In the apartment, Irena said, "We are going to have to hide you two separately. There are a number of families who will take you in but most are only willing to take one of you, so we have to separate you. You are going to have to follow my instructions to the letter. If I say run, you can't ask any questions. You have to do exactly as I say, exactly as I say it. Do you understand?"

Cass nodded.

Thaddeus said, "Yes."

Irena continued, "We heard this morning that the Germans are going to be conducting door-to-door searches on this street tomorrow. They haven't searched here yet, but they might. You boys are in the greatest danger if you are here. I made arrangements for each of you to go to a separate place where you will stay for several days. When the Germans start searching in that neighborhood, you will have to move on. They said to just send you when it is time. Josef will take you tomorrow."

"Okay, Mama," Cass said.

The following evening the boys got into the truck with Josef. They rode several miles and stopped at a town house on a quiet street. "This is where you will stay, Thad," said Josef. "Cass, wait in the truck. I'll be right back. Let's go, Thad."

Josef and Thaddeus walked up to the house. Josef knocked on the door. The door opened, and Cass watched as they went inside. A few minutes later, Josef came back out and climbed into the truck. As he started the truck, he said, "Cass, I'm going to take you to a place that is very different from the church where you were staying."

Josef put the truck in gear and pulled into the street. "That's okay," said Cass. "What kind of place is it?"

"It is a place where only women live. No one will search there because the Germans know that none of the women are Jews."

A few minutes later they arrived at nice house located in the business district. Josef pulled the truck to the curb. The large house was a wooden Victorian structure painted blue. The yard was well maintained. The bushes were perfectly manicured. Cass noticed a young woman looking out an upstairs window. She was joined by a second woman who also looked out the window. Josef looked at Cass. "Are you ready?"

Cass nodded. "What is this place?"

"It is a house where only women live, but they have lots of friends who are men, and they come and visit them."

"Are they psychologists?"

Josef laughed. "I suppose in a way, but not the way you are thinking. These girls have helped a lot of Jews. They will help you."

"Are they harlots?" asked Cass. "Like Rahab, King David's grandmother who saved the spies at Jericho?"

"Exactly like that," said Josef with a startled expression. "Are you ready to go in?"

"Yes."

They went up to the house, and Josef rang the doorbell. A very attractive woman who appeared to be in her thirties opened the door. "Mr. Litynski, come in, please."

As they entered the door, she looked at Cass and smiled. "You must be Cass. I am Gabriela." She took ahold of his shoulders and laughed. "You are an adorable little man. The girls are going to eat you up. I will have to keep my eye on them."

"I will leave you, Cass. You will be okay here," Josef said.

"We'll take good care of him," said Gabriela.

"I know," said Josef. "Call me if you need anything."

After Josef left, several girls came into the living room. One of them was wearing a sheer negligee. Cass was startled. He quickly looked away.

Gabriela said, "Marina, we can't dress like that in front of Cass. He is a gentleman."

"I'm sure he won't mind," Marina said as she walked toward Cass.

"Marina, his mother is trusting us." Gabriela pointed toward a door leading to a hallway.

One of the other girls said, "Come on, Marina."

"Okay," said Marina with a laugh. She turned and went through the doorway and down the hall to her bedroom.

Gabriela said, "Cass will stay in the back den. He won't be out here during business hours. We will always keep the hall door to the den locked during business hours so no one can go back there without going up the front stairs, then coming down the back stairs to the den."

Another girl introduced herself. "Hi, Cass, I'm Valentina. It's going to be fun having you here."

"I'm Tamara," another girl said.

"And I'm Lana," said another. Cass was struck by her youth. "How old are you?" he asked.

"I'm fourteen."

Gabriela said, "Lana is our youngest girl."

"Is there anyone else living here?"

"No, this is all of us," said Tamara. "We have a lot of visitors, but we're the only ones who live here."

They were interrupted by the sound of the doorbell. Gabriela said, "Quick, Lana, take Cass in the den and lock the hall door behind you. Cass, you have to be very quiet. You don't want anyone to hear your voice."

Lana grabbed Cass's hand and pulled him into the hallway leading to the back den. She closed the door behind her and locked it. She led Cass into the den—a large room with two couches, several chairs, and a desk. She walked over to the couch and sat down, patting the seat next to her. "Come and sit with me, Cass. Are you hungry?"

"No, I'm fine." Cass sat on the couch next to Lana.

"How old are you, Cass?"

"I am twelve."

"Oh, you are a little younger than me."

"When did you come here?" he asked.

"We all came here three years ago. I don't take customers. I serve drinks to the men, and I cook and clean."

Cass felt relieved to hear her say that. "Are you going to take customers someday?"

"Gabriela says I don't have to unless I want to. Before she wouldn't let me but she says I am old enough now if I want to. I would make a lot of money."

"I think you shouldn't," said Cass.

"That is really sweet of you to say."

"I just think it will be better if you don't."

"Thank you, Cass. I will remember that."

Marina and Tamara entered the den. "You can't have him all to yourself." Marina laughed.

"Who was at the door?" asked Lana.

"Captain Stossel," said Tamara. "He's with Valentina."

"I noticed all of you have funny names and you speak with Russian accents. Are you from Poland?" asked Cass.

Tamara replied, "No, we're all from Russia. We came to Eastern Poland after the Soviet invasion in 1939. We found that there was better work here because the German officers like us."

"Are you from Russia too?" Cass asked Lana.

"Yes, my real name is Svetlana, but I go by Lana for short. Gabriela is my aunt. She brought me here from Eastern Poland."

"Did anyone tell you how long you are going to stay here, Cass?" asked Marina.

"No. I think as long as I can, but I don't know."

"You could stay here permanently if it was up to me," Marina said. "We could use a man around here."

A short time later Gabriela came in with some blankets and pillows. "The couch you are sitting on is a hide-a-bed, Cass. It opens up into a bed. This is where you can sleep. It's fairly quiet tonight, but some nights it's very busy."

Gabriela continued, "The kitchen is right across the hall, but that door will be kept locked as well so that no one can come in here. Lana will bring food to you. There is a bathroom with a shower right there in the hallway. You can use that one."

"We open for business at seven in the evening, and we stay open until three in the morning. The doors are locked when we're not open, and no one is permitted to have guests until we open at seven the following evening. You have full run of the house when we are closed but don't go outside. No one can know you are here."

"Thank you, ma'am," said Cass.

"You can call me Gabby if you like. It is only nine o'clock now. You can sleep when you want to but if you want to sleep during our working hours then you can be awake all day. It's up to you. The main thing is don't go outside. And don't open the door for anyone. And during working hours you have to be back here."

"Yes, ma'am…I mean Gabby."

In a short time, all the girls left the den because customers were coming in. Eventually, Cass decided to open the hide-a-bed and go to sleep. He closed the den door and locked it as instructed by Gabriela. He awakened around six o'clock the following morning. The house was quiet. When he opened the den door he found a tray of bread and fruit sitting on the table next to the door. There was a note from Lana saying she had prepared it for him. Cass found some books to read on a shelf in the den. He decided to start with *Moby-Dick* by Herman Melville.

By ten o'clock the girls were all up. They unlocked the hall door to the living room and invited Cass to come out. He spent the day talking to them as they lounged in the living room. This routine was repeated daily for weeks. In time, he felt comfortable there. He had grown accustomed to living with the girls, and they enjoyed having him there as well. He had become especially close to Lana given their proximity in ages. He would talk with Lana for hours on end. He was growing fond of her, as she was of him.

One evening, several weeks later, Cass was in the den reading when he heard a man shouting in German upstairs. Then he heard Lana scream and Marina yelling. Although he knew he wasn't supposed to go up, he unlocked the door of the den and slowly walked up the back steps. He could hear someone hitting someone else. Valentina walked into the hall and saw him standing there. "Cass, you need to go back down."

"What's going on?"

"One of the officers is drunk, and he is beating Lana. He said she fixed his drink wrong."

Cass ran up the steps and started down the hall toward the room they were in. Valentina grabbed his arm. "No, Cass. You can't go in there."

Cass broke loose and looked into the room through the door. He saw a man in a German officer uniform striking Lana repeatedly. She was bloodied, and he was not stopping. Cass ran in and instinctively delivered a sharp kick with his heel to the officer's closest leg. The officer's leg buckled. While he shrieked in pain, because of the close confines he was able to stumble forward and fall on Cass, pinning him to the ground. The officer immediately began hitting him. Cass fought back, but despite his unique fighting skills, the much larger man continued to pummel him. Cass finally succeeded in inserting his knee against the officer's torso and gouging his eyes to push him away. The officer shouted in pain as Cass jumped to his feet. In the meantime, Lana had gotten to her feet and struck the man in the head with a brass figurine that was sitting on the nightstand. He fell to the floor unconscious.

"Oh no, Cass," whispered Gabriela, who had come in the room during the fight. She took his arm and pulled him out of the room and down the back steps to the den. "He saw you. Now he knows you are here. And there was another man standing in the hall who saw you when we came out of the room. We need to get you out of here fast. They're almost certain to search for you."

Gabriela picked up the phone and dialed a number. "Mr. Litynski, we have a problem. One of the customers attacked one of the girls, and Cass came to her defense. At least two of them saw him here."

Gabriela paused as she listened to the voice on the other line. Then she said, "We'll have him ready." She hung up the phone and closed the den door. Then she locked it.

"Quickly, Cass, pack everything. We need to get you out fast."

"But I didn't even get to say good-bye," Cass protested.

They heard a knock on the den door. Then they heard a man's voice. "Gabby, this is Major Dougherty. Is everything okay? Who was that young boy? He looked too young to be a customer."

Gabriela opened the window and whispered. "Climb out the window. Go behind the house. Mr. Litynski will pick you up within five minutes. Don't let anyone see you."

There was a second knock on the door. "Gabriela, what's going on?" asked the male voice on the other side of the door.

Cass climbed out of the window. Gabriela handed him his belongings and closed the window behind him. Cass looked back through the window to see Gabriela open the door and an officer come in. He turned and ran to the rear of the house. *I sure hope I didn't get the girls in trouble. That would be awful.*

He waited in the alley behind the house. A short time later he saw a truck turn into the alley. He recognized it as one of the trucks belonging to Josef. The passenger door opened, and Josef said, "Jump in, Cass, quick."

Cass jumped in on the passenger side and saw Rajmund and Josef. As the truck pulled away he looked in the rearview mirror and saw several soldiers looking up and down the alley behind the house.

"What happened, Cass?" asked Josef.

"One of the customers was beating one of the girls. I had to help, or he was going to kill her."

"I understand," Josef said. "Of course, that means you can't stay there now."

"Do you think it will cause problems for the girls?"

"No, I don't think so. They will probably just say you were a young-looking customer or just someone who showed up trying to see one of the girls. We are going to have to take you to another house, though. There is an old couple who previously said they would take you in. We will see if they will still do that."

After driving for about a half hour Josef pulled the truck up to the curb in front of a small house. "Wait here," he said. Then he got out and went up to the door. He returned a few minutes later and said, "Your mother called and told them you are coming. Everything is fine."

Cass got out of the truck and followed Josef to the door. The house was one of several small houses on a quiet street. The yard was well manicured with no trees. As they walked up the sidewalk to the front door, Cass noticed that the sidewalk was painted red. The house was painted red with white trim around the windows and doors. The door was white. Josef opened the door, and they went inside.

"This is Cass," said Josef. "Cass, this is Mr. Nowak, and this is Mrs. Nowak."

"Hello, Cass," said Mrs. Nowak. "I heard you had quite an ordeal at the last place you stayed. Did you like it there?"

"Yes, they were really nice."

Mr. Nowak chuckled. "I don't know if we will be as exciting as the last place, but you are welcome here. The only real rules we have are stay away from windows and doors, don't open the door for anyone, and don't go outside. Can you live with those rules?"

"Yes, sir."

Cass stayed with the Nowaks for several months. The Nowaks were very kind to Cass and treated him like family. Cass learned that they'd lost their son and grandchildren in the German invasion. Cass enjoyed staying with the Nowaks, but he missed the girls from the brothel. In December he received a visit from Josef.

"Cass, I have some good news. Our plan has worked. We were able to convince the Germans that you and your family are Catholic and are relatives of mine. They haven't the slightest clue that you are Jewish. You can come back and stay with us for the time being. Have you kept up studying the catechism?"

"Yes, I have also memorized some prayers."

"Okay, pack your belongings, and we can go."

While Cass collected his few belongings, Josef spoke with the Nowaks. He explained what was happening and thanked them for undertaking great risk to themselves by taking in Cass. Cass brought out his belongings and thanked the Nowaks for letting him stay with them.

On the way back to the truck repair shop, Josef said, "Okay, there's one last thing that you need to do, and you aren't going to like it, but it is the safest thing to do."

"What is that?"

"Your grandfather, Dr. Szyncer, has developed a method of temporarily reversing a circumcision using invisible stitches and some kind of dental adhesive. It isn't a true reversal of the circumcision, but it looks uncircumcised unless someone actually gets close enough to see the stitches. He has done it for several Jewish men and boys. It holds for months."

"You're joking, right?"

Josef laughed. "Actually, no. You will have it done when we get back to the apartment."

"Does it hurt?" asked Cass.

"He has anesthetics to give you. You won't feel anything. As soon as the Germans are driven out of Poland, your grandpa will undo it. You'll be as good as new."

"I'm not sure I'm going to like this," said Cass.

"You need to do it. It will make it impossible for anyone to suspect you are Jewish. With the knowledge of catechism and the uncircumcision, no one will ever figure it out."

When they arrived back at the apartment everyone was overjoyed to see Cass. Thaddeus was already back and said he had undergone the procedure performed by Grandpa. He assured Cass that it was painless, and it might mean the difference between life and death.

Grandpa Szyncer came into the living room with a long needle, a spool of fishing line, some dental adhesive, and a large staple gun.

"What's all that for?" asked Cass.

"This is what we use for the reverse circumcision," replied Grandpa.

"A staple gun? Where are we going to do it?"

"Right here," said Thaddeus.

"In front of everyone?" Cass looked at Irena. "Mama, Sarah and Helena are in here."

Grandpa said, "Oh, Cass, it has to be a ceremony. When you were a baby, eight days old, you were circumcised in front of the entire congregation. We have to reverse it the same way. It is a ceremony."

Everyone was silent for a moment then suddenly Thaddeus burst into laughter. Everyone else joined in. "I couldn't hold it any longer," said Thaddeus. "Cass, it's a joke. We are joking."

Cass joined in the laughter. "That was mean."

Irena said, "I thought so too, Cass. I was against it, but I was outvoted by the boys."

Later that day, Cass was surprised to learn that he was now permitted to go into the repair shop during business hours with German soldiers walking around. The Germans were now convinced that the Biebersteins were visiting cousins of the Litynskis. Soon, Cass had no fear of being discovered as a Jew. After all, everyone knew his family was Catholic gentiles.

When Chanukah arrived, the Litynskis brought gifts that they gave to the Biebersteins in the apartment. Despite the efforts of their compassionate hosts, the holiday did not bring the cheer it did when the Biebersteins lived in the mansion. As memories flooded back, Thaddeus mustered the courage to ask Sarah about Treblinka. "Sarah, what happened to Rachel? I know she was killed at Treblinka, but how did it happen?"

Cass, Sarah, Thaddeus, and Rajmund were sitting at the kitchen table enjoying breakfast. Sarah leaned back in her chair and looked toward Thaddeus. She kept her voice soft and even.

The room grew silent for a few moments then Rajmund said, "I remember when we used to sit at the dining room table at the Bieberstein house and talk about what we would do if Germany ever invaded Poland. I don't think any of us really believed they would."

"I remember too," said Thaddeus. "I remember that we all said we would fight Nazis if it ever happened."

Rajmund nodded. "In our own way, we all have."

"Do you think we can force the Nazis out of Poland?" Sarah asked.

"Definitely," Cass said. "Without a doubt we will rid our country of the Germans."

"I wonder what it will be like when they are gone," asked Sarah. "Will it be like it was before?"

"I don't know," Rajmund said. "The Germans destroyed so much of the city. When you go up and down the streets, the buildings are in shambles."

"Do you think we will be able to get our property back?" Thaddeus asked.

Rajmund shook his head. "I honestly don't know."

No one knew, but all the Jews shared a concern. When the Germans invaded Poland, their property was confiscated and distributed to those who would purchase it at the best price. Real estate was transferred into the names of persons who purchased with forged deeds. Personal property was simply sold to the highest bidder. The Jews had become inferior beings in the eyes of the Poles. Would the Poles allow them to return to the social status they enjoyed before the war?

In the second week of December, Cass was working in the repair shop. Several German soldiers were walking around in the shop. Cass had crawled under a truck to work on a brake line. He noticed the boots of an officer who had walked up and was standing next to the truck where Cass was working. "How is it looking?" asked the officer.

"I'm just bleeding the line," Cass replied. "Should be done in a few minutes."

"Those larger trucks have air brakes, don't they?" asked the officer.

"Yes, this one has fluid brakes because it is a smaller truck," replied Cass as he climbed out from under the truck. Looking up he saw Major Muller. "Hello, Major," he said.

"How are you, Oskar? Where did you learn so much about trucks at such a young age?" It felt strange to Cass to be called by the fake name that was also the name of the man who had driven them from their house on Pulawska Street. Cass knew the fabricated story well. The entire family would have fake names, a fake story, and fake papers.

"My father taught me before the war. He worked here before he died."

"He taught you and your brother both?"

"Yes, he did, and I just kept working here."

"Is your mother in? I thought I might say hello."

Cass knew the major had a romantic interest in Irena, believing her to be a widow. "I will see if she is here," he replied. Cass wondered if it is possible that his romantic interest in Irena was the cause of the major's willingness to believe that they were not Jewish. He wondered if the major really knew better.

Cass walked into the back apartment and came out a few minutes later with Irena, who walked over to the officer with a smile. "Hello, Major."

"Hello, Celina, you look lovely today. I was chatting with Oskar and thought I would say hello. How are you?"

"Oh, I'm well," replied Irena. "What brings you here today?"

"I stopped by to pick up a car. I thought perhaps if you haven't gotten your Christmas tree, I could take Oskar into the woods to find one."

"Oh, that is very kind of you," she said. "Oskar, would you like to go with the major to find a Christmas tree?"

Cass remembered all the times he went to search for a tree for the Christian servants at the Pulawska Street house. He remembered what to look for, and he remembered how to decorate the tree. The difference is that they did not cut the tree, they removed it by the roots so they would not have a dead tree in the house. When looking for a tree with the major, they would be cutting the tree. "Yes, I would like to get a tree."

"What time do you get off today, Oskar?"

"Actually, I'm finished now," replied Cass. "If you can give me a minute to clean up, I can go now."

"Sure," said the major. "I will just talk with your mother for a while."

Cass took a shower and changed his clothes then returned to the garage ready to go for the tree. He left with the major and returned two hours later with an eight-foot tree. The major had fashioned a frame base using pieces of wood. They brought the tree in and set it in the apartment. The major even stayed to help decorate. The Litynskis came back to help decorate, and they sang several popular Christmas carols the Biebersteins had learned from Father Litynski. The major, who had an extraordinary tenor voice joined in, to everyone's delight.

After the major left, Josef asked Irena, "What are you going to do? The major has taken an attraction to you."

Irena shook her head. "I don't know. It was terrifying to let him take Cass to look for a tree. I knew Cass wouldn't slip up and say anything that would clue him in that we are Jews. But it was still terrifying. I almost said no, but then I realized he might take it as an insult. This is scary. If he keeps coming around I will try to make sure someone else is always around when he talks to me. If he says he wants a romantic relationship, I will tell him that I have been through too much trauma from the war, and I need time. Maybe that will buy time until the Nazis are driven out of Poland."

Major Muller continued to come around several times each week. Finally, after Christmas, he caught Irena alone one afternoon to have the conversation she dreaded. "Celina, I have wanted to talk to you for some time now. I think you know that I am very fond of you. I have been since I first met you several months ago. I was wondering if you would like to go out to dinner with me."

"Major, that is so kind of you."

"Please call me Bryce; that's my first name. I think we can be on a first-name basis now."

"That is very sweet of you, Bryce. You know that I am pretty traumatized from the war. I lost my husband, and we lost our home. It has been very hard."

"Yes, you have been through a lot."

Irena continued, "I think what I am saying is, I believe I am going to need some time to heal. I don't want to say I have no interest because you know I do. I am just asking you to be patient with me and give me time to get over the war and all of the pain that went with it. I appreciate all you have done for Cass." Irena instantly realized that in her nervousness she slipped and called Cass by his real name.

"Who?" asked Major Muller.

"Oh, I mean Oskar. Cass is a nickname he had when he was very little because he was a very strong boy. Sometimes I still call him that."

"I understand what you are saying. Yes, I will give you time."

"If we could just keep it on a friendship level, a very good friendship, I think I will be ready in time." Irena was deeply troubled to lie to the major about emotions, but she felt trapped. If she rejected him outright, he might become angry, which could have serious consequences for her and the family. German officers had been known to be extremely ruthless toward Polish women who rejected their advances.

"Yes," said the major. He gave Irena a hug, and she reciprocated. Then he said, "I need to go now. I have a meeting at four." Major Muller left but continued to come around to see Irena once or twice per week. In time, he came less often, but he still came.

By the spring of 1944, talk of the uprising edged into nearly every conversation. For the first time since the German invasion in 1939, the people of Poland had a new hope. The courage of the Jews in the ghetto shone like a beacon in their hearts and minds. While the Jewish Resistance served as an inspiration for Polish nationals, the question in Cass's mind was whether the respect for the Resistance would allow the Poles to overcome the ethnocentrism that had grown in their hearts over the past five years. The Jews and the Polish nationals shared a common enemy, but would that commonality prevent the Poles from taking advantage of the authority they had acquired over the Jews—and their property—during the German occupation?

During the winter Cass had gained over forty pounds. Working out several hours per day, he had regained the fighting skills he possessed before entering the ghetto. He knew he was ready for the final fight against the invaders. Notwithstanding the underground movement to rise against the Nazis, the Jews were still not able to move freely on the streets. The Germans were still sweeping neighborhoods, searching house to house for Jews. Those found harboring Jews were arrested along with the Jews they were hiding.

By June, word spread that the Red Army was approaching from the east. Through the network of communication, contact had been made with the Russians. Germany was being forced westward from the eastern border of Poland. Hitler had spread his forces too thin, against the advice of his senior officers, who had now begun to see him as a madman. Word quickly spread of the D-Day invasion by Allied forces on June 6, and for the first time since the German invasion, it appeared that the German war machine might be defeated.

As the Soviet Army continued to approach Warsaw from the east, Joseph Stalin began broadcasting radio messages from Moscow, encouraging the inhabitants of Warsaw to take up arms against the Germans. On August 1, 1944, the Poles launched Operation Tempest as a nationwide effort. The objective was to drive the Germans from Warsaw and to assist the Allied forces in defeating the Axis powers. The fighting was fierce, and both sides suffered tremendous losses. Cass, Ari, Yitzhak, Thaddeus, Rajmund, and Helena, all joined in the fighting. The Germans used the same strategy they had used in the ghetto by destroying every building where people were hiding. Going door-to-door, they would arrest the Jews and everyone who was harboring them. Then they would bring in tanks and demolish the building as a warning to others.

CHAPTER

28

CASS, ARI, YITZHAK, Thaddeus, Rajmund, and Helena lined up next to one another, lying prone on the rooftop of a large apartment building on a busy street near the ghetto. They each held a rifle. The red clay tiles were loose on the old building so they had to avoid unnecessary movement. For extra support, Cass braced his foot on a metal pipe that was protruding from the roof.

The fighters knew they had to make the ammunition last because of the limited supply. Thousands of Poles were hiding in other buildings, many of whom were Jews who had survived the previous uprising. They were equipped with a limited number of weapons; the Nazis had confiscated most guns after the invasion in 1939. Nonetheless, the British had promised to drop thousands of guns and ammunition by parachutes from low-flying planes. The Resistance was relying on those weapon supplies.

As they watched up the street, they saw soldiers running into the buildings, searching door-to-door for Jews. Occasionally, they would hear shots fired. Sometimes they would hear a firefight; other times they would only hear one or two shots. They knew the firefights meant the people were defending themselves. One or two shots meant someone had been executed.

As the Germans reached the block of the buildings where the Resistance fighters were waiting, everyone watched for a signal from a former Polish officer named Commander Erlich, who was strategically situated on a nearby building. Ari whispered, "Don't shoot until he gives the signal. If we shoot too soon, we won't hit enough of them."

When the German soldiers were right below them, the Polish officer gave the signal to fire. Shots rang out from all the buildings, and dozens of Nazi soldiers fell in the street below. With no place to run for cover, they retreated while firing back at the Resistance fighters they could not see. When the first wave of fighting was complete, the street was filled with dead and dying Nazi soldiers.

"It's like shooting fish in a pond," Yitzhak said.

"It won't always be that easy," said Ari. "When they find they can't beat us on foot, they'll send in the tanks."

The street remained silent for the rest of the day though shots could be heard in other nearby locations. For two days, no troops were seen from the roof.

On the third day, again lying on the same roof, Ari said, "This isn't working. We aren't doing enough. People are being rounded up and killed, and we are just lying up here on the roof."

"What can we do?" asked Cass. "We can't run through the streets going to where the Nazis are. There aren't enough of us. We would be exposed."

"I know," said Ari. "I just wish there was something more we could do."

"Why do you think the soldiers haven't come back after the first day we had our battle?" Helena asked.

"Too much resistance here. They are going to areas where the people aren't fighting back. They will come back for us later," Rajmund said.

"I wish there was a way we could go to them," said Helena. "I feel helpless up here on the roof. We might as well wait inside the building."

Ari replied, "That's probably right. We've waited up here for three days, and they haven't been back since the first battle. Let's go inside. It will be more comfortable there. We can watch from the windows."

They all slid down the roof to the window they had used to get onto the roof and started to go inside. Just as they began to enter through the window, they heard a sound of low-flying airplanes. They sat on the roof looking in the direction of the sound. Cass pointed to his right and said, "Look over there."

The first thought was that the planes were Nazi bombers coming to destroy what was left of the city as punishment for the uprising. As the planes got closer, Ari said, "Those don't sound like Nazi bombers."

"They're coming this direction," Rajmund said. "They're really low. Hey, look—they're dropping something from the planes. Something in crates with parachutes."

"Those are British planes. It's the weapons drop," Ari said. "They are dropping the weapons they promised."

They watched as the planes flew just a short distance above the building. The pilot tilted the wings and waved at them. After flying over the building, the plane dropped a large wooden crate suspended by a parachute. The crate landed in the street below with a thud. Immediately, the street was filled with Poles who ran to the crate to break it open. Cass and his companions ran down the steps and joined the others in the street. The boards were ripped off the crate and inside were hundreds of rifles.

One of the Polish soldiers said, "These are British Enfield rifles. They are great guns. Everybody grab one."

"Where are the bullets?" another fighter asked.

"Look! There is another crate falling. Maybe they're in that one," said another as a second crate landed on the ground just a few feet from the first. Everyone ran over to the second crate and broke it open. Inside were hundreds of additional British Enfield rifles.

"Hundreds more rifles," said the Polish officer. "There aren't any bullets in this crate either. They will probably drop another crate with bullets. Everybody grab a gun. We must have five hundred of them now. Let's get all of the guns out of the street so the Nazis don't know we have them."

After all of the guns had been taken into the buildings, the fighters came back out and stood in the street waiting for another drop. After thirty minutes it became apparent that the planes were leaving. The fighters stood in the street looking at one another. Finally someone said, "What good are guns with no bullets?"

"Maybe some more planes will come later," Ari said, knowing that it would soon be dark, and it was unlikely they would drop the crates at night.

The fighters stood in the street looking at one another and at the sky. "They aren't going to drop any more today," said Commander Erlich. "I will send word out in the network. They have been dropping these crates all over the city. Maybe the bullets were dropped somewhere else."

On the fourth day, Cass, Thaddeus, Rajmund, Ari, Helena, and Yitzhak were again lying on the roof waiting for soldiers to approach. "I sure hope they drop some ammunition for the guns," said Cass.

"You and me both," Ari replied. "These guns won't do us much good without bullets."

"Listen," Cass said. "I hear something that sounds like a tank."

"Tanks?" Helena said. "Can this get any worse?"

As they lay on the roof listening, the sound grew louder and louder. Suddenly the fighters felt a sense of dread. As they watched, a tank turned the corner and began driving up the street toward the location where the fighters were hiding in the buildings. The tank stopped in the street, pointed its gun at a building on the east side of the street and fired, blowing a large hole in the front of the building. There were no soldiers near the tank. It was just a single tank driving up the street toward them. Several soldiers stood at the corner where the tank had turned onto the street, but they did not advance with the tank.

The fighters watched as the tank slowly moved toward them and destroyed buildings along the way. "How are we going to fight the tanks?" Rajmund asked. "These guns can't fire through the tanks."

"We have to get close to the tanks to plant C-4 on the underside," Yitzhak said. "The problem is we have only a limited supply of explosives, and in this war, it looks like we are going to be fighting tanks. Once we run out of the C-4, then how will we fight them? Even worse, how can we get the C-4 down to the tanks without getting shot?"

"Hey, where's Ari? I just noticed he is gone," Rajmund said. "I didn't even see him leave. You don't suppose he decided the fight was too much, do you? The odds against us are too great?"

"No, Ari would never do that." Cass looked at the tank below them in the street. Suddenly he saw the figure of person run out of a building and into the street in front of the tank. The person had a pipe wrench in one hand and something in the other. He ran directly in front of the tank jumped on it and began banging on it with the wrench. "Hey, look," Cass shouted. "That's Ari there. That's him in front of the tank."

"What's he doing?" Yitzhak asked.

As they watched, the hatch of the tank opened. The head of a German soldier wearing a helmet emerged followed by a machine gun that began firing toward Ari at the front of the tank. Ari dropped down and ran to the side of the tank, jumped on the track, threw his body on the side of the tank, then threw something down the hatch. He leaped off the tank and ran back toward the building from which he had emerged. There was a blast inside the tank. Flames and smoke blew from the hole; the tank remained motionless.

A few minutes after the explosion in the tank, Ari suddenly reappeared on the roof. "That is how we get the explosives into the tank," he said, causing a round of laughter. "That was a potato-masher hand grenade. We have twenty-four of them…well, now twenty-three."

"That was great, but how many times will they fall for it?" Rajmund asked.

Ari replied, "Probably not very many, but anything we can do to get them to open the hatch, even for just a second, is all we need to toss in a grenade."

"What will we do when we run out of grenades and C-4?" Yitzhak asked.

"Hopefully by then we will have more ammunition and weapons from an airdrop," Ari said.

"But they only said they are going to drop guns and ammunition. They didn't say they would drop hand grenades and C-4," Helena pointed out.

"I know, but maybe they will send more than just guns," Ari said.

The tank sat in the middle of the street for the rest of the day. No other tanks came along, and no soldiers arrived. That night they slept in the building. Early in the morning a messenger visited the flat where they were staying and informed them that Commander Erlich had called a meeting in one half hour. "Attendance is mandatory."

"What's this about?" Ari did not particularly like having instructions thrown at him.

"Commander Erlich has important information to give to us."

"Okay," Ari said. "Is anyone going to stand watch for Germans?"

"Commander Erlich has already taken care of that."

Half an hour later, hundreds of fighters were gathered together in a large room of a warehouse. Commander Erlich asked everyone to sit down. When they were all seated, he began.

"I want to thank all of you for coming on such short notice. We have all put our lives on the line. I feel that it would be unfair to keep important information from you. You have the right to know so you can make informed decisions. Unfortunately, I have some bad news for you. Yesterday, we received airdrops from the British of thousands of rifles. These are state-of-the-art guns. We are very fortunate to have them."

"What about bullets?" one of the fighters shouted.

"I'm getting to that," he replied. "I sent messengers to every section where we are fighting to see if anyone got any ammunition for the rifles. There were no drops of ammunition yesterday. As you know, we have contact with Britain via radio transmission and a secret code that they gave us. We asked if any ammunition was going to be coming. We were told that Britain can't spare any ammunition right now because they need it for their own soldiers. They said we will get it, but they can't tell us how soon."

"You mean all we have are the weapons we came here with?" said one of the fighters in a raised voice.

Commander Erlich paced the floor in front of the fighters. "Unfortunately, that's about it. Britain says they will drop the ammunition as soon as they can. They just can't tell us how soon that will be."

The room was silent for a time. Finally someone asked, "What about the Soviets? When will they get here?"

"That is the other thing I need to tell you," Commander Erlich said. "The Soviets have stopped their advance at the river."

"What does that mean?" asked a fighter.

"I don't know yet. They are the ones who told us to start the uprising with their promises that they would invade from the east side of the city as soon as we started. I have been told by our Soviet contact that Stalin issued stand-down orders from Moscow."

"Who's your contact?" asked Ari.

"His name is Yurik. He says he knows you. You helped them map out the sewers."

Ari nodded. "Yes, we met him once about a year ago but haven't seen him since."

"It was in large part because of the information you gave them that Russia decided to proceed with the invasion of Warsaw."

"So what happened? Why are they standing down?"

Commander Erlich shook his head. "We don't really know. It almost seems like Stalin set us up. We all know what an ass he is."

"What are they doing?" Ari asked.

"They stopped on the other side of the Vistula River and are just sitting there," Commander Erlich said. "That's the reason I wanted to have this meeting. I wanted to tell everyone what is going on and give everyone a chance to decide if he wants to keep fighting."

One of the fighters said, "We have to keep going now. If we stop, the Germans will just kill us. Also, if Russia sees us back down, they will think we are an easy mark and will try to occupy us after they force out the Nazis. But if we hang on and fight this to the end, the Soviets will see how strong we are, and they will think twice before they decide to bring us under their control."

Commander Erlich nodded. "If anyone wants to leave, no one will think badly of you. If you want to leave, you are free to leave now. But if you stay, we will count on you, and you are in it to the end. Think about it until tomorrow morning, and let me know then."

Commander Erlich looked around the room. "I do want to mention one thing that happened yesterday. Many of you saw Ari Levine throw that grenade into the tank that is sitting out there in the street. That is the kind of courage we need to have. He didn't hesitate for one moment."

"Levine? Did you say Levine?" asked one of the fighters. "He is a Jew? I didn't know that. I have never seen Jews fight. Usually they just walk like sheep to the slaughter."

"You don't know your Bible very well, do you?" Commander Erlich replied. "The Jews were the best fighters in the Bible."

"Oh yeah," another fighter said. "I didn't think of that. Ari Levine, isn't he the guy who has been killing Nazis over the past five years?"

"Yes." Commander Erlich continued. "Because we did such a good job of wiping out the Nazis a few days ago, when they were on foot, I expect that they will use tanks more often now. The only way we can fight the tanks is with explosives. Our guns are useless against tanks. We only have twenty-three grenades and a small quantity of C-4. Does anyone know where we can get more explosives?"

The room remained silent for a time. Finally Ari said, "We can make Molotov cocktails."

"What are Molotov cocktails?"

"Bombs made out of petrol."

"Where will we get petrol fast and cheap?" Commander Erlich asked.

"I can get it from my dad's truck repair shop. We have fuel pumps," Rajmund volunteered.

Commander Erlich nodded. "That's great. We can't drive around with Molotov cocktails in the back of a truck, but if we can bring a truck here, we can make them in this warehouse."

After the meeting adjourned, Rajmund and Thaddeus walked to the repair shop and brought back a truck with a tank loaded with petrol. Everyone found as many bottles as they could and brought them back as well. By the time they had used all of the fuel in the tank, they had made over one thousand Molotov cocktails. Rajmund and Thaddeus took the empty truck back to the repair shop. Cass, Ari, and Helena carried two hundred Molotov cocktails to the building where they were staying.

That night Cass reflected on everything that had happened that day. They didn't know when they would receive ammunition for the guns that had been dropped, and the Soviets were not advancing to provide ground support. *This is going to turn out like the Jewish uprising last year*, he thought.

CHAPTER
29

T HE FIGHTING RAGED for weeks, with the Resistance
suffering far greater losses than the Germans. Though they fought
bravely and with skill, they were outnumbered and outgunned.
Cass, Ari, Thaddeus, Helena, Rajmund, and Yitzhak continued to use the
same building as their base. The disabled tank remained in the middle
of the street where Ari had tossed the grenade into the open hatch. The
Germans thought it was too dangerous to retrieve the tank with foot
soldiers. Some of the Resistance fighters had crawled into the tank and
thrown the burned bodies out onto the street. They took turns pretending
to drive the tank, though it was inoperable.

By the fourth week the Resistance was growing tired. Food was in
limited supply, and it had become too dangerous to make frequent ventures
in search of supplies. There had been no Nazis on the street in front of the
building for weeks, and the team had decided to fight the battle wherever
the fighting broke out. They would listen for gunfire and run to the
location of the fight along with other Resistance fighters.

On September 3, 1944, Cass, Thaddeus, Helena, Rajmund, Ari, and
Yitzhak ran up the street toward the sound of rifle fire. They turned the
corner of a building to find themselves in close-quarter combat with
dozens of Resistance fighters and Nazis. Ari drew a sword from his belt and

immediately ran into the crowd thrusting and striking five Nazi soldiers within thirty seconds. Untrained in the use of the sword, the Germans were no match for Ari's incredible skill and speed. Helena also drew her sword and ran into the midst of the fight, striking every Nazi she could see. Cass did not have a sword, though his rifle was equipped with a bayonet. He found the gun and bayonet cumbersome for close-quarter fighting, but it was all he had. He took the butt of his rifle and thrust it forward into the chin of a German soldier, who looked down at him with a puzzled expression. *That didn't go well*, thought Cass. As the soldier bolted toward him, Cass turned as if he was going to run. He suddenly thrust the bayonet under his left arm into the stomach of the Nazi. As the Nazi fell forward, Cass pulled his weapon from the body of the falling soldier and looked around for his comrades. For a moment, he could see no one he knew. Then in the distance he saw Helena swinging her sword violently. Cass noticed that she was surrounded by Nazi soldiers, and they were closing in on her.

Realizing that Helena was in peril, Cass ran as quickly as he could toward her. He saw her knocked onto her back on the ground. Then he saw one of the soldiers point his pistol at her. Knowing he could not reach her in time to stop the Nazi from shooting her, Cass dropped to his knee, pulled his rifle to his shoulder, sighted the Nazi with the gun, and pulled the trigger. Notwithstanding his heroic effort, Cass was not quick enough to shoot the Nazi before he could shoot Helena in the chest. As the Nazi fired his gun he was immediately struck by the bullet from Cass's rifle. Cass cocked the gun repeatedly, firing and shooting two more Nazi soldiers.

The Nazis scattered as Cass ran toward Helena. Ari, who had turned to see who had fired a gun, saw Helena on the ground and ran toward her. Arriving at her side at the same time as Cass, Ari placed his arm under her head as she lay dying. Cass held her hand. She looked up at Cass and said, "Thank you for saving me."

Cass shook his head. "I wasn't fast enough."

"You were fast enough, Cass. You were fast enough for me to know you did your best. That's all that matters."

Helena looked at Ari, who was glancing around to be sure no Nazis were approaching. She said, "Ari...I have to tell you. I am not going to make it, but...I have to tell you...I love you. I hoped I could be with you, but you have a wife somewhere. I hope and pray she is still alive."

Helena's speech slowed as she lost orientation. "I hope and pray...that..." She paused, looked at Ari, closed her eyes, and stopped breathing.

Cass and Ari both knew she was gone. Ari held her momentarily. He then gently laid her head on the pavement and stood up. Brandishing his sword, he screamed and ran through the crowd striking and stabbing as many Nazi soldiers as he could see. By this time the Nazis had begun to retreat. Cass slowly stood up and began looking for Thaddeus, Yitzhak, and Rajmund. He found them one street over where they had ambushed a group of Nazi soldiers who were beating a Polish woman. When they saw him, Thaddeus asked, "Are you okay, Cass?"

Cass shook his head. "Helena was killed. A Nazi shot her with a pistol. I shot him, but I was too late."

Thaddeus, Yitzhak, and Rajmund stood silently for a moment looking at Cass. Finally Yitzhak said, "Where is she?"

"This way." Cass began to lead the others to Helena's body.

The three men followed Cass. "We should have stayed together. Maybe we could have protected her," Rajmund said.

"I don't think so," replied Cass. "It all happened so fast. We were standing together when Ari ran into the middle of the fight. Helena was following behind him with her sword. She was swinging at everything. A soldier knocked her down and pointed his pistol at her. I fired as fast as I could, but he shot her first."

"Is he dead?" Yitzhak asked.

"Yeah, he is dead too."

When they arrived at the location of Helena's body they found Ari sitting on the ground next to her. He said nothing as they approached. The boys sat down next to Ari and remained silent for several minutes. Finally Ari said, "We need to bury her."

Rajmund asked, "Where are we going to bury her?"

"There is a grassy area over by the building where we have been staying. I think it would be fitting that we bury her in the yard of that building," Ari said. "She has no family, so what better place to bury her? We were her family."

Everyone agreed. They lifted her body and carried her several blocks to the building where they had been staying. Cass retrieved several shovels from the garage, and they buried Helena in the yard. Ari went into the garage and found pieces of rebar that had been left from some construction work. He also found a gas welding torch. He heated the rebar and welded it into the shape of a star. He threw it in the yard to cool. When it had cooled sufficiently, he placed the star above the grave of Helena.

That evening they sat in the upper room in the building. Yitzhak said, "It will be strange not having Helena to fight with us and to cook for us and to do all the things she always did."

Cass nodded. "I still can't believe she is gone."

Rajmund asked, "Are you okay, Ari?"

Ari nodded. "I'll be all right. I really miss her."

The men remained silent for several minutes. Finally Ari said, "Well, it looks like the Soviets aren't going to be helping. And we still have never received the ammunition for the weapons that were dropped by the British. It doesn't look like that's going to happen either."

Thaddeus nodded. "I think this is it. We aren't getting any help."

By mid-September the Resistance was clearly losing ground. The Nazis had brought in troops from both the eastern and western fronts, causing them to suffer greater losses from the Allies on both fronts. The German troops destroyed thousands of buildings as they plowed through neighborhoods with tanks, blowing up structures and killing everyone they saw. Wherever the Resistance was fighting, all of the buildings in the neighborhood would be destroyed. Food was in short supply, and Nazi patrolling was so heavy that it was nearly impossible to obtain supplies, except by traveling in the sewer system. Even this route was known to the Nazis, who had begun patrolling the sewers too. Having previously experienced severe hunger, Cass was prepared to experience it again if necessary to continue the fight against the Nazis. After the loss of Helena, their fighting took a more serious approach. They no longer joked as they had when Helena was with them. Perhaps it was Helena who had kept their spirits up with her ability to find humor in even dire situations. Now, Ari seldom talked at all. Perhaps it was his silence that caused the others to withdraw into their own thoughts of tragedy and loneliness.

September 15, 1944, was a Friday. The team always tried to rest for Shabbat but often had no opportunity due to the intensity of the fighting. That morning a slight drizzle dampened the streets and sidewalks. The air was warm, and Cass enjoyed the fresh smell of the rainy air. Around eight o'clock they heard the sound of fighting about five blocks away. Equipped with MG42 machine guns they had taken from dead Nazi soldiers, they were ready for the fight. Cass was pulling a wagon filled with Molotov cocktails and several potato-masher hand grenades covered by a tarp to keep them dry.

As they neared the fighting, they could hear machine guns and occasional blasts from a tank. Soon they could see the Nazis firing their weapons up the street. They ducked into a building to obtain a vantage point above the fighting so they could use the Molotov cocktails. They took the tarp off the wagon and laid it on the floor. They put the Molotov cocktails and hand grenades on the tarp. With one person at each corner of the tarp, they ran up four flights of steps. On the fourth floor they found an exit out to a deck. From the deck they could see hundreds of German soldiers in the street. Two Panzer tanks were driving up the street and had just passed the building they were hiding in. They could see no Resistance fighters in the street but could occasionally see shots fired from various locations in the buildings. The tanks were headed directly toward a hospital at the end of the street.

Ari shouted, "Look! The hatches are open on both tanks. There are soldiers' heads sticking out of them. These dummkopfs don't learn, do they?"

They ran to the far end of the deck for a better view of the tanks. The tanks stopped, and the first raised its gun, preparing to fire directly at the hospital. They could see in the upper floor windows of the hospital several hundred patients crowded together on the third floor. Ari grabbed two hand grenades and said, "When I come out that door down there cover me. I'm going to toss a grenade into each tank."

Thaddeus shouted, "There are too many foot soldiers with machine guns. We won't be able to provide enough cover."

"I have to try. They are going to kill everyone in the hospital if we don't disable those tanks." Ari ran into the building and down the stairs. Yitzhak grabbed two grenades and started into the building.

"Where are you going?" Cass asked.

"I'm going with him in case he doesn't make it."

"It's too dangerous," Rajmund insisted.

"We have to try," Yitzhak shouted. "We can't throw it in from here, it is too far." He ran into the building and down the steps.

As they watched the chaos in the street below Ari suddenly burst out of a door on the first floor and ran straight toward the tank that was aiming its gun at the hospital. Cass, Thaddeus, and Rajmund opened fire on the soldiers near the tanks to draw their fire away from Ari. Ari ran up to the front of the tank, jumped on the tracks, climbed to the top of the tank, pulled the cap and drawcord on the potato-masher grenade, and lobbed it down into the hatch. The soldier with his head protruding from the hatch look stunned to see Ari. He tried to climb out. Ari jumped down from the tank as the grenade exploded inside killing everyone, including the soldier who had been sitting with his head protruding from the hatch.

Ari fell but quickly jumped to his feet. Notwithstanding the cover provided by Thaddeus, Cass, and Rajmund, Ari was hit by a single bullet in the leg and fell to the ground. Suddenly Yitzhak, who had been watching from the first floor, burst through the door and out onto the street. Ari shouted for him to go back, but Yitzhak ignored him. He jumped on the tracks of the second tank, climbed up to the hatch, and pulled the cap and drawcord on the grenade, but before he could lob it in, he was shot in his back. Then a second time. As he fell backward off the tank, the grenade exploded in his hand, killing him instantly but doing little damage to the tank. The soldier dropped quickly down into the tank.

Ari shouted as he saw Yitzhak killed by the grenade.

Cass picked up a grenade, pulled the cap and drawcord, and threw it directly at the open hatch on the second tank, which was approximately forty meters away. Perhaps it was a fluke, but as the grenade left his hand, he felt a strange sensation that it was going to go into the hatch. Indeed, as the hatch was being pulled shut by one of the soldiers inside, the grenade flew cleanly through the small opening and exploded, killing everyone inside.

Seeing both tanks disabled by Ari and Cass, other Resistance fighters felt a sense of encouragement. Suddenly they ran out of the buildings and burst into the streets, shouting and cheering as they fired at the German soldiers who began running down the street to escape. In less than two minutes, the Germans, who were preparing to fire a tank into a hospital, had been disabled and were now running for their lives. The Resistance fighters were not going to show any mercy as they chased the Nazis for blocks. Cass, Thaddeus, and Rajmund stood on the deck with submachine guns, firing as quickly as they could to eliminate as many fleeing soldiers as possible.

Once the fighting had stopped, the three boys ran down to the street to see how badly Ari was injured. Notwithstanding the successful fight against the Germans, there was no celebrating for these young men. They had recently lost Helena and now Yitzhak. Ari was badly injured and would not be able to fight again, assuming he lived. This was not a time for celebration.

"Ari, what do you want us to do?" asked Cass. "We should take you to the hospital."

Ari grimaced in pain. "They won't take me in. I am a Jew."

Rajmund replied, "You just saved them from being blown to bits. They'll take you."

"That doesn't really matter to them," replied Ari. "They would not even let us fight alongside them."

Rajmund replied, "Then let's give you a non-Jewish name. We will tell them you don't have your papers because you have been fighting since the beginning of the uprising, and you lost them."

"That's a good idea," said Cass. "Ari, we will tell the people at the hospital that you are Arnold Gorski. You were born and raised here in Warsaw, and your family was killed in the German invasion in 1939."

Rajmund said, "What do you think, Ari? I think it will work. There is no way you are going to get well without penicillin. We have to try."

"Okay, let's try it. It might work, at least until someone recognizes me. I will have to memorize the name Arnold Gorski."

They helped Ari to his feet. Despite the pain, he was able to limp into the hospital. As they entered the front door, several doctors and nurses came up to him. One of the doctors said, "Thank you for what you did."

"I didn't do anything," replied Ari.

"Yes, you did. We all saw it. You saved us from being killed," the doctor said.

Rajmund said, "Can you help him? His name is Arnold Gorski."

"Arnold Gorski? What are you talking about? We know who he is. This is Ari Levine. One of the greatest Jewish Resistance fighters in all of Poland."

"You will help him then?" Cass asked.

"Yes, of course we will help him," the doctor replied. "Let's get him to a room."

The doctor helped Ari lie down on a gurney then jabbed Ari in the leg with a morphine shot. "This will kill the pain. I am amazed at what you did. I have never seen so much courage in my life. You ran into the midst of machine gun fire to blow up the tank. I'm so sorry about your comrade. He gave his life trying to save us."

The doctor looked at one of the nurses. "Take him to the operating room. We need to get that bullet out."

As the nurses wheeled Ari away, another doctor said, "Who was the guy who threw the grenade into the tank from the deck of the building. That was incredible."

Rajmund pointed at Cass. "He did."

"That was amazing. If you can throw like that you should be throwing the javelin in the Olympics."

"Thank you, sir, but it was just luck."

"Luck? I suppose, if you think God is luck." The doctor laughed.

Ari was taken to a room where he was well cared for. The nurses gave the others a pot of food to take with them. Cass, Rajmund, and Thaddeus went back to the tank to see if they could retrieve Yitzhak's body for burial. They soon realized it would be impossible to retrieve even part of his body; it had been blown into pieces. They ran back upstairs, retrieved their Molotov cocktails and grenades, and headed back toward their building, dragging the explosives in the wagon.

That night Cass, Rajmund, and Thaddeus sat together in their building. They ate the chicken, potatoes, and corn they were given by the nurses at the hospital. It was their first meal in days. They spoke little as they ate. Finally Rajmund spoke. "It is just us again. Just like before the war."

Thaddeus nodded. "The only ones missing are the girls, Rachel, Sarah, and"—he looked at Cass—"Zofia."

After a few moments, Rajmund said, "I still can't believe that both Yitzhak and Helena are gone. It seems they were here just yesterday, and now they are gone forever."

Cass nodded. "I know."

The boys fell asleep sitting together in the living room of the flat where they were staying. While they were hopeful they would soon be joined by Soviet or British forces and would overpower the Nazis, they were beginning to doubt they would receive any assistance at all. They were becoming aware that they might not be able to defeat the Nazis. It was a sad evening indeed for these young fighters.

CHAPTER

30

T HE UPRISING LASTED for sixty-three days, from August 1 until October 2, 1944. Approximately sixteen thousand Polish Resistance fighters lost their lives and eight thousand German soldiers were killed in the fighting. In addition, two hundred thousand Polish civilians lost their lives, mostly in mass executions. During the fighting, approximately 25 percent of Warsaw was destroyed. After the uprising was quelled, the Germans systematically destroyed another 35 percent of the city. When added to the destruction from the initial invasion by Germany and the first uprising, 90 percent of Warsaw had been destroyed by the end of the second uprising. In every direction as far as the eye could see, the buildings were in rubble. *So this is war*, thought Cass. *This is modern war.*

After the fighting subsided, Thaddeus, Cass, and Rajmund decided to remain in the flat for a few weeks. The Germans were systematically going from building to building looking for Jews and destroying every building along the way. Early one morning, the boys went to the hospital. There they found the doctor who agreed to take Ari in and help him. "Where is Ari?" asked Rajmund.

The doctor shook his head. "He's gone."

"He died?" Rajmund asked. "We didn't think he was hurt that bad."

"No, he didn't die," replied the doctor. "He just got up and left one day. He told us he was going to leave. We told him he wasn't well enough yet. He said he was concerned that if the Nazis discovered we were hiding a Jew, they would arrest us all. He was probably right. The nurses went into his room early one morning, and he was gone."

"Do you know where he went?" Thaddeus asked.

"No, we have no idea."

Thaddeus, Cass, and Rajmund searched for Ari for several days but were unable to locate him. No one seemed to know where he had gone. Eventually, they made their way through the sewers back over to the Litynski garage where they had been staying before the uprising. Once inside the garage area, the family came out to see them.

Irena beamed at Cass. "My little boy. Come here and hug your mama."

Cass hugged his mother, who didn't seem to care that he was dirty and had not bathed in weeks. Irena then hugged Thaddeus and said, "I am so happy you made it through the fighting. I was so worried."

The three boys went into the showers and came out wearing clean clothes. They each had a large bowl of stew and some freshly baked bread. It was the first real meal they had eaten since the chicken, potatoes, and corn they had been given by the nurses.

The family was thrilled to see them alive and well, but saddened about Helena and Yitzhak and worried about Ari. For months the Nazis searched houses all around the neighborhood but never searched the Litynski property. There were so many German soldiers around the garage, all of the time, that it never occurred to any of them that the Litynskis might be hiding Jews. This was a time when there was nothing for the Jewish guests to do except remain hidden. During the time they were living there, Thaddeus and Cass learned how to repair truck engines. In this way they were able to earn the room and board they were receiving from the Litynskis. They also became experienced mechanics, and Cass decided then that he wanted to become an airplane mechanic if they ever got through this troubled time.

Other than the searches and the raids that occurred after the 1944 uprising, there was little military activity in the neighborhood around the Litynski truck repair shop. Nonetheless, German soldiers were in the repair shop on a daily basis, dropping off and picking up trucks.

Although the 1944 uprising had been quelled, hope remained that the Poles would eventually obtain freedom from the Nazis. There were rumors that the Soviets were still planning to invade Warsaw and expel the Nazis, but many worried that the Soviets would be just as bad or worse than the Nazis. Yet, the belief was that any change would be better than no change.

By December of 1944 word began to spread through Poland that the Nazis were losing the war. Given the lack of support exhibited during the uprising, many doubted the rumors. In January of 1945, the Soviet and the Polish armies launched a massive offensive in Poland in an effort to terminate the Nazi occupation. Early one morning Josef and Rajmund came into the back apartments. Thaddeus and Cass were getting ready to go to bed, having worked through the night in the garage.

Josef said, "Cass, Thaddeus, there's someone here to see you."

"Who could that be?" Thaddeus asked.

"Do you remember meeting two Russian spies in the sewer a few years back?" Rajmund looked at Cass.

"Yes, I remember. I don't remember their names. They told us Russia was going to invade Warsaw, but it never happened."

"It's happening now," Josef said. "Those spies are here to see you."

"How did they find us?"

Rajmund replied, "Apparently they have been in contact with Ari. They said Ari has been fighting with the Russian army."

"What were their names?" Thaddeus asked. "The spies, I mean."

"Gustaw and Yurik," Rajmund replied.

"That sounds right," Cass said, "but I'm not sure. How do we know this isn't a trap?"

"I think they know too much about Ari for it to be a trap," Rajmund said. "They must be in communication with him. They said he told them how to find you."

"The more I think about it, I do remember their names," Cass said. "Those are the names of the Russians we met in the sewer."

"Do you want me to show them in?"

"What do they want?" Thaddeus asked.

"They want to know if you want to fight with the Russian army against the Nazis," Rajmund said.

"Why don't you go ahead and bring them back?" Cass asked.

"I will get them." Rajmund left and came back a few minutes later with two men. Cass could not recognize them because he had only seen them for a few minutes in the dark sewer.

One of them said, "Cass, do you remember us? I am Gustaw, and this is Yurik. We met you in the sewer a couple of years ago when you were with Ari, another guy, and a girl."

"I remember meeting you, but I didn't really see what you looked like."

Thaddeus asked, "What can you remember about the meeting? Maybe if you can recall some details, Cass will know it is you."

"You aren't sure it's us, are you?" Yurik asked.

"I can't be sure. The Nazis use all kinds of tricks to find people," Cass replied. "How many people were down there with us?"

Gustaw said, "I think there were four of you. Three men and one girl. There were two Nazis and us as well. Ari threw a knife at one of the Nazis and used his bayonet to kill the other. We had never seen anyone fight like that before. It was insane."

Yurik said, "We ran, and Ari tackled us. Then we told him we were Russian. After we talked, he gave us a map of the sewers. The Russian army has been using that to get into the city."

Cass said, "Okay, I'm convinced it is you. What did you come here for? How is Ari?"

Gustaw replied, "Ari is doing well. He is fighting with us, and he asked us to come and see if you want to fight with us to take back Warsaw."

"To fight with the Russians?" Cass asked.

Yurik replied, "Yes, to fight with us. He said you're both very good even though you are young, and you know the city very well."

Irena walked into the room where they were talking. "What's going on?" she asked.

Rajmund said, "These men are Russian spies. They have been fighting alongside Ari. They were sent here on a spy mission, and Ari asked them to stop here to see if Cass, Thaddeus, and I want to join the Russians in fighting the Nazis."

"No more fighting," Irena said. "I just got the boys back a few months ago. I don't want them leaving again."

Cass replied, "I need to do this, Mama. I have been restless all the time I have been here. I need to get back into the fight."

Irena sat in a chair. "Oh, Cass, I just want you to think about this. Before when you fought, it seemed we had little chance of surviving. Then it seemed that you might as well be fighting because we were all going to die anyway. But it is different now. Now the Nazis are losing. Soon we may be free. We have a great chance of surviving. I don't want you to do this."

"I have to do this, Mama. It's my reason for living."

Irena shook her head. "Thad, are you going to go too?"

Thaddeus replied, "No, Mama. I have had enough fighting."

"How about you, Rajmund? Are you going to fight?"

"No," said Rajmund. "I am like Thad. I think we've fought enough. The Russians have a huge army. They don't need us."

Cass said, "You have to let me go, Mama."

"When will you leave?" she asked.

Cass looked at Gustaw and Yurik. Yurik replied, "We can come back in two days to pick up Cass."

"Cass, you are only thirteen years old now."

"That's right, Mama. That makes me old enough to fight if I want to. Many countries recruit fighters at the age of twelve."

Grandpa and Grandma entered the room. Irena looked at them. "These men are here to recruit Cass to fight with the Russian Army against the Nazis."

Grandpa asked, "Where will you be stationed?"

Gustaw replied, "He will be here in Warsaw."

Irena looked at Grandpa, "Papa, should I let him go?"

"I think he's old enough to decide. He is a young man now. Many young men join the army at age twelve."

Irena replied, "Cass, you grew up too early. I know if I tried to stop you, you would just slip out at night and be gone. I would rather have you leave knowing that you are leaving than to have you run away at night. I can't stop you."

"I will be careful as always, Mama."

"Okay, we will be back on Tuesday to pick up Cass," Yurik said.

"I will be ready," Cass replied.

Two days later, before daylight, Yurik and Gustaw stopped by in a black Volkswagen Beetle to pick up Cass. Gustaw was driving. He parked behind the repair shop. Cass came out the back door carrying a German

MG42 in his left hand with a seventy-five-round drum magazine attached and a duffel bag with clothing and ammunition in his right. He was wearing a military trench coat and military-issue boots. He set the gun and the duffel bag in the rear seat of the car. "I'll be right back," he said as he started back to the building. He returned a few moments later with a large ammunition case. He set that in the rear seat of the car as well. Irena stood by the rear door and waved at Cass. He jumped into the rear of the car and waved back. Gustaw put the automobile in gear and headed up the alley to the street.

As they drove, Yurik said, "Where did you get the MG42, Cass?"

"I took it off a dead Nazi during the uprising."

Gustaw asked, "You have plenty of clothes in the bag? It is going to be cold out here."

Cass replied, "I'll be warm. I have the heavy coat I'm wearing. In the bag I have a second pair of pants, underwear, and shirts. I am wearing military boots and I have on two pairs of wool socks, and there's another pair in the bag,"

"Is there anything else you need?" asked Yurik.

"I wish I had a pistol and holster. Something like a Luger that I could use for close-quarter fighting. This MG42 goes through ammunition too fast."

Yurik replied, "You should use your MG as a single shot. How many rounds of ammunition do you have in that case?

"Five hundred."

"That's a lot," said Gustaw. "If you use it sparingly that will last a long time."

As they drove toward the east side of Warsaw, they saw a checkpoint up ahead manned by two soldiers.

"How are we going to get through this checkpoint?" asked Cass.

"Cover the gun and the ammo box with your coat," said Yurik.

Cass took off his coat and placed it over the ammo box and gun. As they pulled up to the checkpoint, one soldier walked to each side of the car. Gustaw and Yurik rolled down their windows. The soldier on the driver side asked, "Where are you going?"

Cass saw Gustaw tap Yurik's knee. Suddenly, both Gustaw and Yurik opened fire with pistols. Gustaw put the car in gear. Yurik shouted, "Let's go." Gustaw let out the clutch and sped away just as the lights of another vehicle were approaching from behind. It soon became apparent that the vehicle behind was following. Suddenly a large spotlight shone on them from the vehicle. "That's a German military truck," said Gustaw.

Yurik said, "How far to the river?"

Gustaw replied, "Not far. A couple of blocks."

"Step on it."

Gustaw pushed the accelerator to the floor. "There it is," he said, as the car suddenly drove down a steep embankment. At the bottom of the hill were German soldiers positioned behind iron plates facing across the Vistula River where the Russians were positioned. In front of them was the river, frozen over. The soldiers jumped back to get out of the path of the speeding VW. At the bottom of the embankment the car sped out onto the frozen river at 120 kph and began spinning in 360-degree circles across the ice. The German soldiers began firing at the vehicle. Yurik shouted, "Cass, let me borrow your MG."

Cass handed the machine gun to Yurik who leaned out of the front passenger window and began firing at the Germans on the bank who were firing at the car. On the other side of the river, the Russian soldiers recognized the VW and began firing at the Germans to provide cover for the VW. The VW stopped spinning, and Gustaw regained control. The bank on the other side of the river was much more level, and the VW was able to drive up on shore and behind a concrete wall for cover. Soon the shooting stopped.

"Wow," said Cass. "That was a crazy ride."

Gustaw and Yurik began laughing. Cass looked at them momentarily then started laughing too. "Welcome to the Soviet way of fighting," said Yurik.

"Do you guys ever get killed doing this crazy stuff?" Cass asked.

Gustaw replied, "I've never been killed. Yurik, have you ever been killed?"

"Not that I know of."

All three of them laughed. "You know what I mean," Cass said.

Gustaw said, "Actually, we don't have too many deaths in this unit. What we do is so crazy most people don't anticipate it. Think about it. How many times have you heard about enemy soldiers driving through a

German checkpoint and attacking the guards? No one expects that. So we have the advantage of catching them off guard."

That day they stayed in a warm house on the east side of the river. They laughed and joked and ate good food. Gustaw and Yurik drank a vodka called Stolichnaya. "Here, Cass, have some of this," Yurik said. "If you are old enough to fight you are old enough to drink vodka." Both Yurik and Gustaw laughed.

Cass felt awkward. "No, thanks. I want to always be alert."

Yurik and Gustaw laughed again. "That is why we drink Stoli," said Yurik. "You can't buy this stuff in the stores. It is only available to the army. It is made by the Moscow State Wine Warehouse number one. Here, take a big gulp. If you don't like it, you don't ever have to drink it again."

Yurik handed a pint bottle to Cass, who took a huge gulp. He swallowed and immediately began coughing. "Augh, what is that stuff? It tastes like dog barf."

"When have you eaten dog barf?" Yurik asked.

"I haven't, but I know what it tastes like," Cass said.

Yurik and Gustaw burst into laughter. "That is the Russian man's drink," said Yurik. "Every Russian man drinks it."

"I'm glad I'm Polish," Cass said with a laugh. He continued, "I remember hearing that you are actually Polish but were captured when Russia first invaded Poland way back in 1939. I think you said it in the sewer, and I think I heard a Resistance fighter say it too. Is it true?"

Gustaw nodded. "That's right."

"Why did you join the Russian army?" asked Cass.

Gustaw nodded. "It was either join the army or go to a labor camp. They killed a lot of Poles. Others were sent to labor camps. Some of us who were younger were given a chance to join the army."

"Russia doesn't sound much better than Germany," Cass replied. "Why did Russia invade Poland in 1939? How is Russia any better than Germany?"

"Russia really had no choice," Yurik said. "Britain and France were reluctant to anger Hitler, so they constantly attempted to appease him. Russia was forced to do the same. So Stalin entered into a pact with Hitler. Under that agreement Germany invaded Poland from the west on

September 1, 1939, and Russia invaded from the east on September 17, 1939."

"I think I heard of the agreement," said Cass. "Was it called the Molotov Pact? I heard about it when we were in the ghetto."

Yurik nodded. "Molotov-Ribbentrop Pact."

"I thought that was a funny name for an agreement," laughed Cass. "That's what we call homemade bombs."

Gustaw replied, "The agreement was named after the man who drafted it, Soviet Foreign Minister Vyacheslav Molotov. The Molotov cocktail was also named after him."

As they sat in the comfortable house with the fireplace burning throughout the day, they could occasionally hear gunfire. "Where's the shooting?" asked Cass.

"That's down south on the river," Gustaw told him. "There's a German officer down there who thinks he looks tough if he starts skirmishes. He doesn't know it, but he is the first one we are going to eliminate when we cross the river."

"When are we crossing?"

"As soon as we get word from Moscow," Yurik said.

Later in the day the men were joined by several other soldiers who came in to eat and get warm. They sat with Yurik, Gustaw, and Cass, playing poker and checkers. As evening approached some additional soldiers entered the front door of the house. As they talked, Cass recognized one of the voices as Ari's. He went into the living room and saw Ari standing by the door. Ari saw him and started laughing. "Cass, you made it." He walked toward Cass with a noticeable limp and gave him a hug.

"How's your leg?" asked Cass.

"It's better, but it looks like I am going to have a limp from now on. I can't run as fast as I used to, but that's the hazard of war. Did Thaddeus and Rajmund come with you?"

Cass shook his head. "No, they said they'd had enough fighting."

Ari nodded, "I can understand. It takes a certain kind of crazy to do what we do."

"What's it like fighting with the Russians?" asked Cass.

"Much easier than the uprisings."

"Why is it easier?"

Ari threw his coat on a hall tree. "For one thing, we always win. The Germans are always running. We never have a shortage of ammunition, and we always outnumber them when we attack."

"So when will we attack?"

"Tomorrow morning we are heading across the river."

"Tomorrow?"

"Yeah, you guys didn't know?" asked a soldier who had come in with Ari.

Gustaw and Yurik walked in. "Tomorrow, what?" Yurik asked.

"At eight o'clock tomorrow morning, we are crossing the river. After crossing we are going to move right across the city until there are no more Nazis," said Ari.

Cass sat down on a couch. *So it really is going to happen. We are finally going to drive the Nazis out of Poland.*

The following morning the Russian army began crossing the river, just as Ari had said. Initially, they opened fire on the Germans, using machine guns and heavy artillery. Within minutes the Germans were scrambling to get up the embankment and away from the Russians. The Russian army swept across the river, chasing the Germans, who were in full retreat. As the Russians reached the top of the embankment on the other side, they realized that the Germans had regrouped approximately one hundred feet ahead and were now shooting back. They charged the hill and a number of Russian soldiers were shot, but it seemed that each one was replaced by ten. As Cass looked up and down the river in both directions he realized that this was the largest number of men he had ever seen assembled in one location. As far as he could see in both directions, there were thousands of Russian and Polish soldiers climbing the embankment and firing at the German soldiers.

The Germans had held Poland for six years and had secured strong fortifications. Even so, the Russians proceeded across the city, notwithstanding the significant loss of life. Within a matter of days, the Russians had taken Warsaw and were advancing westward toward Germany. The progression was sporadic as the Germans frequently stood their ground and then retreated. The constant advancing and retreating movement proved frustrating for the Russians. One problem was the inability to see the sudden shifts in the position of the Germans, rendering it impossible to anticipate their sudden reversal and attacks. It was decided that the Russians needed a scout to view the terrain with binoculars and to report back by radio. They needed someone small and difficult to see, but dedicated. Sitting around a campfire one evening, Yurik said, "What we need is someone to hide in a tree, high enough that he can see for several miles, and report back by radio what he sees."

A soldier asked, "Who would we use for that? It would be very dangerous."

Yurik said, "It would have to be someone inconspicuous, maybe someone small who could wear camouflage and not be seen."

"What camouflage? There are no leaves on the trees yet."

"I can do it," said Cass. "I am small enough to hide behind a tree limb, and I can report back what I see."

Everyone remained silent for a moment. Finally an officer said, "That might be a good idea. Cass might be the perfect scout."

"I can do it. Let me try."

Yurik said, "I say let him try. He is a good warrior. If anyone can do it, Cass can do it."

It was decided. The following morning, a 750-cc BMW R75 motorcycle, driven by Yurik, carried Cass close to enemy lines on the western front. The motorcycle thundered across the open field toward a wooded area several miles from the German line. Upon reaching the woods, they followed a path to the edge of the opposite side of the wooded area. The branches of trees along the side of the path brushed against Cass as they sped through the woods. Slowing, they searched for a tree suitable for climbing. An old oak tree was selected for Cass to use as his observation post. He was given a three-day supply of food rations, a pair of binoculars, a handheld two-way communication radio, a rope, a pistol, and several brown blankets.

"We're counting on you, Cass," said Yurik. "Be careful. We will be less than a mile away. If they see you, we'll be here within ten minutes to get you out."

"You promise?" asked Cass.

Yurik nodded. "I promise. Here is an extra battery in case your battery dies. Turn the radio on only when you need to call us. Otherwise, keep it off."

Cass nodded.

"Okay, can you climb the tree?"

Cass stood on top of the motorcycle seat. He grabbed the lowest branch on the tree and pulled himself up. Once he was on the branch, he turned around, held his hand out, and said, "Okay."

Yurik tossed the binoculars up to him along with the radio and a pistol. "You may need the pistol," he said.

Cass put the binoculars around his neck by the strap. The radio he placed in his pocket, and the gun he put in his belt.

Yurik tossed up the blankets. Cass threw them over his shoulder. Yurik then tossed up a ten-foot rope. "That's it," he said. "Find a good solid limb that goes up like a 'V.' Sit on the limb with your chest against the tree. At night wrap the rope around you and tie it to the tree so you don't fall out when you sleep. You will probably be up there several days but we will always be a short distance away. Remember, if you are spotted, call us on the radio immediately, and we will be here within ten minutes."

Cass nodded. "Okay." He began to climb higher up the tree. Yurik watched as he climbed. When Cass was approximately twenty feet up the tree, he found a limb like Yurik described. He straddled it, his chest against the tree. He was reminded of the tree blinds from his younger years when he would hunt in the mountains overlooking Warsaw.

"Are you all set?"

"All set." Cass waved.

"Okay, remember keep the walkie-talkie off except if you need to call us. That way the battery will last longer."

"Got it."

Yurik started his motorcycle, waved at Cass, and sped away.

In the distance Cass could see German troops. With the binoculars he could observe the movements. As the tanks began moving, he used the radio to inform the Russian ground forces. This practice continued as the Germans moved westward and slowly retreated toward Germany. As the troops moved, Cass would follow them, find another tree, and climb it. Yurik would show up every third day to bring Cass fresh supplies.

One morning Yurik brought chicken and potatoes for Cass. "I'm too far away," said Cass as he sat on a log in the woods eating his meal. "I need to go behind enemy lines."

"That's too dangerous," Yurik said.

Cass shook his head. "I need more detail about what they are doing."

"How are you going to get behind enemy lines without being seen?"

"I will walk in at night."

Yurik insisted, "That's too dangerous. You need to keep your distance."

After Cass finished eating, Yurik got on his motorcycle to leave. "Remember, don't go behind enemy lines, Cass. I don't want to take a corpse back to Warsaw."

Cass did not respond. Yurik started his motorcycle and shouted, "I will be back in three days." He waved, put the motorcycle in gear, and drove away.

That evening Cass decided to go behind enemy lines, notwithstanding the warning he had received from Yurik. Using the moonlight, he walked for several hours until he knew he was deep in German-occupied territory. He could see German troops both north and south of his location. He was within a mile of troops to his west. Behind him were the Russian troops.

Cass found a tree that seemed as if it would provide good cover. He could see well enough in the moonlight to locate the lowest branch on the tree though it was out of reach. Throwing the rope over the branch Cass took ahold of both ends. He pulled himself up onto the branch, then climbed onto the next until he was approximately twenty feet up in the tree. He tied himself to the tree to sleep through the rest of the night.

Cass awakened the following morning to voices speaking German. Looking down he saw two German soldiers walking in a northerly direction approximately three hundred feet in front of the tree where he was hiding. He remained perfectly still as they walked out of sight. Using the binoculars, he looked toward the location of the troops. Canvassing all around, he saw German troops in every direction except directly behind him where he could see the Russian troops. He realized that he had gotten in closer than he thought. He could hear the clanking sound of metal pans as the Germans prepared their breakfast. He reached for his radio and called the Russian troops. Talking softly, he gave his location then informed the Russians that the Germans were eating breakfast. He saw supply trucks arrive with ammunition and explosives, and he relayed this information to the Russians.

"Stay where you are, Cass, we are coming in," said the voice on the other side of the radio.

Approximately forty-five minutes later, Cass could hear gunfire behind him as the Russians were shooting toward the Germans. The Germans began firing back with 88-mm guns, rifles, and tanks. Cass held perfectly still, hoping he would not get shot. As he looked through the binoculars he saw a German officer looking back at him with binoculars. *I wonder if he saw me*, thought Cass as he leaned into the tree. He continued to watch with the binoculars as an 88-mm gun, sitting on wheels, was pointed directly toward him. Deciding he had better climb down and take cover, Cass loosened the rope. Suddenly he heard a loud crack as a missile from the gun struck the trunk of the tree in which he was hiding. The thrust threw him backward out of the tree. He landed on his buttocks on the ground and momentarily lost consciousness.

Cass awakened to the sound of guns firing and of people talking near him. He felt himself being lifted on a stretcher and placed in the back of a military truck. He looked up and saw Yurik. "You're going to be okay, Cass."

"What happened?" asked Cass.

"That tree you were in—it is lying on the ground over there. It got hit by an eighty-eight millimeter."

"I saw them aim it directly at me," said Cass. "The officer was looking at me through his binoculars."

"We saw you go down," Yurik said. "The Germans were coming toward you, but we got here first. If they had captured you, they would have tortured you for information. We are taking you back to a field hospital. They will take care of you."

"When will I be back?"

"I don't think you will be fighting anymore in this war, unless you want to fight from a wheelchair. Your hip is broken. We are only about a week from taking Berlin, so the war will probably be over before you are back on your feet. If I don't see you again, it has been great fighting with you. Everyone on the Russian side knows what you have done for us. They call you our little hero."

Cass was taken to a field hospital behind the Russian lines. He was placed on a gurney in a room with a hundred Russian soldiers. Eventually a doctor and a nurse came over to him. The doctor looked at his chart, which consisted of scratches on a single piece of paper. "Let's turn him on his right side," said the doctor as he examined Cass. "It looks like you may have a pelvic fracture and a dislocation. I can help you with the dislocation, but there isn't anything I can do about the fracture. I can't perform that kind of surgery out here."

Cass nodded.

We don't have any anesthesia, but I can give you some vodka. The doctor handed Cass a half pint of Stoli. "Drink this," he said. "All of it. I will be back in about a half hour."

Cass took the bottle. "I have had this stuff before. I hate it."

"You need to drink it. By the way, I am an orthopedic surgeon, so don't worry, I can help you."

Cass followed the instructions and drank the half pint of vodka. A short time later the doctor returned with the nurse. He turned Cass back on his side and said, "This is going to hurt." He made a swift and sudden rotating move with Cass's hip then began shoving on it. The pain was excruciating. Suddenly Cass felt a popping sensation. "We got it," said the doctor. "You will be okay now."

"But I am going to be sick from that stuff I drank."

The doctor laughed. "That's vodka." He motioned for the nurse to get a bucket, which he gave to Cass. "This is in case you get sick."

Cass took the bucket but found he didn't need it. He slept much of the day.

The following morning, he was awakened to the gruff voice of a large Russian woman. "I am going to be your physical therapist. I am going to help you walk again."

"No, I don't need physical therapy."

"The doctor said I am to do this for you," the therapist said.

Cass shook his head.

"Well, we won't start for about a week."

"I will be out of here in a week," replied Cass.

"Where are you going?" she asked.

"I am going back out to the battle."

"You can't fight now. Besides, they won't need you now. The war is almost over. Russia is winning."

The following day Cass was walking, albeit painfully, and with a limp. He decided to find a division commander who could take him back to the western front. He saw an officer walking past some tanks. "Sir, can you help me get back to my unit?"

The officer turned and looked at Cass. Then he started laughing. "Where is your unit, young man?"

"I was on the western front when I was shot out of a tree," Cass replied, frustrated that the officer found him amusing.

"You were shot?"

"The tree was shot by an eighty-eight millimeter, and it knocked me out of the tree."

"Oh yes, I've heard about you. You are the Jewish boy who has been spotting for the infantry. Your name is Bieberstein."

"Yes," Cass said. "I want to get back to my unit."

"What is your first name?" asked the officer.

"Cass."

"Well, Cass, I can't let you go back out on foot. You had a serious injury. How would you like to ride in a tank?"

Cass nodded. "I would like that, but what would I do?"

"You are a good spotter. Sometimes you could navigate, and sometimes you could drive."

"Okay, I will do that," said Cass.

"I'm Field Marshal Georgy Zhukov," said the officer. "I know your grandfather, Colonel Bieberstein. Everyone has heard about you. Where are your parents, Cass?" Cass had heard the name Zhukov but was unaware that he was a high-ranking Soviet officer who had been charged with leading the attack on Germany from the east, or that he would eventually become the Minister of Defense of the Soviet Union and a member of the Politburo. To Cass he was just a nice man in a tank who seemed to view Cass as a wounded war hero.

"I don't know where my father is. He left when the war started to go somewhere so he could send for us. Mama is living in a flat not far from here. Do you think we could go there? I want to get some insulin from the hospital for my grandmother. She has diabetes. She has been out of insulin for a long time and is really sick."

Field Marshal Zhukov replied, "The hospital won't have any insulin, but I have some. I am also diabetic. Wait here."

Field Marshal Zhukov walked toward the officers' quarters. Cass walked around the tank, looking at the large tracks, the wheels, and the gun. *This is different from the German tanks*, he thought. As he stood looking at the tank, he heard footsteps behind him. Turning, he saw Field Marshal Zhukov approaching with a bottle in his hand. He gave it to Cass and said, "Let's go." Another tank approached and stopped behind Zhukov's tank. As they climbed into the tank Zhukov said, "There are still a lot of Germans around, so we will bring some backup." He pointed at the tank behind them.

Inside the tank Cass looked at the levers and instruments. There were two other soldiers in the tank. Cass did not know what they did but knew that it involved operating the tank. As the tank started moving, Zhukov climbed up into the hatch so his head was protruding through the hatch. "Climb up here, Cass, so you can direct us." Cass complied.

After driving a few minutes Cass directed them to a small house in a country area. "This is where Grandma is staying now." Cass climbed out of the tank and went inside. He saw his mother sitting at a table with Sarah and Grandpa. Irena looked tired. Her hair was unkempt. She appeared weak. She looked up and asked, "Cass, how did you get here?" She stood up and ran to give Cass a hug.

"I came with the Russians."

"You did not, Cass. How did you get here?" she asked again.

"The Russians brought me," Cass repeated. He motioned for Irena to follow him to the door. She looked outside and saw the two Russian tanks. She raised her voice. "Cass, why did you bring them here? This is dangerous. There are Germans all around."

"I brought insulin for Grandma," said Cass. He ran out to the tank. Zhukov was looking through the hatch of the tank. "This is Field Marshal Zhukov. He knows Grandpa Bieberstein."

"Good afternoon, ma'am," said Zhukov.

"Do you know Colonel Bieberstein? Where is he?" she asked.

"Yes, I know him well," replied Zhukov. "The last I heard, about three weeks ago, he was in Moscow. Doing fine, I am told."

"He is my husband's father," said Irena.

After talking for a time, Cass began climbing back on the tank. "What are you doing?" asked Irena.

"I am leaving."

"Where are you going?"

"I am going back out to fight Nazis."

"I hardly got to see you."

"I have to go, Mama."

"Cass," Irena said with a distressed expression.

"We'll take good care of him," said Zhukov. Though his words provided little comfort to Irena, trying to stop Cass would be futile. She had tried before to no avail. Cass was now even more independent and uncontrollable than before. Irena waved as the tanks pulled away.

The following morning Cass was riding to the western front sitting on top of a tank. Over the next several days, they drove toward Germany. On occasion they found themselves in the midst of heavy fighting and often close-quarter combat. On one occasion they were driving through heavy fighting. As they drove, Zhukov said, "Cass, you have been a great warrior. I want to get you something special to show Russia's appreciation for your heroic efforts. Is there anything you would like as a token of appreciation? A Nazi uniform? Anything?"

"I think I would like a Luger pistol."

"Then you will have a Luger pistol."

About an hour later they came to a small town. As they drove into the town, they saw both Russian soldiers and German soldiers. The Germans were running to get out of town as the Russians came in. The Russians were allowing them to escape simply because taking prisoners was a burdensome task. As they drove through the streets, they came up behind a German officer. The tank pulled in front of him and up to a building, blocking his path. Zhukov pulled out a pistol and shot him. "There is your Luger. Go take it from him, and take the holster too."

Cass obediently climbed off the tank, walked over to the officer, removed the Luger, the belt, and the holster. He stopped and looked at the dead officer, wondering if he had a family.

"Don't feel sorry for him. If he had been captured, he would have been shot anyway," said the driver of the tank.

Cass climbed back on the tank and looked at the Luger. He saw an eagle and a Nazi emblem on it. "That is a special gun," the tank driver explained. "The guns with the eagle are given to officers by Hitler himself for outstanding performance in duty. You have a very special gun there. It will be worth a lot of money someday."

Cass felt strange emotions as he looked at the gun. The German officer had been shot in cold blood. He looked at Zhukov, who smiled at him. He remembered this same feeling when they had accidentally severed the motorcycle driver's head with a piano wire. Mama would be upset. He decided he would never tell her how he got the gun. He climbed back into the tank as they took off across the open field and headed toward the German border.

Notwithstanding the fortification, the Germans were no match for the united Russian and Polish armies, and they were forced to retreat again. This process continued all day. This forward motion by the Russian army persisted and within two weeks the Russians had advanced over three hundred miles. By now it had become apparent that Hitler had spread his forces too thin, and it was just a matter of time before Germany would be defeated. The fighting ended on May 7, 1945, when Germany surrendered to the Allied forces.

The war was over.

At the end of World War II, Poland was left decimated. The population of Warsaw, 1.3 million before the German invasion in 1939, had been reduced to 150,000 people. Of the 350,000 Jews living in Warsaw before World War II, at the end of the war, there were only 11,500 Jews remaining in Warsaw. Ninety percent of the buildings in Warsaw had been destroyed. In an effort to ridicule the Polish people because of how easily they were conquered, the occupying forces had begun the practice of telling "Polack jokes," which caught on throughout the world and would taunt the Polish people for decades. An entire nation of people had been left in ruins, and certain ethnic groups were all but completely destroyed, most notably the Jews. Even so, there were a few Jewish Holocaust survivors. Cass Bieberstein was one of them.

CHAPTER
31

FTER THE LIBERATION of Warsaw in January 1945, it appeared doubtful that the city would rebuild. Now under Soviet rule, the new communist government considered moving the capital of Poland to Lodz and leaving Warsaw in ruins. However, immediately after the Nazis fled Warsaw, the Poles who had left the city began to return, and without the assistance of any government, they began to rebuild the city on their own. Meanwhile, in preparation for the Yalta Conference, Stalin decided that rebuilding the city as the capital of Poland would favorably affect his image. For this reason, the national council passed a resolution calling for the rebuilding of Warsaw as Poland's capital, and on February 14, the Office for the Reconstruction of the Capital was formed. The communist Polish Committee for National Liberation, later known as the Lublin Committee, had been formed during the war, and immediately upon the liberation of Warsaw in January, it became the governing body, with Soviet oversight.

After the war, Cass returned to the house in the country, where his mother, grandparents, and Thaddeus had been staying. Sarah had remained with the Litynskis. They all returned to the apartment behind the Litynski truck repair shop so the Litynskis could help them get back on their feet. Ari returned to the ghetto to search for his wife. The Biebersteins never saw him again. Gustaw and Yurik were recalled to Russia and were also never to be seen again. Initially planning to return to the mansion on Pulawska Street, the Biebersteins discovered through Josef that the mansion was now inhabited by several families. The house had been confiscated by the new government, and the families had been assigned to live at that location. When Josef spoke with authorities, he was told that no one needed a house that big. The Biebersteins could live there as well, but they would have to share the home with five other families. Furthermore, they were no longer the owners.

In August, Josef drove the Biebersteins to the house so they could move in. They were devastated to see how severely the home had been vandalized by the new tenants. Irena, Cass, Thaddeus, Grandpa, and Grandma got out of the truck and walked up to the door. They found the front door locked. Thaddeus knocked on the door, which was opened by a large dirty man smoking a cigar who was clearly intoxicated. "What do you want?"

In the house Cass could see a dozen people walking around. Several came up to the door.

"We're coming home," Thaddeus said. "This is our house."

The people near the door burst into laughter. "You must be the Biebersteins," the man said gruffly. "You stupid Jews. You don't own this house anymore. It now belongs to the people of Poland. Get out of here." He waved his hand toward them. "Go on."

Cass reached into his pocket and took ahold of the Luger, ready to draw it and shoot. Irena looked at him and shook her head slightly. "We'll go."

"Not so fast," the man replied, looking at Irena. "You can stay, but the rest have to go."

"Let's go," Irena said softly. The rest of the family followed her down the front porch steps.

"Didn't you hear me? You can stay. It's better than living on the streets, isn't it?"

Cass turned around and glared at the man as he took ahold of his Luger again.

"What are you going to do, little man?" the man asked, laughing.

"You don't want to find out. There is nothing you can do that is worse than what I have already seen, but I can show you some things you have never seen."

Seeing Cass's hand in his pocket and hearing the sternness of his voice gave the man pause. Yet he had to save face with the others in the house. "Go along with your mama."

"Come on, Cass, let's go," Thaddeus said.

Cass followed the instructions of his older brother, though he likely would have ignored the same instructions if they had come from his mother and would have shot the man. The Biebersteins went back to the truck and told Josef what had happened.

"Okay, get in. I expected as much, which is why I didn't leave," Josef said as the Biebersteins climbed back into the truck. Josef put the truck in gear and drove back toward the truck repair shop. As he drove he said, "You can stay in the apartments as long as I own the building, though I am expecting to have my property confiscated as well. This is the new government. It is communism, and it is just as bad or worse than Nazism."

Josef was correct. In the fall of 1945, he was told that his businesses now belonged to the people of Poland. He could stay as the manager as long as the businesses served the government's purpose. Fortunately for the Litynskis, the mechanics were very skilled at truck repair, and the military was pleased with the service.

It was no longer legally necessary for the Biebersteins to conceal that they were Jews, though it was practically necessary. Hostility toward Jews by Polish citizens, possibly the result of six years of Nazi indoctrination, was as severe as when the Nazis were in control. The safest option was for the Biebersteins to remain in the apartments behind the garage while Cass and Thaddeus worked in the garage repairing trucks.

In late 1945, Irena received a letter from Sigmund. He was living in New York and was in poor health. He had been working to arrange the family's passage to America. He said that the family would be contacted by human rights workers from Switzerland; they would help them find a place to stay in Europe until immigration to the United States was possible.

Uncle Bernie Szyncer had also relocated to America. He and three other engineers, Selma Gottlieb, Harold Pitcairn, and Agnew Larsen, had formed a partnership and designed a prototype for a helicopter called the Szyncer SC-VI. Pitcairn and Larsen left the partnership in August of 1945, and Bernie secured a contract with Intercity Airlines of Montreal to design the prototype helicopter. The Canadian Helicopter Company was to market the helicopter, but the helicopter was eventually built by a subsidiary of BF Goodrich in Montreal called Engineering Products of Canada, Ltd.

Bernie's political connections enabled him to persuade officials of several governments to assist in bringing the Bieberstein family to America, though he knew it would not be easy. The immigration plan presented several concerns, the first of which were rumors that Poland planned to close its borders prohibiting anyone from leaving the country. The second was that the United States would only allow a limited number of immigrants each year. These conflicting interests created a dilemma. The Biebersteins wanted to get out of Poland as quickly as possible, but it would take time to obtain entry into the United States even with refugee status. Finally, a plan was developed whereby they would first emigrate to Sweden. Then, when possible, they would enter the United States and become US citizens. The primary implementers of this plan were Swiss human rights activists.

In the spring of 1946, arrangements were made for the Biebersteins to travel to Sweden via air transportation. There was some concern that the Polish militia would stop them at the airport, though they passed through without incident. They remained in Sweden where Cass and Thaddeus were able to work as mechanics for a short period of time. Finally, in 1947, using his political connections, Bernie was able to obtain passage to the United States for Cass, Thaddeus, and Irena. Grandpa and Grandma Szyncer decided to remain in Sweden where they would live with Grandma's cousin.

Irena and Thaddeus took an earlier flight, and Cass was supposed to follow on the next flight. The flight on which Cass was initially scheduled to travel was overbooked, and as a result he had to wait another day. Ironically, the overbooked flight crashed, and all the passengers were killed. Cass took a flight the following day and arrived in New York two days after Irena and Thaddeus.

Irena, Sigmund, Thaddeus, and Bernie were waiting at the airport to pick up Cass. In his luggage was the Luger he had been given by Field Marshal Zhukov. As he came through customs, he was asked if he had anything to declare. Before he could reply, Thaddeus said, "He has a gun in his luggage." The customs officer confiscated the gun and said that Cass could retrieve it in ten days. When they came back to pick up the gun ten days later, the gun could not be found, and the customs officer no longer worked there.

Due to the possibility that Nazi sympathizers might seek retaliation for his activities as a Resistance fighter, Cass changed his name from Bieberstein to Biebers. He went by that name for the rest of his life, as did his children.

Cass spent the next few years living in New York with his family. However, as a result of his history of fighting Nazis in Poland, he was volatile, making assimilation difficult. He was also skeptical of people who attempted to befriend him out of concern that they may have been sent by Nazis to assassinate him. As a result, he often fought with others in the community. In an effort to keep him from getting into trouble, his parents sent him to Canada to live with his uncle Bernie for several years.

Cass returned to New York, where he attended the Vaughn College of Aeronautics and Technology. He found a position as an airplane technician at Newark Metropolitan Airport (today known as the Newark Liberty International Airport). During his young adult years, Cass had one failed marriage, which resulted in two children, Dorothy and Debbie. Eventually, he met a United Airlines flight attendant named Elsie Joyce MacGregor, who also worked out of the Newark Metropolitan Airport. They married and had two children, Tom and Irena. Tom is the coauthor of this book.

Cass passed away on April 7, 2014. At the time of writing this book, Joyce is living in San Diego, California. Given his concern that someone might seek to injure his family if his true identity was known, Cass seldom spoke about his experience during the Holocaust except to his closest family members and friends, until he was interviewed for the Shoah Foundation Project in 1996. Even in the interview, he was reluctant to disclose many details about the fighting during the uprisings in 1943 and 1944, though he did provide limited information about his role in the Russian invasion of Poland in 1945.

Sigmund reunited with Irena when she arrived in the United States. By then he was suffering an illness that took his life in 1960. Irena did not remarry and passed away in 1973. To this day, her descendants attribute the family's survival in Poland to her constant vigilance and protection of the boys. She made the plans about where they would stay, how they would eat, and when they would take certain actions. Cass in particular always remembered the time he was standing in line in the ghetto with other children to be taken to Treblinka for extermination, when his mother spoke to the guard and saved his life. She never told him what she said to the guard, but he knew it saved his life.

Thaddeus attended the Massachusetts Institute of Technology and became a successful businessman in New York, opening a business called Plywood Distributors. He passed away in 2011. Bernie married a famous singer-actor named Katharine Sergava from Georgia in Europe. She was best known for her role in the play *Oklahoma*.

Colonel Szymon Bieberstein, Cass's paternal grandfather, stayed in the Soviet army until his death. After World War II, the Soviet Union closed itself off to the rest of the world, and there was no communication with the outside world until the 1980s. During this time of Soviet isolation, known as the Cold War, the family lost contact with Colonel Bieberstein. He died long before the Cold War ended, so they were never able to reestablish a relationship with him.

Grandpa and Grandma Szyncer remained in Europe after the war. They felt it would be too difficult to relocate in America due to their age. They had family members still in Europe. The family was in contact with them, though they both passed away not long after the war.

Due to the isolationist policy of Soviet countries during the Cold War, Cass and Thaddeus were not able to maintain contact with Rajmund Litynski or his father. Cass often wondered if Rajmund and Sarah married, but he did not ever contact him to find out. For the most part, Cass wanted to forget that part of his life until he was very old, when he decided to tell his story.

For many years Cass and Thaddeus remained in litigation with the government of Poland and others as they attempted to recover damages for their financial losses from the confiscation of their property first by the Nazis, and then later by the Polish government. Their settlement in 2014 of several hundred thousand dollars was a small fraction of the family's actual financial losses, but as it was for many Jewish families who suffered through the Holocaust, "reparation" was just a word of token gratuity.

EPILOGUE

O N MARCH 19, 2014, I met with Cass and Tom Biebers at BJ's Restaurant and Brewhouse in Temecula, California, to discuss this book project. Cass was across the table from me, and Tom was seated to his left. Cass looked around the room as he took in the ambience of the early twenties decor. This was one of numerous meetings during which I interviewed Cass concerning his experiences in the Holocaust. I asked him what he would like to communicate to the world about his experiences.

He said, "I hate the image the world has of Jews in WWII. Movies always show them walking like sheep in lines to the slaughter. They are seen as cowards who never fought back. What the world doesn't know is that the reason many didn't fight back is that the first thing Hitler did after invading was to confiscate all guns. The Jews had nothing to fight with. In addition, the Jews were told they were going to work camps, where they would have plenty of food and would live in comfort. They believed what they were told. But some of us knew better. We knew we were going to extermination camps. When you corner an animal and give it only the option of death, it becomes the fiercest form of life on earth. That was what we had become.

"The Nazis were very foolish. They did everything like clockwork. The patrols would come through at exactly the same time every day. It made it easy for us to ambush them, throw their bodies in the sewers, and keep their weapons. And the stupid Nazis always thought the soldiers had deserted because it never occurred to them that a Jew could kill a Nazi.

"I want you to tell the world the truth about the Resistance. Let the world know that we fought back, and we fought well. Many of us died fighting, but we had nothing to lose; we were going to die anyway. But we were going to die on our terms, and not without a fight."

I asked Cass about his impression of Oskar Schindler. "You described Oskar Schindler as someone substantially different from the hero portrayed in *Schindler's List*. It is known that at the beginning of the war, he took advantage of the Jews, and you mentioned how he took your family's property and shot your dog. Supposedly toward the end of the war, he fell in love with a Jewish woman and changed his thinking toward Jews, even helping many of them survive the war by allowing them to work in his factory. Do you believe he changed?"

Cass replied, "I don't know. I can't tell you what is in another man's heart. I will say that when I met him, what he did to my family and to me was horrible. I tried to convince Steven Spielberg not to make the movie *Schindler's List*. I felt there were others who had never mistreated Jews who were far more deserving than Schindler. People like Irena Sendler, Anne Frank, or Mordecai Anielewicz. I wanted to know why he had to make a movie of someone who had hurt so many Jews. He just felt that Schindler was a good candidate for recognition because of what he did for Jews toward the end of the war."

Cass passed away on April 7, 2014, a short time after I met with him at BJ's. His funeral was attended by hundreds of people of many different faiths. There was a common bond that brought them together. That bond was that we will never forget, and we will never let something like the Holocaust happen to anyone again.

Writing this book was an enlightening experience for me. Instead of viewing the Holocaust from afar, I have been allowed to see into the midst of it in a way I never had before. After working on this project for years, distant images are now a reality, and the atrocities are ever more real. It has been an honor for me to write this book, not only because of the opportunity to tell the story of this hero, but also because my maternal great-grandfather was a Bieberstein.

ABOUT THE AUTHOR

D.W. DUKE IS an experienced California trial attorney who earned a bachelor of arts from the University of Michigan and a juris doctor from Washington University School of Law. He holds a fourth-degree black belt conferred by the World Tae Kwon Do Federation in Seoul Korea, is a freelance editor for Oxford University Press, and is the author of six books.

Thomas Biebers is the son of Casimir Bieberstein, a Holocaust survivor and member of the Jewish Resistance. Tom is an actor and a businessman who served in the Marines and attended California State University, Long Beach. Since then, he has built an impressive foundation of experience both in front of and behind the camera.